JB

The Autobiography of a Twentieth Century Mennonite Pilgrim

Cover and book design by Gail Enns, Fresno, California

Printed by Dumont Printing, Fresno, California

ISBN: 1-877941-04-2

JB

The Autobiography of a Twentieth Century Mennonite Pilgrim

J.B. Toews

Center for Mennonite Brethren Studies
Fresno, California

Table of Contents

Foreword

At Mennonite Brethren conferences, J.B. Toews had a knack for being the last person to speak on an issue. Some of us wondered: was it exquisite timing that gave him the final word at the microphone? Or was it just that after he had spoken there was nothing left to say?

This book may be JB's "last word" to his beloved church. In the first instance it is a personal testimony, a memoir of his life. But it is more than that. It is a particular kind of life, a life lived *as a Mennonite Brethren.*

I first met JB in 1964 when I was a college student in Fresno and he was president of the seminary next door. He clasped my hand warmly and proceeded to ask about my home, my church, my lineage. "So you're the grandson of...." I didn't know it then, but this was not mere chit-chat; what we were doing was laying out the relational coordinates. A sense of history was being invoked.

Two decades later I had the good fortune to occupy an office next to JB. At the end of a day he would linger at the door and muse about some issue of concern in the Mennonite Brethren Church. I looked forward to these daily benedictions. A comment I heard often was, "A church that forgets the past cannot understand the present and lacks direction for the future."

In this volume, a companion to his earlier book, *A Pilgrimage of Faith*, JB's life is a lens that projects a fresh view of our Mennonite Brethren past. The book purports to be autobiography, but JB's passion for the church is so all-consuming that the lines between denominational and personal history are not always sharp.

Early in his life JB felt called to serve God through the Mennonite Brethren Church, and for six decades he followed that call with unflagging zeal. Little was allowed to get in his way: not comfort, not profit, not even family. You won't see JB bouncing his boys on his knee. You won't read much about family outings to the beach. You won't learn about his favorite foods or what he likes to do on a day off. But you will read about a tireless pursuit to build the Mennonite Brethren Church.

No one of our generation has experienced JB's measure of Mennonite Brethren history. He is the last of those who overlapped with the first generation of our fellowship. He has presided over and helped shape our collective experience through most of this century. In some ways he *is*

Mennonite Brethren history. His life, spent in devotion to the church, is a microcosm of the swirling changes that have buffeted and burnished our pilgrimage together.

Today, JB is slowing down, no surprise for someone who is nearing ninety. But his vision for the church remains keen. As you'll see here, he remains a caretaker of our heritage and a critic of our vagrant spirit.

About the title: The shorthand of initials was common in earlier times when biblical names like Abraham, Jacob, John and Peter would cover most of the men in a Russian Mennonite village. Initials like AH, BB, JJ, JA, and HH were a kind of conference code that brought instant recognition.

J.B. Toews is one of those. Throughout the Mennonite Brethren Conference he is affectionately known as, simply, JB. There's no confusing him with anyone else because he's one of a kind.

We'll never see another JB

Wally Kroeker
Winnipeg, Manitoba

Preface

The twentieth century has been described as a time of "breakneck changes." It has been "the most troubled, unsettling, costly, adventurous and surprising time ever. More has changed and faster, more has been destroyed, more accomplished than in any comparable interval in five thousand years since recorded history."[1] The story of this book reflects events and experiences of just one life in the context of this turbulent and most progressive century of history.

It is a personal story. It spans two world wars, breathtaking scientific breakthroughs, clashes of world views and political struggles ending in the searching question: What next?

My story is but a glimpse of the sovereign providence of God revealed in the life of an individual. It is a testimony to the faithfulness of God in the various circumstances of an exiting journey so well expressed in the testimony of Moses at the end of his life's journey: "I proclaim the name of the Lord; ascribe greatness to our God. He is a rock, his work is perfect; for all his ways are justice, a God of truth and without injustice; righteous and upright is he" (Deut. 32:3-4).

The story reflects human weakness and imperfections in the context of God's provision of love, grace, patience and long-suffering. It is a record of memory substantiated by many of my contemporaries who were consulted in the process of writing the story.

The publication of the book is made possible through the kind and capable assistance of several individuals. Wally Kroeker, a long and dear friend edited the manuscript. Paul Toews and Kevin Enns-Rempel of the Center for Mennonite Brethren Studies carried it through the process of publication. Laurene Peters, in a spirit of service, has again typed and retyped the manuscript. I am indebted to all who contributed to the publication of this autobiography.

In the Beginning

W here does one begin the story of a life? With the first drawn breath, the earliest flicker of consciousness? With parents, grand parents and distant ancestors? We—you and I—are products of so much that has gone before us. We are shaped by our genes and environments; by our struggles with events and circumstances.

Now, in the late evening of my life, I am more convinced than ever that our human search to understand the mysteries of existence, the universe, and our place within it, leaves us groping in darkness unless we accept the most basic of formulations—"In the beginning God ..." (Gen. 1:1). There is no other key to unlock the secret of being. John, the author of the Gospel, reflects on this mystery when he writes, "In the beginning was the Word . . . and the Word was God. He was with God in the beginning. Through him all things were made. . . . In him was life, and that life was the light of men. The light shines in the darkness, but the darkness has not understood it" (John 1:1-5 NIV).

Our personal stories cannot be detached from the eternal "In the beginning." Psalm 22 says, "Yet you brought me out of the womb; you made me trust in you even at my mother's breast. From birth I was cast upon you; from my mother's womb you have been my God" (vv. 9-10). My story is part of a larger panorama in which God is the beginning and the end, the first and the last.

The landscape of my own story gained texture and definition from the sixteenth-century Reformation, particularly the birth of the Anabaptist movement. That cataclysmic event, distant as it seems, informed and shaped my pilgrimage in a decisive way.

Though I only recognized it at the age of thirty-six, my spiritual heritage is that of the Anabaptist movement, which spread like a prairie grassfire through Switzerland, Germany, Austria and the Netherlands. The story of the Dutch wing of the Anabaptists—the Mennonites—is my story. Their landscape, like mine, is one of spiritual mountaintops of joy and devoted witness to the Christ who redeemed us. It is also a landscape of ravines and valleys, the kind that prompted this blunt message to the early church at the close of the first century: "You have forsaken your first love. . . . I know your deeds, that you are neither cold nor hot. . . . You say, `I am rich; I have acquired wealth and do not need a thing.' But you do not realize that you are wretched, pitiful, poor, blind and naked" (Rev. 2:4; 3:15-17).

From the outset the Anabaptists, also called Mennonites after their Dutch leader Menno Simons, sought to be people of unflagging faithfulness to Jesus Christ. Martin Luther's main emphasis on justification by faith was not sufficient for them. They clung to a more rigorous definition of salvation by grace which is expressed in Menno Simons' legendary declaration:

> For true evangelical faith is of such a nature that it cannot lie dormant, but manifests itself in all righteousness and works of love; it dies unto the flesh and blood; it destroys all forbidden lusts and desires; it seeks and serves and fears God; it clothes the naked; it feeds the hungry; it comforts the sorrowful; it shelters the destitute; it aids and consoles the sad; it returns good for evil; it serves those that harm it; it prays for those that persecute it; teaches, admonishes, and reproves with the Word of the Lord; it seeks that which is lost; it binds up that which is wounded; it heals that which is diseased and it saves that which is sound; it has become all things to all men. The persecution, suffering, and anguish which befalls it for the sake of the truth of the Lord is to it a glorious joy and consolation.
>
> All those who have such a faith, a faith that yearns to walk in the commandments of the Lord, to do the will of the Lord; these press on to all righteousness, love, and obedience. These prove that the Word and will of our beloved Lord Jesus Christ is true wisdom, truth, and love, is unchangeable and immutable until Christ Jesus shall come again in the clouds of heaven at the judgment day. These will not make light of God's Word as does the ignorant world, saying, What good can water do me? But they diligently try to obey the Word of Christ in every particular, even if it leads to death for the body.[2]

Adhering to this vision brought them heart-rending persecution, well described in the *Martyrs Mirror*.[3] They became pilgrims and strangers, scattering throughout Europe in their search for religious tolerance. A group of Dutch Anabaptists found their haven of safety in the Vistula Delta of present-day Poland, where they settled for more than two centuries. They were joined by small groups of believers from Moravia, Bohemia and Austria. Their competence as tillers and tamers of land gained them a degree of acceptance.

In time their life became too comfortable, their faith a mere tradition. They ceased to be a pilgrim people "in the world but not of the world." When government restrictions again threatened their earthly well-being, they began to cast about for greener pastures.

These they found, for a time, in the wide-open grasslands of South Russia. The promise of religious freedom, economic opportunity and continued cultural isolation provided unprecedented possibilities to develop large colonies and fashion a "Mennonite paradise." Despite difficult beginnings, the region prospered and became known as the breadbasket of the world. By the mid-nineteenth century it was the showcase of the Russian Empire in agriculture and industry.

As so often happens, material success took its toll. The climate of comfort and economic prosperity sapped their spiritual vitality. This had already begun to happen during their years in the Vistula-Nogat Delta. In the Mennonite colonies of Russia, things only got worse. Mennonite identity became a matter of ethnicity, not vibrant faith. Simply being born a Mennonite entitled one to church membership, not to mention the privileges guaranteed by Russian law. Faith had been domesticated and acculturated.

The faithfulness of God in sending renewal through the work of the Holy Spirit did not bypass the Mennonite colonies in South Russia. Seeds of renewal were planted in the early nineteenth century. Spiritual hunger grew, and was nourished through Bible study groups, the influence of western Pietism and various literary and educational programs. One expression of this earnest searching for new life was the birth of the Mennonite Brethren Church.

The secession document signed by eighteen heads of households on January 6, 1860 was sincere in its motive but not without fault in its content.[4] The fissure between the fledgling new group and the mother church widened. Rejection and persecution ensued. Yet the new movement, a decisive response to a long-brewing spiritual crisis, survived.

The new church was still young when, in 1878, my father, John A. Toews, son of Aron A. and Justina Toews, was born in the village of

Alexanderkrone, of Molotschna. The spirit of intolerance had not yet vanished when he, twenty years later, became a teacher in the village of Neukirch. He would never forget the rejection he experienced from others when, after years of struggle in his teens, he found new life through the efficacy of the cross. To profess assurance of personal salvation was no small test for a young teacher struggling for acceptance in the village, since other who had made similar professions had been removed from their positions.

Such was the milieu into which I was born.

First Steps

In Neukirch, at the age of twenty, my father found the sweetheart of his youth. She was Liese Janzen, an orphan girl reared in the home of her uncle, Peter Warkentin.

My father's autobiography records five years of happy marriage. They were blessed with three children, Aron, Liese and Justa. Their move from Neukirch to Alexandertal, where there was a Mennonite Brethren fellowship, added to their spiritual enrichment.

But the joy of their marriage was short-lived. On April 9, 1903 the young mother and dearly beloved wife of my father died after a brief bout with tuberculosis.

In the midst of his shattering grief, a new and unexpected dimension surfaced. Leaders of the Mennonite Brethren Church had carefully observed the young teacher from Neukirch-Alexandertal. They were impressed by his consistent Christian testimony and his evident gifts of leadership and teaching. In keeping with Mennonite Brethren practice, they called to him to accept affirmation as a minister of the gospel. He was ordained that spring on Pentecost day.

Margaretha Janz, a young woman from Konteniusfeld, was aware of the teacher from Alexandertal. He had visited the Mennonite Brethren Church in the adjoining village of Sparrau. She had heard him preach and had been impressed with the sincerity of his message. The news of his wife's passing was known throughout the colony. Margaretha, then twenty-two, felt a special burden for the three children who had been left without a mother. She wondered if it should be her task to respond to their need.

A fellow minister in Konteniusfeld, Klass Enns, felt led to suggest that the widowed teacher consider Margaretha Janz as a possible replacement for his loss. After much prayer he agreed and on September 28, 1903 my father married for the second time. Margaretha Janz became the mother of the three youngsters and the wife of the teacher in Alexandertal.

There had been no courtship. She did not experience the romance of youthful love. Her marriage, according to her own testimony, was an act of obedience to a call that had come to her on the day of the children's mother's funeral. Aron, Liese and Justa and a lonely husband, became her family. Within a year, on July 26, 1904, she became the mother of her own first child, a daughter named Lenchen (Helen). Two years later I was born.

My life began in 1906 as the fifth child in the family. My mother told me later that my beginning was clouded with difficulty. A few days after birth my body broke out in a rash that soon developed into festering sores. My tiny body was kept in a large cloth because I couldn't be handled without touching the sores. My condition became so critical that my parents prayed that God might relieve my suffering by taking me to himself.

But I was destined to live. After weeks of agony, healing began. The nightmare was over, though its scars would continue to haunt my early childhood.

Hardship and premature death were frequent visitors in those days. My first conscious memory was the funeral of my baby sister, Mariechen, who was born in 1908 and died at the age of two. Her funeral procession and burial registered on my four-year-old memory. I have no recollection, however, of the death of my half-sister, Justa, a year earlier.

Life in the Village

Alexandertal, the place of my birth and childhood years, was one of the sixty villages of the Molotschna Colony in South Russia. The population consisted of eighteen family units known as full farmers, owners of 175 acres of land, and eleven smaller farms with 82 acres. The support population for the village included a school teacher, a storekeeper, the blacksmith, the owners of a large three-story flour mill with its employees, a windmill owner, a shoemaker, a tailor, carpenters, farm workers, house servants and the night watchman. The landless lived in smaller houses on the outskirts of the village.

The main street of the village ran east to west, parallel to a small tree-lined river named Tschekrak, a tributary of the Yushanlee, which in turn was a major tributary of the Molotschna River. Several other villages dotted the same stream: Schardau, Pordenau and Mariental to the east; Elisabethtal and Steinbach to the west. Looking south, across the primitive bridge that spanned the river, one could see a beautiful rolling meadow that every spring would erupt with wild flowers.

A tree plantation at the west end of the village marked the border between Alexandertal and Elisabethtal, the birthplace of the Mennonite

Brethren Church in 1860. To the south of the plantation in the middle of a large meadow was a lake, formed by a dam across the Tschekrak River, which served as a watering place for village cattle as well as a swimming pool and baptismal site.

The main street was lined on both sides by neatly kept farm yards. The houses differed from each other mainly in size. A corridor led from the house into the attached barn for cattle and horses. A large shed attached to the barn in an L shape provided room for implements and wagons, as well as storage for feed, hay and grain.

Each farm maintained a large orchard with abundant varieties of fruit: apples, pears, plums and several kinds of berries. Behind each farmstead was a spacious garden full of vegetables for family and servants. My father owned a "half" farmstead, across the street from the school, which he purchased through an inheritance from his first wife's family.

The school, a landmark in the middle of the village, was a big, imposing building with a large classroom to the west and the living quarters for the teacher and his family to the east. The complex included a barn with stalls for three cows, two horses, a pen for calves or sheep, a large feed storage room with a hayloft and a shed to house additional hay, a pig pen and room for a wagon. A second house provided storage for school equipment, an outside kitchen and a small jail.

Like the farmsteads, the teacherage had a lush orchard and vegetable garden of sufficient size to meet our family's food needs. I have especially fond memories of two great walnut trees in the orchard, which provided shade to play and branches to build treehouses.

In the middle of the spacious schoolyard was the well, eighty-five feet deep. Water for our family and for the students and cattle was pulled up in a bucket with a long rope on a winch. The village government was formed by the landowners. Those owning 175 acres had one vote; those with only 82 acres had half a vote. Those who owned no land had no vote.

The mayor was elected for a three-year term. He, together with the assistant mayor and secretary, composed the executive body responsible for all affairs related to village life. The village council, consisting of all voting members of the village, met periodically as circumstances required.

Everyone in the village, except farmhands and house servants, was known by their first name. Strangers were easily recognized. Keeping order in the community was in the hands of assigned overseers chosen from the landowners. Those who broke village rules faced the discipline of a leather strap administered in the village office.

Each farm had men and women servants from the Russian villages. Some of them came long distances to find work in the Mennonite colonies. Like many homes, we had a housemaid to handle much of the washing, ironing, cleaning, gardening, milking, butter-making, dishwashing and food preparation. In summer, when school was out, we also had a second maid, usually a teenage or elderly woman, to serve as a nanny for the children. The men servants looked after chores related to horses, cattle, milk cows, sheep and general farm maintenance. During spring and summer many farmers had two farmhands to help them and their own grown boys with the heavy fieldwork of tilling, seeding, planting, weeding and harvesting.

Servants' wages were low. I remember one nanny, a teenager, who looked after us one summer. Her wages for the four summer months were two dresses that mother bought for her and five rubles per month, plus meals. The men servants slept in a small room at the entrance to the barn, next to the corridor connecting the house with the barn. The women servants slept in the kitchen.

The village servants constituted a social unit of their own. On Sundays and holidays they would congregate where they could—in one of the larger barns, among the trees of the plantation or simply on the street. They had little or no access to the living quarters of the family during leisure hours.

Many servants felt keenly their "have-not" status, and this would come back to haunt the Mennonites. Some of the men servants who felt they had been mistreated later joined the revolutionary army and returned to their former places of work with a spirit of revenge.

School Days

The school classroom was governed by strict rules. Speaking to a classmate, even in a whisper, during instruction time was forbidden. Violators had to stand in a corner facing the wall. Repeat offenses brought corporal punishment with a rod or a strap. Conformity to rules in school as well as in the wider community was strictly enforced.

The Alexandertal school was home for my entire youth. During my first fourteen years we lived in the school house; for the next six we lived on a farmyard across the street.

My earliest playmates were Jacob Wall and Hans Suderman. Born within a week of me, they were our immediate neighbors at the Alexandertal school, Jacob to the east and Hans to the west. We spent many hours together playing (and, as youngsters do, quarrelling) in the schoolyard sandbox. To minimize tension during the week (as a minister he was gone most weekends) my father would keep me in the classroom while he taught. So even at the age of four and five I would spend the better part of the school day in the class drawing pictures and observing the process of elementary education. I became a student before my time. At the age of six I joined the first year's students.

Our family, meanwhile, was growing. Lydia came along in 1911 and Jacob in 1914. We employed a Russian nanny to help my mother with the endless family demands. She became our chaperon, responsible for all of us children.

Jacob Wall and Hans Suderman were major factors in my development. Jacob, a husky boy much taller and stronger than me, and Hans, superior in wit, kept me continually aware of my feelings of inferiority. Being smaller, I was always out-maneuvered in the competitions so typical of early childhood.

The Wall and Suderman families each owned 175 acres of land. Mr. Wall served as the village mayor and so the village office was in their home. Jacob, as one of the younger children, enjoyed privileges that I had to forego. His father frequently took him along when he went to the district meetings in Gnadenfeld. Such opportunities were important.

Mr. Suderman had a crippled left leg and walked with a crutch. A very talkative man, he frequently came over to regale us with endless stories about his children, horses, cows and dogs. My father would often fall asleep from boredom.

Summers with Grandparents

When school was out my father would spend the summer months travelling as an itinerant minister to the Mennonite colonies scattered throughout the Russian empire. To make things easier around home during his absence, I was sent to my grandparents, Benjamin and Helena Janz in Konteniusfeld. My grandfather, a miller, landowner and beekeeper by occupation, had plenty of activities to harness my restless spirit. I spent my summers with them from the time I was seven until I was fourteen.

Grandfather Janz had come to Russia from the Vistula Delta as a teenager. His speech, mostly Low German with a strong Polish-German accent, was mild and relaxed. Even when upset he remained calm, but very specific in his orders. He would give me low-key instructions to stay awake when assigned to watch the bees in the swarming season, but if he found me asleep, sitting in the hot summer sun, I would have a painful awakening.

Very kind by nature and emotionally soft, he would often be moved to tears during the Sunday sermon. He was known throughout the village for his kindness. Many of the landless poor of the village would come to him when in need. I often saw him give flour to a needy mother, or feed grain to a poor neighbor to fatten the family's hog before slaughter. It was the generosity of Grandpa Janz that kept our family from starving during the famine of 1921-1922.

Grandma Janz was a good complement to her easygoing husband. Many of her family, the Penners, had migrated to the United States when she was a teenager. She and Grandpa had fallen deeply in love and her devotion to her husband-to-be was stronger than her own family ties. She was a strong, independent woman who basically "ran the family ship." With very few words and never in anger, she communicated the policies of the home. When I would go out to play with the neighbor children she would frequently remind me: "Hans, never forget that you are the son of a minister. You cannot bring shame upon your family; behave properly." I chafed under these continuous admonitions. Why did I need to be different from other children?

While I spent many summers with my Janz grandparents, I spent little time with my other grandparents, Aron and Justina Toews of Alexanderkrone. I did not learn to know them intimately. I remember Grandpa Toews as a very quiet man. He was highly regarded locally, having various responsibilities with the village government. I was impressed by his beautiful horses. He took great pride in having a meticulous farmstead and the best horses in the villages of Lichtfelde, Alexanderkrone, Kleefeld and Friedensruh. I was also impressed by his large orchard on the banks of the Yushanlee River. Whenever we visited Grandpa and Grandma Toews we could count on abundant fruit of various kinds.

Grandmother Justina Reimer Toews was a very tender person. She, too, was a woman of few words, but very effectual. As a youngster of four or five I would love to sit on her lap. She would cuddle me and put cookies in my pocket when we were ready to leave for home.

My most vivid images of the few family gatherings I remember in Alexanderkrone are of my father's youngest brother, Peter. He would gather all the nephews and nieces under a big tree behind my grandparents' house and entertain us. He would perform baffling tricks with hands and yarn, and tell fascinating jokes and fables. Sometimes he'd play ball with us. Whenever we visited Grandpa and Grandma Toews Uncle Peter was the focus.

Unforgettable, too, was the death of Uncle Abram's first wife. Uncle Abram had taken over Grandpa's farm, and his family lived on the same yard as my grandparents. His wife died in childbirth and left two orphan girls behind. I recall standing at her coffin and seeing the baby, who also died in the birth struggle, in her arms. This is the second funeral I remember from my early childhood. The first was that of my baby sister, Marichen.

CHAPTER 3

Growing Up

A very trying chapter of my childhood opened in July 1914, the beginning of World War I. Father, a teacher and minister, hoped to be exempted from the general military mobilization. In October all exemptions were canceled. All men from the ages of twenty-one to forty were called for induction. Our family was no exception.

I have indelible memories of the October night when Father bowed over the cradle to kiss the sleeping baby Jacob. Shaking with emotion he embraced each of us, than sobbed as he put his arms around Mother. Who knew what the future would bring? Deep loneliness came over us as he and the other men from our village were taken away in the middle of the night.

Aron, fifteen, the oldest of the family, was in his third year of high school (*Handels-schule*) in Alexanderkrone, the village of my father's birth. Grandpa and Grandma Toews gave him a home away from home. His brilliance, perception and deportment put him ahead of all his classmates, and he completed high school at age sixteen. In Father's absence we were deeply concerned for Aron's future.

The wealthy Johan Federau family of Halbstadt learned of this exceptional student. Needing a companion for their son Jacob, who was the same age, they offered Aron a home a full scholarship to attend college (*commerz-schule*) in Halbstadt. What a provision of God in a time of war!

My father spent three years in Moscow as a chaplain to the thousands of Mennonite young men who served under the Red Cross, caring for the wounded brought in by special trains from the battlefields.

During these three years we saw my father only twice when he came home on two-week furloughs. My mother found it taxing to have complete responsibility for the family, two boys and three girls. Liese, the oldest daughter in her early teens, and Helen, who was ten, took charge of the younger siblings and the household demands. The separation from Father affected Mother's health. She developed a critical eye disease. For weeks we children were alone while Mother was in Berdyansk, a city on the Azov sea, to get help from an eye specialist. I remember her sitting for weeks and months in a darkened room to avoid the light which increased the pain.

During this time I developed deep feelings of insecurity as a result of Mother's prolonged suffering, the absence of my father and the necessity of spending summers with my grandparents in Konteniusfeld. I found myself afflicted with a nervous condition that expressed itself in twitchings in my face, shoulders and arms. My walk became unsteady. All efforts to get medical help failed. My peers in school and church rejected me. I became a very lonely boy at the ages of nine, ten and eleven.

My health problems did not affect my academic work in school, however. I surpassed Hans Suderman and Jacob Wall in my grade three, four and five standing. Meanwhile, my older sisters Liese and Helen dropped out of school after finishing their fifth grade to help care of the family and ease the pressure on our ailing mother.

The Family Reunited

Father's return from Moscow in 1917, when I was eleven, marked a significant shift in my development. The social isolation because of my twitching problem had left me very lonely. Father's return to the classroom for the last year in grade school boosted my depressed self-image.

As a boy, I yearned to have a horse of my own, since horse racing was a popular village sport in springtime. Without my parents' permission, I frequently went to nearby farms where Russian farmhands, without the knowledge of the owners, let me ride the horses. These often were the young horses that were not yet trained. Other boys were afraid to ride the untrained horses, so here was my chance to regain some self-esteem. Taking daring chances made me feel like a hero. Frequently I was thrown off and sustained bruises, but no broken bones. The danger didn't matter: I could do what other boys did not dare to do!

Somehow Mother learned of these boyish pranks, and was not pleased. Doctors had prescribed rest, as excitement always increased my twitching and brought on insomnia. The punishment, accompanied by Mother's tears and prayers, had no effect on my behavior. I needed a way to excel and compensate for my feelings of social inferiority. After years of being the smallest in my age group, unable to compete with my peers, these dangerous exploits on frisky untrained horses became my way of balancing the scales.

It was a great day then, when Father finally recognized my need and consented to buy a horse. Abram Dueck, in the village of Elisabethtal, had a bay mare known for her speed in competition. What a day when the bay mare was brought home! I fed her very carefully, only oats and hay to keep her slender for racing.

In spring I entered the village races and won repeatedly. What a great feeling for a boy of eleven! A year later the mare gave birth to a colt, a perfect picture of the Arabian stallion that had sired him. My excitement had no measure. Here I was, a freshman in high school; at the age of twelve, I was the proud owner of a fast mare and a beautiful Arabian colt named Major.

Revolution and Anarchy

The joy of our family solidarity was short-lived. The Russian Revolution of 1917 dramatically changed the panorama of life. Central government control broke down, leaving only the provisional local government, and even that in a state of flux. The Russian peasants in the surrounding villages, with some noble exceptions, felt their day had finally come. Soldiers by the thousands who had deserted from the military joined thousands of common villagers in a loosely organized movement. They poured into the colonies to target the wealthy landowners whom they had served as laborers. There was looting and killing as ravaging masses terrorized our villages.

Only the arrival of German troops managed to stem the tide. From April 1918 until November 1918 these troops occupied our colonies and provided temporary order and security. Their arrival was marked with a special reception held in our village because of its central location. Garlands of flowers, carried by selected girls from several villages, were presented to the commander of the troops. For the moment they were our saviors from the roving hordes of bandits who had plundered our homes and killed many people.

The German occupation brought to the surface the divided loyalties of Mennonite and German colonists in the Ukraine and the Volga region. The presence and influence of the troops revived a sense of German patriotism that had been preserved in the system of education throughout the colonies over more than a hundred years.

As a boy of twelve I was deeply impressed by the discipline and efficiency of the German army. I developed significant friendships with soldiers stationed in our village. Their marksmanship, marching precision and patriotic faith in German superiority left a notable mark on me, so much so that I developed a degree of identification.

I was in my last year of elementary school and prepared for the examination. High school entrance requirements, based on the German model of education adopted from the beginning of the founding of the German colonies, were quite stringent. We had to pass three days of oral and written examinations before an examining board that did not include our own teacher. I passed with a superior grade and felt greatly encouraged. During the same year a private high school was established in Alexandertal.

My academic performance, along with the temporary stability of the brief German occupation and the return of my father, restored some of my personal equilibrium. My twitching and inward tension decreased. As an early teenager I recaptured status with my peers, felt less isolated and developed more zest for life.

Fighting Back

During the German occupation the historic peace position of the Mennonites faced a critical test. Vivid memories of the recent wave of terror, accompanied by pressure from the German army, generated much debate about forming a Mennonite militia, known as the "*Selbstschutz*" (self-protection). Barely in my teens, I favored some form of self-defense. My concern was to protect my two sisters who in 1917, before the German occupation, had to hide in the hayloft to escape the ruthless rape that many young women experienced. I was ready to protect my own family even if it meant violating a cherished Mennonite principle.

The German army withdrew. In no time an organized wave of terrorism led by Nestor Makhno began to move into the colonies.

The fledgling Mennonite militia was no match for the thousands of terrorists. We were helpless. My father and several church leaders called for an all-night prayer vigil to seek divine intervention. Never will I forget that sacred night.

By mid-morning a detachment of five or six hundred men invaded our village. They looted homes and confiscated some horses, but no one was killed. That noon hour is forever etched in my memory. We as a family were ready to eat dinner when a tall soldier with red hair approached the school house, strode in and commanded that no one move. With a sword in one hand and a pistol in the other he pushed Father against the wall and with a loud voice ordered: "Do not move if you want to live."

For twenty minutes he ransacked every closet and drawer in the house looking for valuables. He took Father's watch, my parents' wedding rings, some new cutlery and whatever money we had. When he finally left we remained paralyzed with shock. Would he return to harm us? Gradually our composure returned.

By late afternoon the detachment was ready to move on. Before they left the commanding officer demanded to see the elders of the village. In a harsh voice he said: "We came here with orders to kill. Something in your village kept us from doing what we came for." That evening the whole village gathered again in the church to acknowledge the divine intervention, the only explanation for the marauders' change of plans.

This event shattered my sympathy for the *Selbstschutz*. Though very young, I had gotten personally involved by standing watch during the night with a rifle. But the clear evidence of divine intervention led me to repent. I became committed to nonresistance and declared my change of position to the other members of the militia. This position would be severely tested as many of our people were subjected to the cruelest atrocities. For the time I was able to stand by the principle of biblical nonresistance without processing its implications. I was troubled without end by the idea of the sovereignty of God in the midst of beastly human behavior. Only years later, in the context of biblical and political history, was I able to process my youthful decision "to be obedient to the teachings of Jesus," as my father called it.

Horse Thieves

By early summer the White Army, loyal to the old regime, fought the revolutionary Red Army, forcing a temporary retreat. Major engagements of the civil war were fought in the villages of the Molotschna. The offensive of one army and the counter-offensive of the other lingered in our villages until late spring of 1921. Our area changed hands eighteen times. All food resources were devoured by the armies. They confiscated our cattle for meat. They took our horses, the only power for agriculture.

It is difficult for me to describe my pain when a lieutenant walked into our barn, saw my bay mare, untied her and led her away to serve in the cavalry. I never saw the beautiful horse again.

Her colt, however, nearing a year old, was left. He developed beautifully. To protect him from the eyes of the army I hid him in the hayshed behind a wall of straw bales. In the darkness of night I would lead him to the orchard behind the school to exercise. A black stallion, he was a picture of beauty. When he was a year-and-a-half I started to ride him. One spring day when he was nearing his second birthday, there was a prolonged calm in the villages with no military occupation. After surveying the surroundings to make sure there were no military scouts around, I decided to give Major some exercise. I chose a road through the forest on the south side of the neighboring villages of Schardau and Pordenau, in my judgment the safest road where I could ride without encountering any military outposts.

My judgment was wrong. Out of the blue I heard a sharp call: "Stop." Glancing to the right I saw three soldiers on horseback. "Stop or we will shoot," was the command. There was no escape. I stopped. "Get off your horse," they ordered. I couldn't believe it; this was only a colt, too young for their purposes. The three soldiers had surrounded me. Again the command, "Get off the horse." I froze. There was no escape.

One of the soldiers got off his horse to pull me off Major's back. He and a second soldier took the saddle from one of their horses, an old brown gelding with crooked front legs, and put it on my beloved Major. Then they vanished into the forest.

The center of my joy and excitement was lost. Stunned and devastated, I rode the old gelding back to the barn.

Loss of A Brother

My brother Aron, seven years my senior, was my idol. He completed pre-medical school in Halbstadt by the age of eighteen. His intellectual brilliance made it possible to complete a four-year program in two years and pass his entrance examination to the medical faculty at the University of Simferopol on the lower coast of the Crimea peninsula. The distinction of a governor's gold medal as the outstanding student of the province helped pave the way to become the youngest student ever admitted to the medical school. While in Halbstadt he had met Sara Dyck, a few years his senior, the daughter of a wealthy estate owner. They became engaged but agreed to postpone their marriage until he finished medical school.

Aron's scholastic distinction continued. At twenty-one he was awarded the doctor of medicine degree, the youngest in the history of the university. This was in December 1920.

Our area was separated from the Crimea by the struggling armies of the revolutionary war. Sara, Aron's fiancee, had gone to stay with her brother, also a medical doctor on one of the family estates in the Crimea. She and Aron were looking forward to be married.

Aron planned to spend the Christmas vacation with Sara and her brother's family on the estate. First, however, he decided to undergo minor surgery to remove a festering sore from behind his right ear. With just a light bandage to cover the wound, he boarded a train on December 23 to travel to the Dyck estate. Underground spies of the Red Army had dynamited a bridge that the train needed to pass some twenty miles from his destination. Aron had no alternative but to walk the distance on foot facing a sharp freezing wind. He reached the estate in the late evening hours.

On Christmas Day he preached a message to the small congregation on the estate. That evening he developed a high fever. The diagnosis of Dr. Dyck, his brother-in-law to be, was serious blood poisoning. For political reasons he could not be taken to the hospital, nor was medicine available to combat the infection. He died December 30 and was buried on January 2.

Aron's last letter to the family, dated December 20, 1920, reached us in mid-January. It described the surgery as follows:

> Six days ago I had surgery on my bone behind my right ear to remove a mastoid which was festering. They scraped the bone to remove the cause. The surgery was performed under anesthesia. I still go around with my head bandaged, because the wound is not completely healed. The surgery and hospitalization was given to me free, as a member of the staff.

A letter from Sara, delivered around the same time by a soldier who had escaped and crossed battle-line, brought the message of Aron's illness. Only on February 1, again via a letter carried by a soldier from the battle-line, did we learn of Aron's death.

We were devastated by the news. Aron had been a hero to all of us. Only fourteen and still suffering from insecurity and twitching, I found the loss especially difficult. I resolved to take up the cause he had not been allowed to complete. I would become a medical doctor.

CHAPTER 4

Spiritual Stirrings

D espite the devout atmosphere of our home, my father's example of faith and the influence of the private high school, I was not known in the village for my piety. My pent-up energies found a release in playing pranks. Cats and dogs, for example, were not safe from me. Armed with a sling and smooth stones from the river, I was a deadly threat to them.

Sometimes I set my sights on human prey. One of these was Mrs. Berg, wife of a major landowner in the village. She angered me by repeatedly commenting negatively about my twitching. I thirsted for revenge. She frequently walked past the schoolhouse after visiting her mother who lived east of the school. I devised a plan. One section of sidewalk had a tree on one side and a thick hedge on the other. I tied one end of a long string to the tree and ran the rest of it across the sidewalk and through the hedge. Hiding behind the hedge in the dark I waited for Mrs. Berg. As she approached the string, I pulled it tight. She tripped and fell. Luckily she broke no bones. I had my revenge.

These pranks were my way of acting out adolescent frustrations. By today's standards I was not an evil child, but I was a loner who was haunted by a deep sense of sin and unworthiness, much of it instilled by my mother.

Mother was the central force in our household. With Father gone so often, she was left in charge of rearing—and disciplining—the family. Even though she loved me, she considered me a problem child, and I found her disapproval a crushing burden to bear. From the ages of seven to thirteen I received many spankings, all preceded by intense admonition and prayer. Toward evening I would be overcome by guilt when our Russian maid, gesturing to the corner of the house where my mother customarily balanced the behavior account of her son, would say, "Well Hans, will you and Mother need to visit the large room behind the oven again?" In my own mind I had become a "bad boy," and the pain of my low self-esteem ran deep.

My father, on the other hand, was gentle and tolerant. When he returned from his travels his warmth and love would be like a balm to my soul. But even his affirmation could not completely overcome my wounded self-image.

Meanwhile, our lives were facing threats of a different sort. The months of military occupation, the lack of proper food and inadequate medical provisions led to a serious epidemic of typhoid. Many people in the village died, among them my childhood friend Jacob Wall. His death affected me deeply. I lost a dear pal who had befriended me more than other boys.

Before long, however, I gained a new friend, somewhat older, who would become a pivotal influence in my life. He was David Reimer, son of the village blacksmith. A newly married young man, he took an interest in me in my early teens and guided me through my struggle with the social rejection I felt so keenly.

He invited me to his home for conversation as we would watch his two children together. He made no mention of my twitching problems or my isolation from other youths of my age. His pleasant personality relieved some of the family and high school tensions I felt. His deep understanding of the needs of a teenager gave me the confidence to share my struggles openly. Among other things, we discussed my relationships in the family. He pointed out how privileged I was to have a father who was so highly regarded for his exemplary devotion and lifestyle. I developed a sense of gratitude for what I had, for my performance in school, and for who I was as a person.

Our relationship was such that I was able to discuss my sense of guilt for being the black sheep who had caused my mother much pain. I felt comfortable expressing these feelings to my new friend. David gently suggested that the change I needed could only come about if I closed the past in repentance and accepted forgiveness. On a Sunday afternoon under the shade trees of the church yard, he pointed me to Jesus as the Savior. I experienced a conversion.

It was difficult to confess past wrongdoing to Mrs. Berg and several neighbors whose dogs and cats had been the target of my slingshot. But the humiliation was wholesome.

I applied for baptism in the summer of 1920. Because of my past and my young age there was a long deliberation in the congregation. Had Hans Toews really been born again? Was he a new creature? Wasn't he too young to be baptized? Adolf Reimer, who led the meeting, asked: "What will you do if the church says you are too young to be baptized?" I was ready with an answer: "Jesus tells me I must be baptized to tell all the people that I have become a follower of Christ. If the church says that I am too young, then they shall have to settle that with Jesus."

I was then asked to leave the meeting while my request was discussed. Later I was told that Mr. Reimer had asked the congregation, "Who is willing to answer Jesus, who has told Hans to be baptized?" No one responded. Family and friends testified on my behalf, and an affirmative decision was reached. I was baptized at age fourteen, perhaps the youngest person in the Mennonite Brethren Church of that day. A new chapter in my pilgrimage had begun.

A Caring Church

As a youth I experienced the church as a very caring community. The congregation, aware of my background as a loner, gave me much attention. After baptism I received instruction concerning lifestyle. The church membership covenant was quite detailed. Many things, such as tobacco and alcohol, were directly forbidden. I was instructed to love and to live a simple and exemplary lifestyle. Older brethren often took me aside to encourage me in my Christian walk. I joined a Sunday school class for young people and took my place in the weekly Bible study groups.

The church was concerned when I graduated from high school at age sixteen and prepared to enter college (*Agroschule*). Several other young men from the community planned to attend the same school. Would we young believers maintain a faithful testimony?

The church program provided many opportunities for young people to participate. I was sixteen when first asked to read Scripture and make comments as an introduction to the prayer meeting that preceded Sunday morning worship.

Services often went into the afternoon because the membership of the Alexandertal church was scattered over several villages (Elisabethtal, Steinbach, Schardau, Pordenau, Mariental, Rudnerweide and Grossweide) and transportation depended on horse and buggy.

The practice of church discipline touched me deeply. Every effort was made to maintain a strong testimony before the world. There were tears and sorrow when people were excommunicated. Simplicity of lifestyle was a major emphasis.

The revival meetings that became so prominent among North American Mennonite Brethren were unknown in Russia. Instead we had regular Bible conferences known as *Bibelbesprechungen.* Church leaders would gather in a central location and prepare the schedule for all Mennonite Brethren churches in the Molotschna Colony—Rueckenau, Blumenort, Tiege, Waldhcim, Sparrau, Alexandertal and Grossweide. Each church was assigned a portion of Scripture from the Gospels or the Epistles. The conferences lasted three or four days, including the weekends. People from neighboring churches would attend as possible, especially ministers, deacons and others carrying congregational responsibilities. Sessions were held mornings, afternoons and evenings.

Each session began with hymns and prayer. The standing or kneeling congregation would pray for enlightenment and openness to accept the Word. One of the ministers would lead the study, providing an overview of the entire passage under consideration and then leading verse-by-verse an exegetical study. The local ministers and those from other churches would join in the process of exposition. Sometimes the evening service would vary slightly, with one or two leading ministers expounding on a section of the passage selected for the occasion.

Visitors from a distance were lodged in the homes of local church members. Where facilities were suitable the noon meal was provided at the church, mostly consisting of *Zwieback,* some meat and coffee.

The *Bibelbesprechungen* were significant highlights in the life of the larger church. They provided understanding of biblical teaching and strengthened social and spiritual relationships in the church and in homes. Host congregations were often renewed with expressions of confession, repentance, cleansing, praise and rejoicing.

As a young man in my late teens I witnessed evenings of confession and cleansing that lasted to the early mornings. In times when there were no conversions the question would be asked: "Is there something in the life of the church that is hindering the Holy Spirit from convicting sinners and bringing them to repentance?" Church purity was seen as a prerequisite for an effective gospel witness. A popular passage was 1 Peter 4:17, "For it is time for judgment to begin with the family of God; and if it begins with us, what will the outcome for those who do not obey the gospel of God?"

Midweek meetings called *Bibelstunden* (Bible study hour) were a regular feature of local church life. Families took turns inviting the believers of their village to their home, usually for 7:30 on Wednesday evening. Some leader, not necessarily the host of the house, would guide the study and discussion, much like today's adult Sunday school classes. Typically the meeting concluded with participants kneeling for prayer.

Sunday evenings were set aside for youth gatherings. Young people would meet in groups for singing and testimonies, and frequently also for confession and prayer. Teenagers were encouraged to sing in the church choir, or in a special youth choir.

When I was eighteen years old some of the church leaders approached me about my potential for church ministry. Would I be willing to preach in a church service? I agreed, and a date was set for me to preach on a Sunday morning when I would be home for a weekend from the university. My text was Ezekiel 18:23, "Have I any pleasure at all that the sinner should die? saith the Lord God: and not that he should return from his ways' and live?" My sermon vividly depicted the lot of the sinner facing eternal death. Not everyone appreciated my message. A prominent man from the community was so offended he walked out.

The following weekend, when I was home again, David Doerksen, my former high school teacher, asked to go for a walk with me on Saturday evening. I knew what was coming. Kindly and lovingly he pointed out that my message had been too personal and negative. I had dwelt too heavily on the death of the sinner. Other men from the church also came to me with criticism. The admonitions were in order, but I did not respond well. It added to my resolve not to become a minister.

Starvation and Death

Two years of civil war had devastated the colonies. The southern part of the Molotschna had been affected more than the northern villages. The fall and winter of 1921 found us with insufficient food and clothing. The armies had consumed all the reserves.

Grandfather Janz, a miller, had secretly sent us supplies of flour, potatoes and beets. Mother hid the supplies in a secret opening behind a wall in the root cellar—a space that once had been a stairway but was closed during remodelling a few years earlier. A small hole, just big enough for me to squeeze through, gave access to the hiding place. In the evening

I would crawl through the hole to get supplies that mother would prepare for the family.

We would have had enough to last the winter, but Father, forever naive and goodhearted, insisted that the food be shared with the poor who had nothing. He would repeat the story of Elijah whom God sent to a poor widow in Zarephath who said,

> As the Lord thy God liveth, I have not a cake, but an handful of meal in a barrel, and a little oil in the cruse: and behold, I am gathering two sticks, that I may go in and prepare it for me and my son, that we may eat it, and die. And Elijah said unto her, Fear not; go and do as you have said. . . . For thus saith the Lord God of Israel, The barrel of meal shall not waste, neither shall the cruse of oil fail, until the day that the Lord sendeth rain upon the earth . . . And the barrel of meal wasted not, neither did the cruse of oil fail, according to the word of the Lord (1 Kings 17:12-16).

Our secret supplies gradually disappeared. Sharing our food with other people meant that for months our family had been taking very small rations. We were on the verge of starvation, but Father would remind us: "We cannot keep food for ourselves while other people are dying. We must share in their suffering. If other people die, we too must die with them." This was how my father understood the Christian faith.

Some people in the village got so desperate they ate cats and dogs. The day came when we as a family consumed our last remnant of bread baked from the flour of corn milled together with corn cobs, not very nutritious but something to fill the stomach. Jacob, eight years my junior, was bloated, a sign of the last stage of starvation. After this last meal we all knelt to pray, the final preparation for death. My father's prayer went something like this: "We thank you for this hour when we see no way for our survival. Glorify thyself according to thy choosing. You can provide food for us, or you can prepare us to die like many others who died of starvation." My father had often said, "When the need is the greatest, the help of God will be nearest."

In November 1921 we heard of help that was to come from America. Would it come before my brother Jacob died? Uncle Benjamin B. Janz, mother's brother, who was in Kharkov to open the way for American relief, knew of our critical condition. When the first shipment of canned milk arrived in Kharkov he thought of our starving family. In January Alvin J. Miller, an American, together with B. B. Janz, hired an old army truck to drive through the villages to inspect the conditions and prepare a method for food distribution. We never forgot the day when that old truck came to Alexandertal, carrying several boxes of canned milk. A day or two later, a package from Holland with twenty pounds of beans arrived at the post office in Alexandertal. Earlier that fall John F. Harms of Hillsboro, Kansas, who knew my father, had sent money to Mr. Gorter, pastor of a Mennonite church in Rotterdam, Holland, asking that a food parcel be sent to J. A. Toews in Alexandertal.

Jacob, near death, was slowly nourished back to life. Every hour, day and night, the six-year-old was given two tablespoons of milk. The sack of beans, rich in protein, was the beginning of our salvation. By March 1922 the American kitchen opened on the property of Heinrich Goossen, across the street from the school. American relief (the Mennonite Central Committee program) and the food parcels from Holland restored the food supply. Spring brought new life. Father's faith had triumphed.

The Mennonite Central Committee relief effort was of enormous historic significance. It launched a movement in world relief that has not waned to this day. I am still moved today when I read the letters of people who were saved from death, as recorded in David M. Hofer's book, *Die Hungersnot in Russland* (Starvation in Russia).[5] Pages 161-163 contain a letter from my father to the Mennonites in America, recognizing God's mercy in the hour of greatest need and expressing repentance for the Mennonites in Russia, who, despite their wealth, had shared so little with the needy in the world.

End of an Era

Amid the assaults of civil war and starvation, school life continued. In the spring of 1922, at the age of sixteen, I completed my four years of high school and took my exit examination.

The Mennonite colonies went by the European school system whereby students were judged exclusively on the basis of a final examination. The student appeared before an examining board (not including his teachers). Assignments, both oral and written, were written on large paper lots. The student then drew the lots for each subject, covering Bible, church history, mathematics, science, world history, and Russian and German composition. The entire process lasted three days. Despite the crises and interruptions of the last two years, I passed the exams with top grades.

As it turned out, I finished high school just in time. The new regime's anti-religious bias found its way to the Mennonite colonies, and things would never be the same again.

Our school was closed that fall; henceforth, private education would be forbidden. By Christmas my father was out of a job; as a minister he was no longer allowed to teach. Up to then, religious instruction had been central. It included courses in Bible introduction, Mennonite Confession of Faith, and Anabaptist and church history. In 1923 the government purged all religious influence from the schools.

Uprooted from Home

My father's dismissal from his teaching position had immediate implications for our day-to-day lifestyle. For one thing, it meant moving out of the schoolhouse we had occupied for so many years; for another, it meant finding a new means of livelihood.

Some years earlier Father had used money from an inheritance to buy a small farm of eighty-two acres across the street from the school. Since the new communist government had not yet implemented its land reform policies, the property still belonged to us.

A landless family, the Peter Foths, had lived in the house on the farm while the land was rented out to one of the larger local farmers. Over the years the rental income had supplemented my father's meager teacher's salary so that he could give time to spiritual ministry without remuneration.

In one of those reversals that were so common following the revolution, the Foth family now moved into the school to assume janitorial duties, and we moved across the street into the old house on the farmyard.

The house, dating back to the 1820s when the village was founded, was quite a contrast to what we were used to in the red brick schoolhouse. It was a clay hut with a thatch roof, perhaps the oldest and most primitive building in the village.

Church members helped us renovate the dilapidated cottage. The men dug out two feet of earth under part of the house to provide a higher ceiling. In one corner, next to the front entrance, was an unheated room that became my abode and would remain so until our escape from Russia.

My room had a dirt floor, but a wooden floor of six-inch boards was installed in the family room and two other living rooms.

The kitchen, in a corner of the utility room, had no outside window. The cookstove, made of brick with holes for kettles, was fueled by straw or shrubs. A large brick oven extended into the other three rooms to heat the living quarters and serve as a bake oven. It was stoked from the kitchen.

The barn had room for four horses, three cows, a small stall for a calf or a pig, and in one corner, closest to the large shed extending from the barn, a small chicken coop.

Our lifestyle had changed drastically, but Father would have no complaining. Even in these meager circumstances he found reason to be thankful.

Back to the Land

Getting started in agriculture was no easy task. Not only was my father not a skilled farmer, but the economic state of our colonies was in ruins. With few horses left in Alexandertal, much of the productive land could not be tilled. Wheat, barley and oat seed was in short supply. The livestock that remained was poorly fed and weak.

Many farmers had to work together to utilize whatever energy was left. We had the old gelding I had received in exchange for my beloved horse Major, and one milk cow. Heinrich Enns, a missionary to the Russians, had a cow, as did Heinrich Huebert, the owner of the windmill on the hill west of the village. This motley assortment of one old horse and three cows was assembled into a team to till our land. Training them to pull a cultivator or small plow became my difficult task, for I had gained at least some experience during my summers with Grandpa Janz. Neither my father, a teacher, nor Heinrich Enns, an evangelist, nor Heinrich Huebert, a professional miller, had any experience with primitive agriculture.

It is hard to imagine the emotional energy needed to coordinate, motivate and discipline this horse and cow combination. The Enns' cow was most problematic. After a round or two of the quarter-mile long field, she would simply lie down. Nothing could persuade her to get up and cooperate. Quite frequently I would see my father and Heinrich Enns kneel in the midst of the small acreage and pray while I applied every method possible—oral persuasion as well as the whip—to gain her compliance.

Corn—the only seed available—was planted with only the help of a spade. Later in spring seed for sugar cane and sunflower became available.

That crop yielded enough to provide grain for bread, sunflowers for oil, and basic feed for the livestock. Through various quarter, including direct gifts from our deacons and a church family, we now also had an ox, a cow, a year-old heifer, a pig and ten chickens.

Mennonite Central Committee had shipped some Fordson tractors to help families who had lost their horses. In the spring of 1923 they plowed a small acreage of land for families that needed help, and we were fortunate to be included. For the rest of our tilling we relied on our new team of one horse and the young ox, which was easier to train than the three cows.

Grandpa Janz furnished a wagon, a cultivator, a harrow and a threshing stone that could be pulled by one horse. Now we were in business. All of us pitched in. Mother, pragmatic and ingenious, did the planning. My sisters Liese and Helen both got involved. Though I was only sixteen, a recent high school graduate set to enter college in Gnadenfeld in September, I was in charge of operations. Together we sowed the crop in spring and weeded the corn and sunflower fields. Mother and my sisters put in a large garden of vegetables, with a small river flowing through it for irrigation.

Harvest was the most difficult. Several neighbors with horses cut the grain for us. With our old horse and the ox hitched to Grandpa's wagon we hauled the loose grain to the threshing floor we had prepared behind the barn and hayshed. There the horse would pull the threshing stone over the grain to loosen the husks. Then we used a hand-operated winnow to separate the grain from the chaff. The work was hard, but God blessed our efforts. Now we were really farmers!

Conditions improved considerably the following year. Larger sections of land could be tilled. We bought a second horse, made possible through money from Holland and North America designated to assist ministers and their families. People from the church offered more help to compensate for Father's ministry away from home. I came home on weekends and assisted where needed.

All in all the year 1924, in many ways, was much more normal. But now the Communist government tightened its grip. Land reforms were implemented. The future held out little hope for a return life as we had known it, and so the great Mennonite migration to Canada began.

Father's Faith

My father's resolute dependence on God never wavered during these trying times. His faith was as steady as it was simplistic. I have rarely seen its equal. To this day, when I remember my father I am reminded of the words of Jesus to Thomas: "Blessed are they that have not seen and yet believe" (John 20:29). A few examples will illustrate.

As mentioned earlier, our area had been the scene of endless civil strife as one military division after another marched through. Our villages changed hands sixteen times as the armies struggled back and forth between offense and retreat. In the process they stripped our orchards bare of fruit.

Jacob, whom we called Jasch, hungered for an apple during the approaching Christmas season. "Papa," he asked with concern in his voice, "will we get an apple for Christmas?" Father's answer to the six-year-old was, "Jasch, we have no apples, but God can send us apples for Christmas." The two of them then knelt down and asked God for apples.

On Christmas Eve thousands of troops passed through our villages. A military truck, part of a long convoy loaded with produce, was unable to make the grade on the banks of the Yuschanlee River in a heavy rain. A farmer in Steinfeld, a village some fifteen miles to the west of Alexandertal, was called to hitch his horses to the truck and pull it uphill. It worked, and the grateful lieutenant of the convoy offered the farmer some produce from the truck. The farmer, who knew our family, asked, "Is the convoy passing through the village of Alexandertal?" Yes, it was. "In the middle of Alexandertal is a schoolhouse," the farmer continued. "A teacher's family lives there. If you want to reward me for my help you can drop off a box of apples at that schoolhouse."

The convoy reached our village in the early evening. We were bewildered when a military truck stopped in front of our house and the lieutenant lifted off a full box of apples and brought it to our door. He left with no explanation. Now Jasch had apples for Christmas, and we were all duly thankful. Father, of course, did not fail to explain to Jasch the secret of answered prayer. Some time later we learned the background to the answered prayer when the Steinfeld farmer inquired whether we had received apples for Christmas.

In late fall of 1922 a Russian evangelist came to Alexandertal. Our three-room teacherage, already crowded for a family of eight, still had room for the evangelist who needed a place to stay. In the conversation Father discovered that the man had only the shirt he was wearing, and it was torn at several places.

The scene is still vivid in my mind. Father came into the kitchen with the question: "Mother, don't I have two shirts?" Mother, suspecting what might come, did not answer. He asked again, "Mother, don't I have two shirts?" Quietly mother answered: "Yes Daddy, you have only two shirts and you need them to change when you go on your next trip to a Bible conference." "But Mother, the Russian brother's shirt is falling apart and I still have two. Will you get one so I can give him a shirt." Mother had tears in her eyes as she went to a drawer in the next room and brought a shirt. But my father wasn't finished. "Mother, I have one old shirt and one new shirt. Is this the old or the new one?" "But Daddy," she protested, "you have only one shirt left." "But Mamma," he countered, "does not the Bible say you shall give to God the best? I cannot give the brother the second best."

Mother went back to get the new shirt and handed it to my father. "Here, she said, "this is the new one, but what will you do when you are far from home and need a change?" "Mamma," my father answered, "can't we trust God to provide a shirt?"

When my father was released from his position as a teacher just before Christmas 1922 he accepted it as divine providence. Now all his time could be devoted to spiritual ministry. The timing seemed ideal, for in 1923 there was a great spiritual revival in response to the tragedies of starvation and civil war. In spring of 1923 a commission requested that father and Aron Dick from Prangenau spend several months on a mission assignment to the Mennonite churches in the Omsk and Orenburg settlements. Father, with only one shirt, was inadequately clothed for the assignment.

Meanwhile a shipment of clothing had arrived from MCC in America. One of the deacons from the church, who helped distribute the clothing, came to Mother to ask about Father's shirt size. "There are several shirts and I thought your husband, who is often away from home, and might need some."

Two new shirts were brought to our house. When Father was told about this unexpected gift he said, "Mamma, don't you see now, we gave away my one shirt, and the Lord gives us back double."

Shortly before Father's departure to the east one of our two cows became ill and died. The loss was a terrible blow to the family. Typically, Father gathered us together for prayer. We desperately needed another cow to provide milk for the family. This, along with the need for additional clothing, became a matter of concern. He wondered: Was it the Lord's will that he spend several months in Siberia? Father announced to the family that the Lord needed to confirm his will with regard to the Siberian assignment. He would pray for a cow and for adequate clothing. One week before the planned date of departure two deacons bought a cow from the Wiebes in Schardau. What a moment when these men turned into our yard leading a cow that had just freshened!

Only three days before the date of departure a new shipment of clothing from America arrived in our village. The shipment contained two woolen army blankets. A deaconess from the church knew Father needed a suit. She told Mother of the two green army blankets: could they provide the cloth for a suit? Three women came to the house to help Mother, and in two days they had sewn a suit. So one day before Father's departure there was the new cow, a source of milk for the family, and the new suit. We all rejoiced together. Once again, Father's faith had been vindicated.

The tangible evidence of my father's answered prayers had a powerful impact on my spiritual development. On the one hand, it appeared that God really entered into issues so mundane as apples, beans, the family cow and an army blanket suit as the affirmation of his care. On the other hand, I struggled to reconcile this with the larger issues of the carnage of war, starvation, and the typhoid epidemic that claimed the lives of many villagers including the revered missionary Adolf Reimer, father of my dear friend Daniel.

Reflections

Illness, family separation, death, civil war, starvation—these were the dramas of my first sixteen years. My life was being shaped in ways I did not yet understand. As Scripture says, "It is good for man that he bear the yoke in his youth" (Lam. 3:27).

Our family had varying responses to the buffeting circumstances. The younger boys, Jacob and Henry, may have seen it all as an adventure, as did my younger sister Lydia, who was always on top of things and ready for excitement. My half-sister Liese, the oldest and the one who struggled with symptoms of tuberculosis inherited from her mother, reflected a melancholy outlook that was common at the time. Helen, always the sparkle of the family with the guitar under her arm and a voice like a nightingale, provided hope in our darkest hours. My father's unswerving faith provided an anchor for us all. My mother undergirded us with an ingenuity that always saw a way out of any dilemma. All this was working together to produce in me a particular kind of clay, pliable enough to be molded, yet firm enough to hold shape.

CHAPTER 5

College . . . And More!

The agricultural college in Gnadenfeld was a new venture established by the Mennonite colony. Its campus was the buildings of the colony's former district offices, which had been dissolved by the communist regime. The major emphasis was agriculture, virtually guaranteeing the approval of the government, but there was also a strong science department, my major interest. The death of my brother Aron, as a young physician, had sparked my resolve to study medicine and take his place.

During this time the communist regime took full control of all colleges and universities. Gnadenfeld became a satellite of the university in Kiev. A political instructor was assigned to Gnadenfeld to integrate our college into the system of communist indoctrination.

A girls high school that had been closed by the communists provided dormitory facilities. I was fortunate to get a tiny room, sufficient for a bed, a small table and a chair. Clothing, of which I had only the bare necessities, was kept in a box under the bed. A small pantry served as a storage place for food, which students had to provide themselves.

I earned money for rent, books and incidental expenses by working five hours per day, five days per week in a sunflower oil processing plant about half a mile from the college. Since Gnadenfeld was only a three-hour walk from Alexandertal, I could go home on weekends for food supplies. Our diet, following the 1922 starvation, consisted mostly of black bread my mother baked, some vegetables, carrots and red beets, plus occasional apples, prunes and pears. Sunflower oil, which I could get cheaply at the processing plant, served as a dip or sop for the bread. Even though the menu lacked variety, the food was good. Of course, after the years of starvation everything tasted good. The Janz grandparents, my second home in Konteniusfeld, were only a ninety-minute walk from Gnadenfeld and served as a second source of food.

The daily schedule during the week was quite uniform. From 7:00 a.m. to noon I attended lectures. From 1:00 p.m. to 6:00 p.m. I worked at the oil processing plant, running the presses. I would return to my room at 6:30, eat my evening meal, and then study 7:00 p.m. until midnight. The academic demand was much more stringent than what I would later find in colleges and universities in North America. On weekends, with some exceptions during exams, I walked three hours on Friday night so I could spend Saturday helping around the home. In spring, for seeding time, I would take off a week or ten days to put in the crop, than make up the academic work later.

My health gradually improved. I had a growth spurt and finally reached normal height. I became physically stronger. My nervous twitchings lessened, depending on the state of my emotions. The academic demands presented no problem.

Consolidation of Communism

The victory of communism was followed by a rapid process of consolidation. Land reform and the educational system were first priorities. As noted earlier, my father was released as a teacher because he was a minister. Radical restrictions were placed upon estate owners. Numerous families from the estates were killed; others fled to the villages of the mother colonies. They were stripped of their wealth and their social structure dismantled. A people of will and ingenuity was crushed. Many became refugees. As early as 1921, petitions were made to emigrate. The book *Lost Fatherland: The Story of the Mennonite Emigration from Soviet Russia, 1921-1927* by John B. Toews, my nephew, documents well the conditions affecting the social and economic life of Mennonites in the post-revolution era.[6] The first group of 726 emigrants left for Canada on June 22, 1923. Larger groups left for Canada in 1924 and 1925. Among them were some people from Alexandertal.

My father promoted emigration for those who could leave, though he personally did not feel the liberty to consider this option. As a minister he felt an obligation to those who didn't qualify. The shepherd, he said, does not leave the flock. He felt bound by the words of John 10:11: "the good shepherd giveth his life for the sheep."

Faculty and students at the college felt increasing pressure to conform to the doctrines of communism. In 1924 this became a direct order. It became clear that only those who identified with the ideology of communism would be able to enter the graduate programs required for a professional future. The communist anthem was introduced as the theme song on all university campuses. Those of us who professed to be Christians could not sing along with the words: "There is no help from higher beings, no God, no Czar, no Potentate. We are the people of the future, the past we will destroy and build a people's future" (free translation).

I came back for the fall of 1924, my third year. On a balmy Sunday evening I had joined a group of students on a stroll through the woods on the south side of the college campus. The conversation drifted to a discussion of our future plans. My family identity was well known to my comrades. When my turn came to share my future plans I boldly declared my resolve to go into medicine, to remain true to the legacy of my brother Aron.

"You, a medical doctor," sneered one of the students who was known to be sympathetic to the new ideology. "You are a preacher's kid and you too will end up as a preacher," he continued sarcastically. My honor was hurt. Without any serious thought I snapped back, "I swear, I will never become a preacher." I made the oath with an uplifted fist.

Later in the evening, back in my small room, I came under deep conviction for what I had said. I considered myself a Christian. What if God's will for me would be different?

Plunging into a Coma

Monday morning I was one of several students assigned to help the agricultural department thresh some stacked grain. In the process a problem developed with the straw stacker. A rope on a pulley attached to a pole some forty feet high was used to pull the straw net up so it could be emptied on top of a straw stack. On the other end of the rope was a team of horses to pull the straw net up. The rope had slipped off the pulley, stalling the whole operation. Someone needed to climb up the forty foot pole and force the rope back onto the wheel of the pulley.

The foreman called for volunteers, but everyone was hesitant. Finally I stepped forward and climbed the pole to correct the problem. As I was working on it the team of horses suddenly lurched forward, squeezing my hand into the pulley. I screamed and plunged forty feet to the ground, landing on my head. I was limp and unconscious, but still breathing. The university doctor examined me and declared the injury to be fatal. Her diagnosis was a broken neck.

The following sequence was reported to me when I regained full consciousness eight days later. A rider on horseback was dispatched to notify my parents. Father and Mother arrived in late afternoon, only to be told by the university doctor that the injury was fatal and there was no hope that I could survive.

My parents had come on a borrowed "drugge," a long flat wagon used for hauling merchandise. I was carefully placed on the wagon and taken to Alexandertal. After consultation with a village nurse, I was taken to a Doctor Bitner in Alexanderkrone, the village of my Grandparents Toews. Dr. Bitner examined me, confirmed the diagnosis of a broken neck, and refused to touch the problem.

For several days I lay unconscious in the house of my Uncle Abram Toews whose second wife, Tante Lena, was a trained nurse. I would regain consciousness for short periods, then slip back again.

I particularly remember one moment of consciousness. I noticed my mother kneeling next to my bed. I heard her plead with God to let me die because if I lived I would be too brain damaged to think properly. She was my first perception in the week-long coma. The second perception was to recall my angry vow, "I swear, I will never become a preacher." As my consciousness returned in successive intervals, I kept remembering that vow.

Dr. Heinrich Wiebe, a bonesetter (chiropractor) lived in Lichtfelde, the neighboring village to Alexanderkrone. He came to examine me, and confirmed the diagnosis of the other doctors. According to the report of my mother, Wiebe was reluctant to attempt any treatment. "The chances of success are very narrow," he said. "He may die under my hands if I attempt to set the bone in his neck."

My family waited another few days and watched my chances for life continue to fade. After much prayer they finally reached a decision: "Hans cannot live in the condition he is in. Wiebe's fear that he may die in the attempt to adjust the broken neck is the risk we must take." Surrounding my bed with Uncle Abram, Aunt Helen and the nurse, Father and Mother then committed me to God—for life or for death.

I was transported to Wiebe's office in Lichtfelde. The experienced bonesetter made careful preparations. He placed two planks across two sawhorses with a space in between for him to work from below in the attempt to set the broken vertebrae. Ropes were attached to a harness around my head and feet. Four strong men were selected, two at my head and two at my feet. Wiebe knelt under the planks. Upon his command the men pulled with all their strength to straighten the vertebrae. As they pulled, Wiebe managed to shift the broken bones into place. At that moment I suddenly regained full consciousness, opened my eyes and looked around, like awakening from a long dream.

The neck was carefully braced. I was moved back to Aunt Helen's house for a few days. Then, lying flat on the "drugge," my parents transported me back to Alexandertal.

I healed remarkably quickly. Within five weeks I went back to the university wearing a neck support. Students and faculty helped me make up the work I had missed. I passed the Christmas exams.

My vow against the ministry remained central in my thoughts. I began to regard the accident as a providential act of God for it forced me to recognize my rebellion. After much struggle I came to an inward concession to be open if God called me to the ministry. But it was a conditional concession that I serve as a doctor of medicine, or some other profession, so I could be independent and not subject to the poverty we had experienced in my youth. I was open to the ministry as long as I could remain economically independent.

Pressure to Conform

In 1925 the pressure on society and especially the church to identify with communism intensified. All administrative posts in the colonies and villages required an open identification with communism. Membership in a church became a disqualifying factor for any office in civil service. I was shaken to see some men, who held leading positions in church, withdraw from the fellowship. Father, as a minister, was stripped of all citizenship rights. He could not participate in any function or vote that related to the social life of the village. A tax was imposed on churches for every recognized minister who continued in active service.

Mother's brother, B. B. Janz, who at the time served as representative of all Mennonites before the government, had been urging his family, including my parents, to prepare to emigrate. His brother Jacob Janz had already gone to Canada in 1924. We as a family submitted to a medical examination to determine our eligibility to also migrate to Canada. Jascha, Helen and I were found to have trachoma, a highly contagious eye disease. People with this disease were disqualified for Canadian immigration.

Political conditions became more and more threatening for the church. Father began to question his own church involvement because any official relationship with a minister was becoming a liability for the people. Uncle B. B. Janz continued to urge Father to consider leaving.

Arrested!

Meanwhile, a sudden crisis at college pounded home the reality of how vulnerable our lives had become. Dr. Ernst Schrill, a zealous communist from the University of Berlin, was assigned to the Gnadenfeld campus as a political instructor. All students were required to attend the three lectures per week intended to indoctrinate us. The focus of the lectures was to continuously discredit Christian beliefs and promote a humanistic worldview. Christian students were singled out for special attention. During the Christmas recess I seriously weighed whether to return for the concluding semester.

In January of 1926 I received notice to report for induction into the Red Army at the close of the school year. My claim for conscientious objection resulted in a call to appear before a court in Halbstadt to defend my position. I prepared my case very carefully and became one of the few conscientious objectors to be granted an exemption. Others from our group were denied this privilege. A number of them who continued to refuse to bear arms when inducted were court-marshalled. Some went before a firing squad. Others perished in Siberian labor camps.

The school year was drawing to a close. I was to complete my last year with specialization in science as a prerequisite for the medical faculty.

Dr. Schrill's lectures continued. He openly defied any belief in God. He would bring a Bible to class and make a show of standing on it while challenging the existence of God and revelation. He devoted a series of lectures to the process of evolution. He described a mysterious process of rotating atoms producing friction that resulted in extreme heat, giving birth to the first cell of life.

After many hours of enduring what I considered nonsense, I ventured a question: "Dr. Schrill, do you have any explanation for what you call an unknown cause?" Visibly irritated by the question coming from someone known to be a Christian, he replied in anger, "No one can answer your question; only God in heaven knows that." The whole class erupted with laughter. His intended slur had instead wiped out the basic assumption of his lectures. Furious, he strode out of the lecture room with the student body still laughing.

Earlier, Dr. Schrill had made cynical reference to his pious mother who was praying for her wayward son. Evidently his subconscious retained some spiritual vocabulary from his childhood teaching. What was intended as a curse had instead undermined his own argument.

Within thirty minutes I was arrested, accused of spreading counter-revolutionary propaganda on campus, and held in a room adjoining the office. The entire student body immediately rose to my defence. The debacle, they said, was Dr. Schrill's own fault. They demanded my release. After a few hours I was set free.

The incident put a big question mark over my future. The next day the campus physician advised me to disappear from campus to escape further indictments. But how could I leave just before the final exams? A few days later she again took me aside. She had gotten wind of plans to charge me as anti-revolutionary, a most serious indictment for those days. "Your health is not good," she said. "I can give you a pass to leave campus for an extended sick leave in need of climate change." In retrospect, I can see that Dr. Manja Kaschanska saved my future. I left my belongings on campus, as if to indicate that I would be coming back. Then I went home to consult with the family.

Carefully we planned our next move. Helen and I would travel to Kharkov, ostensibly to have an eye specialist treat our trachoma. While there we would consult with Uncle Benjamin. Our timing was providential, as we were able to help our uncle make his own escape. Now, some seventy years later, it seems like a plot from a mystery thriller. At the time it was terrifying.

Secret Messenger

As the advocate for Mennonite emigration, which required continuous negotiations with senior government officials, Uncle Benjamin's position was growing ever more precarious. He had quietly been making his own preparations to leave. He secretly obtained a visa from the German Consulate in Kharkov. Under the pretense that a Mennonite representative needed to negotiate agricultural and economic exchanges with the West, he also obtained a Russian passport and an exit permit.

During our visit, events moved swiftly to a climax. In the early morning of May 31 a message showed up mysteriously at our uncle's office. It warned that the secret police (G.P.U.) planned to arrest him the next night. No one knew who delivered it.

Uncle Benjamin continued his regular schedule in the Mennonite offices. At noon he packed his most needed documents and belongings. David Reimer, my mentor from Alexandertal, happened to be in Kharkov. He planned the escape for B. B. Janz.

While the office followed its usual routine, Reimer bought a ticket on the courier train that was to leave for Moscow in the early evening. A coded telegram was sent to C. F. Klassen, then the Mennonite representative in Moscow. Supper was served at the regular time so the housemaid would not suspect anything. The railroad depot was within walking distance.

As darkness fell on the city, Uncle Benjamin put on an old overcoat with a hood to hide his identity. He used a cane and leaned heavily on it while my sister Helen, disguised as an old woman, walked at his side, supporting him. David Reimer took the suitcases to the depot by taxi. I went to the depot separately. My sister and Uncle Benjamin, looking like a feeble old couple, entered the station. When the train came in, David Reimer took the baggage aboard as if he were a passenger. Then, just before the train started to leave, Reimer stepped out, passed the ticket to Uncle Benjamin, helped him onto the train, and stepped back off just before the train moved into the night.   In Moscow C. F. Klassen was there to meet B. B. Janz. With the exit permit and visa for Germany in hand, covert arrangements were made to leave Russia. On June 4 he made it safely across the border.

The secret note had been correct. During the night of Janz's departure the police came to arrest him. But they were too late; he was out of their reach. B. B. Janz's family, for whom he had also secured the necessary documentation, followed him into Germany a few weeks later. Our mission accomplished, Helen and I returned home.

Our Turn to Leave

Uncle Benjamin's escape was our clear signal to leave. I no longer had a choice in the matter; I could not stay after the confrontation with Dr. Schrill. Even Father had by now concluded that his leadership of the church was no longer viable. His brother, Aron Toews, had already left with his family the year before.

Passport applications were filed for my Grandparents Janz, my uncle Abram Toews and his family, and our entire family. My grandparents, the Abram Toewses and my oldest sister Liese were all cleared for emigration to Canada. But there was still our problem with trachoma. Helen, Jacob and I made several appearances before the Canadian Doctor Drurie, but were not given clearance.

My stay grew more precarious by the day. The Gnadenfeld college expected me back to finish my degree. David Reimer accepted the responsibility to negotiate my passport. This would require 250 rubles, which Grandfather Janz paid. Everyone else except my father also received passports. While passing through Europe Uncle Benjamin arranged with the Dutch Mennonite Relief Committee to issue an entrance visa for our family to enter Holland, where trachoma was no hindrance.

My father's oldest brother, Jacob Toews, lived in Pordenau, the second village east of Alexandertal. His daughters Sara was a very close friend of Tina Driedger, whose family were members of our church in Alexandertal. Our frequent visits at Uncle Jacob's home led to a close relationship with my cousin Sara and her friend Tina.

As I prepared to leave Russia my feelings for Tina came to the surface. With everything up in the air, I felt this was not the time for romance. The closer the day of our planned departure came, the more I was led to consider our relationship. We spent a few evenings together and discussed what course to take. Should we become engaged, as my sister Helen and David Pauls were planning to do?

My status—and future—was in question. Would I be caught while trying to escape? The uncertainty was too great to make any life commitment. We mutually agreed that this was not the time. After I was safely across the border we would review our relationship more objectively.

On September 4, 1926 the church held a farewell for Helen, Liese and me. As planned, the engagement of Helen to David Pauls, who also was waiting for a passport, was announced.

In Alexanderkrone we met the Grandparents Janz. Uncle Abram's family was also ready for departure. The next day we left for Melitopol, the closest railroad station to the east of the colony to board the train for Moscow. Accompanying us was Daniel Reimer, my childhood friend with whom a close bond had developed as we became young adults.

Our train for Moscow was scheduled to leave Melitopol at midnight. Because I was subject to the military draft, I had to secure a police permit to travel, with a specific address where I could be reached. In mid-afternoon I went to the police headquarters to register my future address in Moscow. Of course, I said nothing of my intent to leave Russia.

As I emerged from the police office into a large hall of the headquarters a huge shock awaited me. Suddenly I was face to face with my nemesis, Dr. Ernst Schrill.

"What are you doing here?" he demanded. "Stay right here and don't move."

As he turned into the police office from which I had just come I dashed through a back door into the alley. Without looking back I ran through the alleys to the hotel where the family was waiting to go to the railroad station.

We held a quick strategy council and decided the group would head for the station but I would split off a few blocks before we reached it. The train was due at midnight. Daniel Reimer and I would watch the station from a distance until the train came, noting which car the family was boarding. When the bell rang to signal the train was leaving I would climb aboard at the last minute.

Shortly before the train arrived Daniel and I knelt in a dark alley and prayed together. The train came in. The plan was followed. I boarded the train just before the signal for its departure.

The trip to Moscow was uneventful. Here we parted from the Abram Toews family, Grandpa and Grandma Janz and our sister, Liese. C. F. Klassen, whom David Reimer had wired after I was safely on the train, met us. When we related our experiences of the last few days in Melitopol he recognized the seriousness of the situation.

A problem remained. The police office in Melitopol had the number of my passport. Alerted by the angry Dr. Schrill, they no doubt would notify police in Leningrad where we were to board a ship to Riga, Latvia. Klassen suggested the following strategy.

I needed a new passport number. He knew some officials who could be trusted but the process would take at least a week. In the meantime I had to hide. Helen and I were given rooms in the attic of a three-story house. My parents, who had been with us in Melitopol, were very conscious of the precarious situation. Now back in Alexandertal, they were in continuous prayer.

After eight days of waiting, I received a passport with a new number. A different border crossing was assigned. A night train took us to Sebej, a small border crossing on the way to Riga.

Grandfather Janz, always very frugal, had accumulated a few thousand rubles. Because there was no banking system in the colonies, he kept the money hidden in fifty and one hundred ruble bills. After the revolution the money had no value. I asked Grandfather to give me a few hundred rubles as souvenirs. On the train from Moscow to the border I remembered that the bills were in my suitcase. Helen urged me to throw them out of the window of the moving train so I wouldn't get caught with them. But I wanted to keep them, so I hid them behind a partition next to a window, where I was sure they'd be safe. After the inspection I would retrieve them.

When we reached the border everyone was ordered to detrain. Each passenger was searched. Some had to undress. I had a guitar with me. Even though I had acquired a permit to take it across the border, one of the inspectors questioned me about it repeatedly. He suspected I had something hidden inside. Just then two heavily armed guards strode in holding my hidden bills! They stopped at each passenger seeking a confession of ownership. I froze in fear.

As they came closer I continued to argue with my inspector and suddenly smashed the guitar open to prove there was nothing hidden. In the intensity of the moment the other guards passed by to question someone else.

The tour of inspection seemed endless. Would they come back to question me? I tied the broken pieces of the guitar together. Helen had been taken to a separate room and was searched to her underwear. Finally, all who were to cross the border were lined up and marched to the train. Helen, not knowing that the money had been discovered, thought we should go back into the same car. But instead I took her arm and insisted we go to the one farthest away.

The guards made one more pass through the cars. As the train began to crawl the Russian personnel stepped off and Latvians came aboard. Slowly the train pulled away from the border.

A Latvian conductor came into our car and gave us a friendly greeting in German. The tension was broken. Helen burst into tears. "Don't cry," the conductor said. "You're free now. You're in Latvia." By morning we arrived in Riga.

Our first task in the morning was to write our parents that we had safely crossed the border. We spent the next few days in a migrant house. All passengers and their belongings were disinfected because of lice and other insects. On the second day we were free to go into town. We were amazed at the new world. The stores were filled with merchandise.

Within a few days we were pronounced ready to proceed. C. F. Klassen had wired Berlin to inform Alexander Fast, who served as host for immigrants passing through Germany. He had met every train from Riga in the past few days, and he was there to receive us as we stepped from the train. He was fully informed of the arrangement with the Dutch Relief Committee. A few days later George DeYoung, a Dutch industrialist, came to Berlin to take us to Amsterdam.

CHAPTER 6

Dutch Interlude

Members of the Doopzgesinde Gemeinde (Dutch Mennonite Church) and their pastor, C. F. Gorter, assumed responsibility for us. I was billeted with the family of George van Tigchelhoven, foreman on the docks of Rotterdam harbor. Their three daughters, all single and at home, were teachers. Their only son Peter was married, had one daughter, and managed a bank in the city.

Helen was assigned as the chambermaid for Mrs. DeYoung. George DeYoung's brother Ferdinand was Minister of Commerce in the Dutch government. We spent one of the first weekends with the DeYoungs on a large yacht on the North Sea. Ferdinand took a great interest in our family background. He learned that my father was a minister and that he had been denied a passport to migrate.

Ferdinand had diplomatic connections with a Russian delegation who bought some purebred stock of Dutch dairy cows. Through them he negotiated a passport and exit visa for my father. Just before Christmas our family was reunited in Holland. Only Liese, who had gone to Canada with the Abram Toewses, and Grandparents Janz were missing.

Arrangements were made for my parents to stay in a hotel. Jasch (Jacob) and Lydia found a home with a young couple, the J. Veendorps, who had no children. Mr. Veendorp was the superintendent of the Rotterdam Zoo. Heinz (Henry), who was eight at the time, was placed in the home of a widow, Mrs. F. Zoote, and her daughter, a high school teacher. Christmas in the hotel, with the family reunited, was memorable.

Helen, Jacob and I were placed in care of an eye specialist who gave us weekly treatments for trachoma. What had been planned to be only a short stopover in Holland stretched to a year and a half.

Our Dutch Benefactors

The families we lived with practiced their Anabaptist commitment very differently than what we were used to. They understood church membership as largely a matter of form with no personal claim to experiential faith. After work Mr. von Tigchelhoven would relax in his easy chair with a thick cigar. He attended church only on very special occasions. His wife and daughters, however attended regularly. Son Peter, the bank manager, followed the practice of his father.

They treated us with great kindness and compassion. Frequently they invited the rest of my family to their home. We shared many meals with them. Whenever they noticed a need that the church relief committee had not looked after, they stepped in and provided. The first suit I ever possessed was a gift from the von Tigchelhovens, purchased from a prestigious clothing store. The other families—the Veendorps, Zootes and DeYoungs—were similarly kind in caring for our needs.

The Doopsgezinde church was an imposing structure hidden in an inner court and surrounded by a high wall, a protective measure left over from the sixteenth century when Anabaptists were routinely persecuted.

The worship services were rather formal. One of the two pastors of the church was a woman. The service consisted of organ music, a few hymns, some liturgy and the sermon.

The interior of the church featured a high elevated pulpit with some less elevated seats for the church elders who would be formally ushered in together with the pastors. The inner wall of the church, decorated with artistic woodwork, had two levels of elevated pews that were owned by selected families. Each end had a gate with artistic carving. An usher would lead the family to its section, open the gate for them and then close it again. The DeYoungs belonged to the class that owned such seats. Common members, meanwhile, sat in chairs in the middle of the church.

During our eighteen months in Rotterdam we sat with the DeYoungs in their private pew. I remember being invited to an informal meeting after the service in the conference room behind the sanctuary. The church board and Pastor Gorter and the woman pastor sat around the large conference table. All except the woman pastor were smoking thick cigars and drinking either beer or wine. In a very congenial atmosphere they asked Father to share with them about Mennonite Brethren life in Russia. For an hour he sketched the historical background of the Mennonite Brethren and described our practices and basic understanding of the New Testament church.

My sister Helen reported that the DeYoungs spoke freely to her, inquiring about her faith and that of the Mennonite Brethren. One incident stands out. The DeYoungs had a beautiful flower garden behind their home. In the evening Helen would frequently spend time there while the

DeYoungs read or chatted in the large family room. One evening, some time before our parents arrived in December, Helen took her guitar to the garden and sang the hymn, "A Wonderful Savior is Jesus My Lord, A Wonderful Savior to Me." When she finished all the verses (she knew 140 hymns by memory and played the guitar well), the call bell rang. Inside, she found Mr. De Young pacing the room. He asked my sister to sit down.

"Helen" he said in his fluent German, "how can you sing, considering your situation. Your parents, two brothers and one sister are in Russia. Your fiance is also in Russia. You don't know if any of them will ever come out. You may never be reunited. How can you sing in the midst of these circumstances?" Helen, open as always, gave her testimony. She had Jesus, she said, and he had promised not to leave nor forsake us. Then, at their request, she sang the song again. Mr. DeYoung continued to pace as she sang. When she was finished, he with tears in his eyes said, "I would give a million dollars if I could have your faith."

The Tigchelhovens would also invite Helen over to play her guitar and sing. Often our whole family would sing along. Our type of faith was often the subject of conversation. It was something new to them. Yet it seemed to strike a deep chord of need in the Dutch Mennonite soul.

A Spiritual Wilderness

The eighteen months in Holland were a time of confused transition for me. On one hand it was a time of calm after a difficult childhood and a tempestuous youth. On the other hand I felt isolated and at sea. I had survived the past but faced an uncertain future.

The Volks University of Amsterdam, only thirty minutes away by train, operated a satellite program in Rotterdam. The teachers of the Tigchelhoven household encouraged me to enroll in some courses. I felt little urge to pursue my aim to become a physician, since my future was so uncertain and my stay in Holland only temporary.

In January of 1927 I enrolled in two courses at the university, One in philosophy of modern thought and one in religion. Rationalism in Europe was in its heyday. Adding that to my pietist training, personal conversion and exposure to atheistic indoctrination in Russia, only made my sense of intellectual and spiritual restlessness more acute.

The time in Holland became for me perhaps what Arabia may have been for the Apostle Paul. I was in a strange land, without close friends, a lonely person bereft of direction or purpose. My father noticed my gradual withdrawal from the family, my melancholy mood, and my groping for moorings. The various assaults on my belief system were taking a toll. Communism vehemently denied the supernatural. Rationalism denied all claims of certainty and limited reality to the realm of intellectual perception. My confidence in God began to waver. In late fall of 1927, a year after our escape from Russia, I fell into depression. What was life, without an anchor? Early one morning, without informing my host family or the parents, I took the train to the beach area known as the Hook of Holland, only forty minutes from Rotterdam. I spent all day wandering by the water, searching for light. I walked so long that I missed the evening train that was due in Rotterdam at 9:00 and had to take the last train of the day, which arrived in the city after 11:30.

By then I'd missed the last streetcar so I began walking the four miles to Belleforstraat 81, the address of my hosts. When I reached the Rotterdam city square I stopped to rest on a bench. I found myself sitting in the shadow of a monument in honor of William of Orange, who in the seventeenth century delivered the Netherlands from the oppression of the French.

In recognition of his deep religious commitment an open Bible was placed under glass at the foot of the monument. A spotlight illuminated the page, open to Psalm 119:89. In bold Dutch script I saw the words, "Forever, O Lord, thy word is settled in heaven. Thy faithfulness is unto all generations: thou hast established the earth and it abideth."

It was midnight. Under the monument of William of Orange in the city square of Rotterdam I found the answer to my search for an absolute. There God convinced me that there is an absolute and the mystery of this absolute rests in him. It was like a spiritual rebirth, the new beginning of a long spiritual, pilgrimage. The patience and faithfulness of God had persisted. In the words of Jeremiah, the potter continued to work the clay, hoping to form a vessel for his own purpose (Jer. 18:6).

The beautiful monument was destroyed by the Germans in the bombing of Rotterdam during the second World War. But its message to me in my time of need has endured to this day.

Southhampton, England

The Canadian Pacific Steamship Line and Canadian Pacific Railway (CPR) had contracted with the Mennonite Board of Colonization to transport Russian Mennonites on credit. Like so many migrant families, we did not have the means for the ocean voyage or the railroad fare within Canada.

Immigrants who did not pass the test required by the Canadian Department of Health but had already left their homeland (Russia, Poland, Romania, Bessarabia) were detained in a CPR camp in Southhampton, England. In most cases the problem was trachoma. The camp was administered by Dr. Benjamin Unruh, brother to A. H. Unruh, who would later become my colleague. Dr. Unruh suggested our transfer from Rotterdam to Southhampton. Among the more than two hundred detainees there were many children who needed a school while undergoing medical treatment. Our family was well suited to help teach these immigrant children, since Father was an experienced teacher, I had advanced education and Helen could teach kindergarten. Such a move would also relieve the Dutch Mennonite Church from the responsibility of supporting us.

My university class concluded in December. The move to Southhampton would enable us to continue treatment for our trachoma as well as be of service to other immigrants. So shortly before Christmas of 1927 we bid farewell to our Dutch benefactors and crossed the English channel.

During the year and a half in Holland I had continued my correspondence with Tina. (The mail to and from Russia was still fairly reliable.) Our relationship had deepened. She was prepared to follow me to Canada and we would chart our future together. I had sent money to her brother Henry, who had been a fellow student in Gnadenfeld, to buy an engagement ring for Tina on my behalf. A date was chosen and our engagement was announced on the same day in the church in Alexandertal and in Southhampton.

In Southhampton, in the crowded facilities of the camp known as Atlantic Park, I had the good fortune to share a room with Dr. Benjamin Unruh. He occupied the lower level of the bunk bed and I took the upper. We spent the mornings teaching the children. My afternoons and evenings were free.

The opportunities to dialogue with Dr. Unruh were very significant for me at that stage of life. He suggested I read the book *Jesus* by Friedrich Zuendel. I found it very helpful, and reread it several times. It helped consolidate my experience at the monument of William of Orange.

Dr. Unruh was also an ardent student of Greek. Not knowing how long we would stay in Southhampton, I started to study Greek just to exercise my mind. Dr. Unruh was my coach.

In April 1928 Lydia, Jacob, Henry and I all passed our medical tests. Helen did not. Back in Russia, her fiancee, David Pauls, had finally received his passport and passed through England on his way to Canada while we were in Holland.

I had hoped that Tina would get her passport and come from Russia while we were still in England. When she didn't, I wrestled with whether to wait in England until she could come, or proceed to Canada without her.

Our family decided to leave for Canada. Helen, who hadn't yet passed her medical test, would stay back. When Tina came they would come to Canada together.

It wasn't until June 1929 that Helen was finally allowed to follow. But Tina's persistent efforts to secure a passport had failed. Perhaps it was the new regime's way of punishing her for the wealth of her parents.

CHAPTER 7

Starting Over

It was the end of March, the season of stormy seas. The journey was very difficult. For days the waves washed over the deck of our ship, the *Melita*. Most passengers were very seasick, and our family was no exception. What a moment when the ship safely entered the port of Saint John, New Brunswick.

My own emotions were as unsettled as the Atlantic. On the last day when the sea became calm I had sat on the deck most of the day pondering my future. Deep depression again came over me. The events of our recent past could not be erased. What lay in store for us, an immigrant people with no financial resources?

Our destination in Canada was Coaldale, Alberta. Father's brother, Abram Toews and family, together with Grandpa and Grandma Janz, from whom we parted in Moscow in October 1926, were already settled there. Together with the families of B. B. Janz and Jacob Janz, my mother's other brother who had migrated to Canada in 1923, they had bought a 560-acre irrigation farm.

A stopover in Winnipeg on our way west provided opportunity to see Liese, who worked in the city as a housemaid. David Pauls, Helen's fiancee, was in Arnaud, only about an hour from Winnipeg. Many other friends who had preceded us from Russia also lived in the area. Father had a chance to meet a number of his colleagues in the ministry, including A. H. Unruh, who had recently established a Bible school in Winkler. Seeing these many friends lifted my spirits temporarily.

The train took us west to our destination in Coaldale. For hours I stood at the window as we passed through the vast prairies of Manitoba and Saskatchewan. This was said to be a land of opportunity, but at the moment I could see no prospects for a future.

We had to change trains in Medicine Hat, Alberta. It was the second day of Easter, the early days of April 1928. That afternoon we arrived in Coaldale. No one from the extended family was there to meet us. Evidently they had not received the telegram sent from Winnipeg.

A letter we received in England had described the approximate location of the farm they had purchased, two miles east of Coaldale. With the rest of our family staying in the unheated railroad depot, I ventured out on foot to find the farm and contact our relatives. It had rained and the dirt road was muddy. After about two miles I spotted a farm house a bit off the road. Could this be it? I walked toward the house. As I came closer my uncle Jacob Janz recognized me through the window. The three families were all assembled there to observe Easter.

A team of horses was quickly hitched to a large grain tank and two uncles, Abram Toews and Jacob Janz, drove with me to the train station to get the rest of the family with all our belongings. A great celebration awaited us. We talked late into the night, reviewing the experiences of the past several years. Each family had their own story. Five years had passed since we had bid farewell to the Jacob Janz family at our grandparents' house in Konteniusfeld. The day concluded with a prolonged prayer meeting on our knees, thanking God for this reunion.

A Community House

The 560-acre farm, purchased by the four families—our family was included even though we were not able to contribute our share of the down payment—had only one five-room house plus a kitchen. A half-mile from the main farmyard was a second small house with two rooms that had accommodated the farm laborers. The Jacob Janz family moved into the little house. We, a family of six, were assigned to the main house.

To accommodate three families plus the grandparents in one house demanded precise coordination. All had to use a common kitchen. One room was assigned to each family. The younger generation found accommodation in two empty graineries. Washing facilities were improvised outside. The outhouse served all of us, twenty-two persons in all.

We were the poor family in the group. The other three had some means. Aunt Helen would share some food provisions with us. Our diet in the spring and summer was very simple. Potatoes, which were cheap, became our staple food until we could get vegetables from the garden. A sack of rolled oats, also very cheap, supplemented the potatoes. It was a meager beginning. Father, always full of thanksgiving, reminded us daily to remember our escape from "Egypt" and not to dishonor the Lord with complaints.

It was spring. We would need tight organization to operate the farm. The land purchase was based on trust more than money. The owner, a dentist from Lethbridge, had experienced difficulties with previous renters. When he heard of the Mennonite immigrants moving into the area he agreed to sell the farm without much of a down payment. No one of the extended family had any experience in farming except uncle Abe. He became the director of the operation and made all major decisions.

The farm purchase included twenty-three horses and some farm machinery. The ownership of the horses was divided by lot. The equipment was to serve the four families.

The crop of the first year was planted and harvested in joint ownership. By mid-July the B. B. Janz family moved to their own quarters. An old shed that was on their part of the land had been remodeled to make it livable so they could move to make more room for the others. Grandpa and Grandma Janz, who had some finances, purchased a two-room house— basically a shed with a slanting roof—in the small town of Coaldale.

I was not anxious to spend my time farming, but with Lydia only sixteen, Jacob fourteen, and Henry (Heinz) ten, my parents could not be left alone in these difficult circumstances. My first duty in Canada was to assist the family.

My First Job

A golden opportunity to earn extra money by clearing land opened up to us. The CPR owned large tracts of virgin land that it wanted broken up for farming so that Russian immigrants could settle on eighty-acre tracts. The CPR designated a major tract of land to us and offered us a good price per acre to break the ground and prepare it for farming. Stepping out in faith, with a very small down payment, the family group bought a new 15-30 McCormick-Deering tractor. I was assigned to operate the tractor, since I had earlier taken a mechanical course in equipment operation at the university in Gnadenfeld. So from May until the beginning of fall harvest I drove the tractor from early morning until late at night.

Grandfather Janz, who claimed one of the twenty-three horses and hitched it to an old buggy, served as courier. Each day at noon he would drive six to ten miles, depending on the location of the field I plowed, to bring a supply of fuel, water, food and encouragement to the young man of twenty-three who sat on the tractor uncertain about his future. Then he would pick up the plowshares, which had to be changed every day, and take them to the blacksmith to be sharpened.

The long days on the tractor provided plenty of time to ponder the trauma of the recent past and to think and worry about Tina, whose letters, now sporadic, reported repeated denials of her application for a passport. By the end of 1928 no more letters came through.

For the first year the four families—Benjamin Janz, Jacob Janz, Abram Toews and John A. Toews—operated the farm jointly. Each day the fathers of the families and the boys received their various assignments. It was no small task for Uncle Abe to coordinate the operation. The crops consisted of sugar beets, wheat, barley and oats. Each family was assigned a plot to plant their own garden. While the four mothers tended their gardens, the young women worked in Lethbridge as house-maids for modest wages to help support their families.

The tractor brought in good money and provided a major boost to the farm operation. In September, McCormick-Deering sold us a threshing machine, again with a very small down payment. Now we were fully equipped to do custom threshing. With very few threshing crews available, we had a full schedule through September and October. Together, our family group could provide all the manpower. The uncles, Abram Toews, Benjamin and Jacob Janz; my father; the teenage boys, Peter and Victor Toews, Jacob B. and Jacob J. Janz—all carried responsibilities in the threshing operation. Some loaded the bundles and brought them to the machine; others hauled the grain to the granary. I looked after the operation of the tractor and threshing machine. The income was good, but it all went into the common treasury to pay for the equipment, land payment and the farm operation.

More Poverty

The year 1928 was very difficult. Our family was still very poor. A small percentage of the harvest income was divided among the four families. Grandfather Janz bought a cow and gave us half the milk for providing the pasture and doing the milking. Our menus were very simple: mostly potato dishes and, as the summer came, vegetables from the garden.

Jacob and Henry went to school. Every morning a horse-drawn van came past the farm and took them to Coaldale.

Father, as always, encouraged the family to trust God and have faith. He worked in the garden and looked after the sugar beets, our cash crop. He thanked God for the rabbit I caught in the beet fields; it was the only meat we had from spring until mid-summer.

Father had faith that the Lord who provided bread and meat for Elijah when he was hiding from the wrath of Queen Jezebel could also provide meat for us. That August his faith and prayers were answered. Jacob Dick, a farmer and a deacon in the church who had come to Coaldale a few years earlier, raised pigs for market. One evening he came over to tell us to come by the next morning and get a pig. The Lord had told him we had no meat. That evening there was thanksgiving in our home for the pig the Lord had provided.

With the help of Uncle Abram and some money from Grandpa Janz we began to build a house on the half section designated for us and the Jacob Janz family. It was forty-eight by thirty-two feet. The structure was very simple: A two-story shell, a roof and a few windows downstairs, with no interior partitions at first. We moved into the shell to escape the congestion in the community building. There was no barn for Grandpa's cow and the horses. A crude fence would do.

In mid-summer of the first year Father received an invitation to teach at the new Hepburn Bible School in Saskatchewan. The school had begun in 1927 in the facilities of the church, with just one teacher. Now Jacob Penner of the Hepburn church had purchased an old public school building. They planned to introduce a two-year program. No set salary was offered, but it was an opportunity for service.

For Father this was an answer to prayer. He would go to Hepburn for the six winter months. Mother and I would stay in Coaldale and work on the house. The boys, Jake and Henry, were in school. Lydia, only a teenager, would look for work in Lethbridge.

In fall there still were no windows for the upstairs of the house. The front door and the downstairs windows were in. We were grateful to have a roof and food.

In September Father went to Hepburn by train. The boys were in school. Lydia found a position as a housemaid with a wealthy family in Lethbridge. Mother and I remained to build the house, look after the four horses and Grandpa Janz's cow, and tend to the general operation of the farm.

Liese (Eliesabeth) who had preceded us to Canada in 1926 with Grandpa and Grandma Janz and the Abram Toews family, was in Winnipeg working as a housemaid. She faithfully sent us her monthly earnings of $25, a great help to cover household expenses. Father's first stipend for his work in the Bible school, $45, together with some of the money from Liese, was enough to buy our first cow. Helen sent us $12 from England that she had earned helping in the kitchen in Atlantic Park. Here was the money to buy the first two windows for the upstairs of the house. The sale of the sugar beets gave us enough to buy lumber and hardware to continue work on the house. We cooked and heated the house with coal I gathered from the mines along the Old Man River. A day's work at the mines provided enough coal to last two to three months.

The house had only two outside coverings with a layer of boards, tar paper in between, and then shiplap. Mother and I worked through the winter of 1928-1929 to finish the inside. Occasionally Uncle Abram would come for a day to led a hand. More of a builder than I, he helped put up the partitions and installed the doors and windows.

The Church in Coaldale

Since I had some advanced education I was drawn in to lead the young people's group at church. At Christmas Jacob Klassen, a beekeeper, resigned as choir director. For some reason the church appointed me to succeed him. With my scant musical abilities, this seemed an impossible task for me. Lydia, who came home from Lethbridge every other weekend, became my coach.

The music used by the choir was mostly hymns selected from the *Liederperlen*, an eight-volume compendium of German church music. We would select the songs in advance and practice at home to do the best we could. Our limited musical knowledge, seasoned with a degree of enthusiastic leadership, seemingly was sufficient for that day in Coaldale. I managed to get some training through a music seminar conducted in Coaldale by Franz Thiessen, at the time a music teacher in Winnipeg and later a teacher at the Mennonite Educational Institute in Clearbrook, British Columbia. He gathered choir directors from the Alberta churches and taught the rudiments of choir leadership.

The Coaldale Mennonite Brethren Church consisted mainly of an immigrant group that had come from daughter colonies in Russia, all established at the end of the nineteenth century. That group, not having been part of the progressive cultural and educational programs in the mother colonies of the south, was culturally very conservative. A minority of the church members came from the more progressive Molotschna area. Many of them had professional training. They found it difficult to adjust to farm life and to integrate with the others.

A second consideration that affected all immigrants was educational integration. In Russia Mennonites had their own village schools and had controlled the training of their children. Now all their children had to attend the public school. The new environment and the tensions within the two groups in the church resulted in social protectionism.

The church choir was watched carefully by the congregation. They established rules of dress for the choir members as well as other social standards that the young people found confining. If the choir wanted to present a program at other churches like Grassy Lake, Pincher Creek and Namaka, special travel permission was needed.

On one occasion the choir travelled to Grassy Lake, about seventy-five miles west of Coaldale. We went in six cars, all driven by young people. On the way, a car driven by Helen Enns, an inexperienced driver, had a close shave and nearly hit a road grader. Since I was responsible for the group, I decided to ride in her car on the way back. There were no further problems.

The next week, however, I was asked to appear before the church council. One of the young people had reported that I had sat in the middle front seat of the Enns' car with a girl on each side. My engagement to Tina Driedger was well known in the church, even though she had not yet come to Canada. I was admonished by some members of the council for having set a bad example for the young people.

Despite this and other incidents, my brief time as choir leader in Coaldale, (two months short of two years) was a much-needed therapy. Aside from the quality of music, we had a good time. I never again attempted to meddle with music since I left Coaldale in 1930. The twenty-fifth anniversary publication of the Coaldale church made no mention of my brief tenure with the choir.

Working and Waiting

The struggle for survival as new immigrants in 1928-1929 demanded all the energy I had. I spent little time thinking of my future. I hadn't received a letter from Tina since the summer of 1928. I had some hope that she might be among those who came out of Russia in the fall and winter of 1929 and 1930. All efforts to make contact with her failed. Life had to go on.

The spring and summer of 1929 brought new problems. It was the first year in which each family assumed full responsibility for their own farm operation. We had trouble irrigating the crops. The canal system was inadequate, and I lacked the necessary experience.

Father, who had returned from Hepburn in April, was very helpful in tasks that did not require any procedural decisions. He weeded the beet fields, tended to the irrigation water when it was properly channeled, and nurtured the family to believe God would do the impossible. One example illustrates Father's practical limitations on the farm.

As part of the threshing crew he was given a very tame team of horses and a rack to load the grain sheaves. His task was to bring the sheaves to the threshing machine, pitch them into the separator return to the field for another load.

One morning I had moved the machine to a different location about a quarter-mile away. Father's loaded rack was the first to be at the machine that morning. The evening before he had unharnessed the horses and left the harnesses under the wagon. "Should I come with you to harness your horses?" I asked.

"No," he answered, "I can do it."

After he harnessed the horses I noticed that he was slow in coming, though the machine was already running. In the distance I saw him come walking, but the horses and the load had not moved. I stopped the machine and ran to meet him.

"What is it?" I asked.

"John," he said, "those horses are stubborn; they won't pull. They start but then pull back."

"Daddy," I said, "those horses are never stubborn. They're the most faithful team we have."

"Yes," he replied, "but today they are stubborn. I have prayed and even prayer does not help."

I reached the team. What was wrong? Father had put the collars on the horses upside down. The narrow end of the collar, which goes to the top of the horse's neck, had been put to the bottom. When they tried to pull, they choked. After I turned the collars around the horses pulled as usual.

When I brought them up to the machine Father asked: "What did you do to make them pull?"

"Father, you had put the collars on upside down; you put the upper part to the bottom."

"Does it make any difference how you put them on?" he asked surprised.

My father was a saint. You could not be in his presence without sensing that he was not of this world. He was completely impractical in everyday functions, but a man mighty in faith and prayer. When he was in the pulpit you sensed the voice of God in his preaching. Providentially, he had been given a wife of keen perception in the practical realities of everyday life. They were a God-given team for us as a family.

We Move the House

The building site of our house and the projected farmyard was two miles west and one mile north of Coaldale. Jacob Janz, mother's brother, had built on the same quarter of land only a small distance to the north of us. The original plan was to divide the half section in the middle, with the Janz family farming the east half and we the west half. We soon realized that the layout of the farmsteads was impractical if we wanted room for expansion. It had the potential for disagreements and tensions between the two families. By the fall of 1929 it was clear that one family would need to move a mile to the west. Before Father left for his second winter in Hepburn, the decision was made that we would move east and develop a new farmyard. It involved moving a house that was not yet fully finished, digging a cellar and building new fences and stalls for the animals. In short, it meant to begin again from scratch. Our protests as a family made no difference. "We must avoid the potential of tensions within the family," Father said. Then he left for Hepburn.

Lydia was working in Lethbridge for $25 per month to add to the family support. Liese had moved to Calgary from Winnipeg because her health was not good and she needed to be closer to the family. The boys

Jacob and Henry were in school. The task of moving the house and establishing a new structure of farm operation was left to Mother and me.

The grain harvest with the custom threshing lasted until mid-October. The beet harvest was finished by the end of the month. It was November. Frost had set in.

All alone I started to dig a cellar for the house. The ground was frozen to a depth of two feet, making the task nearly impossible. I worked hard with pick, spade and shovel to dig a cellar forty by twenty feet, seven feet deep. There was no time to lose. The four horses, two cows—we had bought a second cow with money that Father sent from Hepburn—a calf and two pigs, all outside without a decent shelter, needed tendeding. Before we could move I also needed to scrape out a water hole to store water for livestock and household use.

The winter of 1929-1930 remains etched in memory. I was a lonely young man, working desperately in the cold to provide a place to live. There was no word from the Tina I loved and longed to be united with.

In December the cellar was ready. Members of the Toews and Janz clans, along with some men from the church provided the long timbers, and four wagons. The McCormick Dearing tractor provided the power. In two days the job was done and the house stood on its new cellar on a hill a mile east. With the help of Uncle Abram a crude barn was built using old wood from a large shed that had been torn down.

When the horses and cows were transferred to the new location at the end of February, we had not yet scraped out the waterhole. They were taken to the neighbor to water. In March, before spring break, we scraped out a waterhole for the livestock. For the household we continued to haul water from the neighbors until summer of 1930 when we dug a cistern of our own.

Facing An Unknown Future

Was this bleak pioneer existence to be my lot in life? Or did God have other uses for my interests and abilities? The work with the youth in the church, the choir and an occasional opportunity to share a word of Scripture in the congregation provided some fulfillment for my searching spirit. Could I see myself staying on the farm? What about Tina, from whom I had not heard for over a year? Could I make decisions about the future without her?

From time to time I recalled the experience in Alexanderkrone after my fall and injury in Gnadenfeld, when mother knelt at my bedside and begged the Lord to take me to himself because there seemed no hope for healing. There I had confronted my vow never to become a minister. In the miracle of restoration I had pledged my obedience even if it would mean the ministry, but only ministry as a layman. I prayed for direction.

Jacob turned sixteen in April and refused to continue school. He wanted to be a farmer. Uncle Abe was his idol. But he was not yet ready to shoulder the responsibility of a new farm operation.

Helen, after more than a year's wait in England, finally passed her medical test and came to Canada. She had not come to Coaldale to see the family but stopped in Manitoba with her fiancee. In June 1929 they were married. None of the family could afford to travel to Manitoba for her wedding.

I informed my parents that my stay with them was only for the present and they shouldn't expect a long-range commitment. Father's reply was typical: "The Lord will have a way."

Helen sent word in January 1930 that she and David were expecting their first child and that her husband's farming prospects in Manitoba looked doubtful. Further letters mentioned the possibility of them coming to Alberta.

In July Dr. Henry W. Lohrenz from Tabor College in Hillsboro, Kansas, came to speak in the Coaldale church. I led the choir in the service where he spoke. At the close of the meeting he greeted me. Someone had told him about me.

"What are your plans for the future?" he asked.

I replied that our circumstances did not permit planning; for the present I had a responsibility to stay with my parents. "When you are ready, consider coming to Tabor," he said, "we have a good teacher under whom you could study English."

In early August Helen wrote to say that David was interested in coming to Alberta. Her message triggered some hope. Could they assume responsibility for the farm, and thus give me a way out?

By the end of August their plans were confirmed. David Duerksen, a cousin to my mother who lived in a small house on a twenty-acre plot that was part of the complex purchased by the Toews-Janz families, was moving his family to Pincher Creek to acquire land and begin his own farming operation. My sister and her husband could move into the small house, only a mile from us. David, with the help of my brother Jacob, could manage the operation of the extended farm.

I felt a tremendous sense of release from my obligations to the parental family. Once again, Father had been right. The Lord did have a way.

CHAPTER 8

A Student at Tabor

N ow that my bonds to the farm had been providentially loosened, the contact with Dr. Lohrenz became a real beacon of hope. At the end of August I wrote to him and received word that I could come to Tabor when the fall farm work was over. I stayed with the threshing crew until we finished in mid-October.

Not everyone shared my enthusiasm for further studies. When Franz Friesen, the elder of the Coaldale Mennonite Brethren Church, heard of my plan, he came by one evening to admonish me. "You have enough education," he said. "You need to consider your obligations to your parents, who need you. You have responsibilities in the church. You are our choir director, and a leader for the young people. To go on to school, after all the education you already have, could lead you astray. Maybe you are too proud to stay with your family and work in the church."

Elder Friesen's concerns did not change my plans. I applied for the necessary documentation to enter the United States. Inwardly, however, I was unsettled. Since coming to Canada I had received only one letter from Tina and that within the first month in Coaldale. The letter described her efforts to get a passport and noted that her aged parents needed her care. I had sensed a tone hopelessness. That had been two years ago. I had heard nothing from her since.

Adding to my unease was the haunting matter of the ministry. I had not forgotten my recommitment under the monument of William of Orange, nor the inspiration I received from the book *Jesus*, which Dr. Benjamin Unruh had recommended. I felt continued pressure to consider the ministry, but I resisted. Was my father's path of poverty to be my destiny, too?

The choir had prepared a farewell program of songs and well-wishes in my honor. Elder Friesen gave his consent for the program on the understanding that he would handle its conclusion. The parting with the choir was touching. Considerable affection had developed during our nearly two years together.

Elder Friesen used his time at the close of the program to repeat his earlier theme. He read the passage from 1 Peter 5:5, "God opposes the proud, but gives grace to the humble," and delivered a short homily on the need to remain humble. But his was not the final word. Afterward, I was met at the door by two elderly ladies, a Mrs. Born and Mrs. Dueck. "Hans," they said, "we have been praying that you would be obedient and respond to the ministry."

Several times during my two-and-a-half years in Coaldale I had responded to invitations to speak to the youth group on Sunday evenings. On several occasions I had also served as the first speaker on Sunday mornings. Apparently I had shown promise.

I couldn't shake off the words of these two elderly ladies. The last few nights before my departure I was awake much of the time pondering my future. My immediate task was to learn English at Tabor College. But what then? Was medicine still an option? What about the prayers of the two saintly ladies? In retrospect I can see that the Potter was continuing to mold the clay (Isa. 41:25).

The farewell at the railroad station was highly emotional. Father had already left for his third winter at Hepburn Bible School. Mother and Jacob, then sixteen years old, were to continue on the farm awaiting the move of David and Helen. Even though I knew they would be fine with the arrival of my sister and brother-in-law, it felt awkward to leave them alone.

Before I boarded the train, Mother took me aside. She expressed concern that we had not heard from Tina for more than two years. "Is it time that you release her?" she asked. "But if you do," she added, sobbing, "be careful that you don't develop a relationship with an American girl."

Grandfather Janz was also at the train station. He cried as he embraced me. "Hans," he sobbed, "I think I will not see you again." Grandfather was right. On January 3, 1932, while on his way to a prayer meeting, he was struck by a car and killed. It was a tragic ending for such a saintly man.

Grandmother Janz gave me a warm hug and said, "When you come through Germany greet my brothers." No doubt she meant her brothers in Hillsboro, Kansas and Corn, Oklahoma. Geographical perception meant little to Grandma Janz, who had only two years of schooling. Both Germany and Oklahoma were far away.

From Coaldale to Hillsboro

The train to Winnipeg and then Minneapolis conveniently passed through Arnaud, Manitoba, so I took the opportunity for a three-day stop-over to visit Helen and her family. I had not seen her since we left England. Now I also had a chance to see their firstborn daughter, also named Helen.

Uncle Benjamin had written to the city missionary, A. A. Smith in Minneapolis, whom he had met at the Mennonite Brethren General Conference in the summer of 1930, asking him to help me change trains in Minneapolis for Kansas City and Peabody, a station not far from Hillsboro.

When I stepped off the train in Peabody, however, there was no one to meet me. A stranger noticed me standing forlornly with my baggage as the train went on to Newton. He approached me and asked where I needed to go. When he heard my broken English he switched to Low German. Now we were on the same wave length. A friend of Tabor College, he took me to Hillsboro.

A small room had been reserved for me in the student boarding house operated by the N. N. Hiebert family. They occupied a former private hospital of a Dr. David Wiebe. Besides their family of nine, they had fourteen students staying with them. Room and board was $20 per month. My monetary reserve consisted of $75. Some unknown benefactor had paid my tuition at the college.

The name Hillsboro was familiar to me. It was the home of the *Zionsbote*, the first periodical of the Mennonite Brethren in North America, which was well-known in the Molotschna. Its editor, Johann F. Harms, had sent money to Holland to buy beans for our family in 1922. Before my departure from Coaldale Father had impressed upon me that I would meet the one whom God had used to save our lives from starvation.

Late in the afternoon of my first day in Hillsboro, I went on an exploratory walk to see this important place known to the Mennonite Brethren in Russia. On Main Street I passed an old man with a long beard, walking with a cane. I had momentarily forgotten my instructions to establish contact with J. F. Harms.

I greeted the elderly man with the customary "Guten Tag." He stopped, realizing I was a stranger. "Are you a student from Tabor College?" he asked. I said I was. "From where have you come?" he asked. "From

Coaldale, Alberta," I replied. "One of my important friends lives in Coaldale," he said.

Then I remembered the name J. F. Harms. "Are you Onkel J. F. Harms?" I asked. "Yes," he answered. I identified myself as the son of J. A. Toews. At that the old man dropped his cane and embraced me. With deep emotion he said, "You are the son of preacher J. A. Toews!" It was a touching encounter. The legendary J. F. Harms became my first contact in Hillsboro beyond my hostess Susie Hiebert.

J. F. Harms became a father figure and intimate friend during my time in Hillsboro. Ours was a relationship I cherished all my life. Harms, by then a widower, lived in a tiny hut with one room that served as kitchen, pantry and living room, and a small bedroom. Without apology for his primitive lifestyle, he often invited me to his abode. He did not share the narrow worldview so characteristic of the Hillsboro community. He could speak critically and analytically—yet with deep love—of the Mennonite Brethren in America.

Harms would share with me his views on the strengths and dangers of the large influx of Mennonite Brethren from abroad. I learned the inside stories of the Mennonite Brethren Church that had been left out of his book, *Geschichte der Mennoniten Brudergemeinde: 1860-1924.* These included moral failures in the conference leadership, the tensions within the Tabor College administration, the divisions in the church at Henderson, Nebraska, and his deep concerns for the future of the Mennonite Brethren Church at large. Then he would read some Scripture related to our conversation and we would spend time on our knees in prayer. Truly J. F. Harms was a "father in Israel" to the Mennonite Brethren Church of his day.

Hillsboro and Tabor College

Hillsboro, in 1931, was a small country town with a population of 2,000. It reminded me of our village life in the Molotschna Colony. Even though it was a college town, however, I found the people less sophisticated than our Mennonites in Russia.

I was struck by the heavy Mennonite population in the area, nine churches in all. There were three General Conference churches as well as their school, Bethel College, at North Newton, only twenty-five miles to the south. Closer by were three Mennonite Brethren churches, one in the town of Hillsboro and two others, Ebenfeld and Steinreich, in the country. In addition, there were the Gnadenau and Springfield Krimmer Mennonite Brethren churches, and the Church of God in Christ Mennonite, also known as the Holdeman Mennonites.

I found the Mennonite community in and around Hillsboro to be very clannish. The social and spiritual gap between the various Mennonite church communities reflected a kind of spiritual narrowness.

These were troubling times for Tabor College. There was a history of tension with its General Conference neighbor, Bethel College. The Mennonite Brethren communities of Hillsboro and Buhler were not pleased when Dr. Peter A. Schellenberg, a young Ph.D. in psychology, left Tabor in the spring of 1931 to join the Bethel faculty. Dr. H. W. Lohrenz, who withdrew from the Tabor administration in 1932, served one year at the Corn (Oklahoma) Bible Academy and then also accepted an invitation to Bethel. Hillsboro found this very difficult to swallow.

When Tabor closed its doors for the 1934-1935 school year, it would be because of depression economics and the anti-intellectual stance of the local community and the wider Mennonite Brethren Conference of North America. Founded in 1908, the college had been spearheaded by a small minority of progressive people. But in the next twenty-six years it was never fully accepted as an institution of the Mennonite Brethren conference. It would eventually achieve this status, but the endorsement would not be wholehearted. Nonetheless, my experience there was a valuable one in the context of my larger life's pilgrimage.

A Word from Tina

In November, only a month after my coming to Hillsboro, there was a Harvest Thanksgiving Festival in Dorrance, Kansas. Tabor College was to send some students to preach and share in a program for the youth on Saturday. Mr. and Mrs. Adam Ross, who recently had moved to Hillsboro from Culbertson, Nebraska, were to take two students along. Mr. Ross, a retired lay preacher and farmer, was to share in the service. Because of my age, and my fluency in German, I was asked to go along and bring two messages, one on Saturday to the young people and the second on Sunday morning. The second student assigned to go to Dorrance was Bernhard (B.J.) Braun, another immigrant from Russia. We would develop a lifelong friendship.

My two messages apparently were well received. On the way home Mrs. Ross, a sister to N. N. Hiebert, began to ask questions. She wanted to know about my family, my education and my background. Finally she said, "You are a good preacher, but you should be married. The girls do not hear what you say, but they are only interested in you."

I had not shared with her was that I was engaged. But her comments made an impression on me. I should be married. Was I deluded to hold out hope for Tina? I hadn't heard from her for more than two years. I remembered my father's persistent motto: "With God nothing is impossible." Could God also do the impossible for me, and bring word from Tina?

After kneeling in prayer that evening and weeping—very unusual for me at twenty-four—I decided to write again to the address given in Tina's last letter. I needed clarity as to our relationship. My letter was very brief: "I have not heard from you for over two years. Is there any hope that you will get the permit to join me? With continued love, Hans."

Before Christmas I received a letter from Tina. The content was as follows: "My love for you is unchanged. There is no prospect that I will get the needed documents to come. The conditions are very difficult; I cannot leave my parents. My brother has been arrested and taken away. I am the only one to look after my parents. I must sacrifice any hope of you and me ever being united. I release you, though with much pain. You must chart your future without me. Tina." I accepted the message as a special favor from God. Our relationship was dissolved.

I did not hear more of Tina until 1988 when I preached in Germany to an audience of recent Mennonite immigrants from Russia. Afterward an elderly woman approached me with the question, "Are you the former Hans Toews from Alexandertal who was engaged to Tina Driedger?" Fifty-eight years after her last letter I learned of her pilgrimage and that she died in 1976.

Back to High School

Tabor College was not sure how to accommodate me. I had come with an extensive academic background: four years at the University of the Ukraine plus additional graduate work at the University of Amsterdam. However, in terms of formal credentials—degree or diploma—I had only a notarized letter from Gerhard Duerksen, who had served on the university board until 1925 and had emigrated a year before my escape. The letter certified my status at the university and listed the courses I had taken.

Tabor didn't know how to classify me. Because I had no English proficiency and had not completed required subjects in American history and government, they classified me as a senior in the academy (high school standing). They explained that I could not be given college standing without having a high school diploma.

So I took high school courses in English, American History and American Government along with my college courses. Credit for college work was subject to the completion of the American high school requirements. The first two months before Christmas I concentrated on the rudiments of English, attending the classes of English I and II, in addition to reading for hours. For one hour in the morning and 30 minutes in the afternoon I read aloud while Liese Schultz corrected my pronunciations. I looked up the meaning of the words in the dictionary, making a list of the vocabulary and memorizing the meaning.

Under Dr. H. W. Lohrenz I took theology, using *The Christian Religion in its Doctrinal Expression* by Edgar Young Mullins. Also from Dr. Lohrenz I took two years of Greek and Introduction to the New Testament. From Dr. Peter C. Hiebert I took Public Speaking to attain fluency in English.

It was most difficult, even humiliating, for me to be classified as a high school student, but I was told that was the system of American education. I later discovered that other institutions could be more flexible. Eight years later, the Western Baptist Theological Seminary in Portland sent the same certified letter and outlines of courses I had taken in Russia to the University of Oregon. They fully recognized my previous education and gave me bachelor of arts standing, a requirement for acceptance to the bachelor of divinity program at the seminary.

Tabor College academically was a disappointment but it opened some important doors. I developed many acquaintances among the rural American Mennonite Brethren. I now see the Tabor experience as a providential chapter in God's design for my life. For the first time in my academic career I was studying in a Christian environment. H. W. Lohrenz and P. C. Hiebert had a significant impact on me. Lohrenz combined deep piety and respectable scholarship. He was a scholar of New Testament Greek and theology as well as biology and botany. He showed considerable interest in those of us from abroad who were older and more mature than the average college student.

Tabor owed much of its stature to Lohrenz. He was the one responsible for the imposing Greek columns that gave Tabor's architecture its distinctive look. Lohrenz had resigned from the presidency the year before I came to Tabor. I found it hard to understand the decline of his leadership during the years I was there.

Peter C. Hiebert was another figure who loomed above the rest of the faculty. In many ways his personality balanced that of Lohrenz. Less of a scholar than Lohrenz, he was popular among the common people and was accessible to anyone at any time. He was the chairman of Mennonite Central Committee and had travelled widely in the inter-Mennonite world, including a visit to our Russian village of Alexandertal. The unfortunate tension that existed between these two leading men of the Mennonite Brethren Church did not escape the notice of the more mature students.

In my second semester at Tabor, spring 1931, I was appointed to travel with the college quartet as devotional speaker. this experience, plus living in the Hiebert dormitory, provided continued social integration with American young people. Friendships born during this time remained with me for life.

The Hieberts were an example of deep commitment to God and the church. It was a significant sacrifice of privacy for them to operate a dormitory for so many students. Their lifestyle was very simple and their family relationships exemplary. The Hiebert family reflected some of my own family background. Mr. Hiebert was a very pious and devoted man. For many years, was the executive secretary of the Board of Foreign Missions, he spent many weeks and months away from home. Mrs. Hiebert and the family had maintained a small dairy farm in Mountain Lake, Minnesota, before moving to Hillsboro in the summer of 1930 so that Mr. Hiebert could be closer to his missions work and teach in the missions department at Tabor.

Mr. Hiebert was very reserved but very kind. I remember him sitting in the front room with a little typewriter on his knees, writing letters in connection with missions, or writing Sunday school lessons or other articles for the *Zionsbote*. He was not a powerful preacher, but was widely loved for his deep sincerity and compassion. Often he appeared melancholy, perhaps burdened by the endless responsibilities resting upon him.

The household of nine family members and fourteen students ran smoothly under the quietly efficient administration of Mrs. Hiebert. Her practicality reminded me of my own mother, although Mrs. Hiebert was more reserved and withdrawn. The students were a mix of young men and women, mostly from Nebraska, Minnesota and Oklahoma. The exceptions were B. J. Braun and me, both recent immigrants from Russia.

Ben Braun was in Hillsboro for the second year. He also had been classified as an academy student when he came to Tabor. Both of us were in our mid-twenties. He was known at Tabor for his academic ability and leadership, and had served as student body president. The differences in our backgrounds, he being from Siberian and me from the Molotschna, were soon bridged. A deep and lasting friendship developed between us.

Ben and I did not exactly fit in with the other young people. They were mostly recent graduates from high school, jolly and rambunctious quite different from the youth in our villages in Russia or Coaldale. They came from the farms and smaller churches, and college was a place to let loose.

N. N. Hiebert introduced me to the Mennonite Brethren Church at Lehigh, a few miles west of Hillsboro. This contact led to the church inviting me in January of 1931 to preach there on Sundays. The small allowance of $20 per month covered the cost of my board and room. Special gifts of one or two dollars from people of the church helped cover personal expenses. At Hiebert's suggestion the church also provided me with a 1927 Model T Ford to commute to church on Sundays. I would continue to use this vehicle the following year for ministry travels in North Dakota and Montana.

I Meet Nettie

The month of March 1931 was an important milestone in my life. During chapel hour a nurse from the local hospital appeared on the stage and gave a reading titled "The Picture on the Wall," a story of a nurse caring for a young man who had been injured in an accident. His recovery was in question. The nurse, concerned for the man's spiritual condition, sought a way to speak to him about salvation. She hung a picture of Jesus on the wall in front of the injured man's bed to provide an occasion to talk to him about spiritual matters.

The man did not respond to the message. He recovered and left the hospital. The nurse never heard from him. Many years passed. The nurse grew old, became ill and was near death. Her fellow nurses summoned a minister to her bedside. As the clergyman entered the room, he recognized the nurse who now hovered at the gates of eternity.

"The picture on the wall," he said. They recognized each other. "Are you the man I told the story of Jesus?" she whispered. "Yes," he answered, "the picture on the wall pointed me to Jesus." He lifted her head to ease her breathing. "The picture on the wall," she whispered and breathed her last.

A hush fell over the chapel when she finished the reading. Faculty and students were deeply touched. "Who is that nurse?" I wondered, amazed at how she swayed the audience with her touching story. I learned that she was a nurse from the local hospital who was taking a literature class at the college. It occurred to me that I, too, should enroll in the same class. After all, I was there to study English. That was how God brought Nettie Unruh into my life.

CHAPTER 9

Struggling to Obey

T hrough the spring months of 1931 my friendship with Nettie Unruh became very important. She was a very modest person, with a heart for outreach. Information about her background and family had to be coaxed out of her, but she spoke freely about her work at the hospital and the fulfillment she found in ministering to people. On Sunday afternoons she was part of a group that ministered to children who gathered at Tabor. I found myself quite attracted to her and wondered how our relationship would develop.

Open Doors

Meanwhile, the idea of ministry continued to beckon. Tabor students and faculty assumed my future lay in the gospel ministry. During the spring semester of 1931 I joined the college's gospel team, which visited churches on behalf of the school. At the same time I was elected leader of the Tabor College Mission Band. I was invited to speak at morning worship services in the Hillsboro, Gnadenau, Lehigh, Zoar and Ebenfeld churches.

The college administration recommended me to the Mennonite Brethren Church in Jansen, Nebraska, as an interim pastor for the summer of 1931. I responded positively because the people there were willing to provide some support for my continuing English studies at Tabor.

Jansen was a small community. Everyone in the church were farmers except the Ben Rempels, who lived in Fairbury and had a produce business. There was a good group of young people and children and they all affirmed my ministry. The assignment at Jansen intensified my struggle about the future. Was the gospel ministry to be a commitment for life? What about the medical profession to which I had committed myself?

To earn additional money for the next school year, I worked on the farm of the Peter Reimers during the week. I lived with them and was treated as part of their family. I shared the farm work and will never forget the experience of cultivating corn with unpredictable mules. In the evenings I took responsibility for midweek prayer meetings and youth gatherings. Sundays were full, with both morning and evening services.

Despite the pressures of pastoring, I found time to ponder my future as I spent days on the corn cultivator under the scorching sun. If my friendship with Nettie developed further, would she be open to the ministry?

In August, John Krause, an elderly member of the Evangelical Mennonite Church, died. Their house of worship was only two or three miles west of the Mennonite Brethren church. Mr. Krause had a large family. Some members of his extended family came from non-German backgrounds. The funeral was to be conducted in English, but their elder, Rev. John Friesen, spoke only German. The Krause family, knowing of my ministry in their neighboring church, asked that I bring the funeral address. I agreed. Having never before preached in English I worked hard to write out the message. My topic was "Man's search for a purpose to life," based on Ecclesiastes 1:2-6.

Just as the Reimer's and I were ready to leave for the funeral their son, Delmer, had one of the convulsions he occasionally suffered. All our concern focused on the struggling child. Mrs. Reimer decided to stay home. By now it was late, and we drove in hast to the church.

I was ushered to the platform. As I opened my Bible, I discovered to my terror that in the excitement I had left my sermon notes on the table back in my room. What now? My first sermon in English, without notes? In my distress I prayed for special grace.

The introductory music and the congregational song ended. All eyes were on the young preacher who was to speak. I read the text and spoke from memory after rehearsing the sermon over and over again on the corn cultivator. I spoke for twenty minutes. At the coffee hour, following the service, some people expressed appreciation for the message.

The incident would come back to me in the fall of 1952 when I was pastoring in Reedley, California. I was greeting the people after a morning service when a visitor stared intently at me while I shook hands with him. He left for a moment, than turned around and came back. He asked: "Are you the man who preached the funeral message for John Krause in Jansen, Nebraska?" I said I was. "Do you remember," he asked, "the message you preached on `all things are vanity'?" "I remember too well," I said. "That was the first English sermon I preached." With tears in his eyes he said: "That message changed my life. I became a Christian, and that is twenty-one years ago." That noon at the dinner table I shared with my family the story of my first English message. In deep humility I thanked God for his mercy those many years ago. The experience was part of my molding process before I surrendered in obedience for the ministry. The Potter was softening the clay.

Conference Speaker

The Central District Conference in 1931 was at the Silver Lake Mennonite Brethren Church in Marion, South Dakota. The Cornelius Unruh family, including Nettie, were members of this congregation.

The Sunday evening service was designated as a youth rally. The Tabor College quartet was to be responsible for the program and I was to bring the evening message. Ben Rempel, leader of the Jansen church, had provided the transportation to South Dakota.

The conference met under a large tent that was filled to capacity. Afterward I was approached by A. A. Dick, chairman of the Home Mission Committee, as to my availability for a month of renewal meetings in the churches of the Central District the following summer. I was to give my answer the next morning. After a restless night of inward struggle I gave my consent.

The Unruh family was prominent in the Freeman-Marion area of South Dakota. I made some casual inquiries about them. Nettie was well known. She had been the first from the community to leave for studies. She had entered nurses training school, first in Mountain Lake, Minnesota, then in Kansas City, and was now a registered nurse having passed the state board exams. Some referred to the family as "the rich Unruhs." Amid the economic depression of the 1930s they were perceived as wealthy. Rumors were already circulating that I was befriending their daughter.

Developments in the months since I left Coaldale had been too overwhelming. My relationship with Tina Driedger had been terminated. I had entered a new and wider environment of Tabor College and the churches of central Kansas. The trips with the college quartet had given me opportunity to speak in Buhler, Inman, Hillsboro and Dorrance, Kansas, as well as Corn, Fairview and Enid, Oklahoma. And now here I was at the Central District Conference, the first such conference I ever attended. I had pledged myself to a month of services for the following summer of 1932, later extended to six weeks. The ministry opportunities seemed to be coming at a relentless pace.

Inwardly unsettled, I returned to Jansen. The ministry there continued through fall, by travelling there on weekends by bus.

Nettie's Influence

My second year at Tabor was easier. I began to identify with the college community and become reconciled to the school's inability to extend appropriate academic recognition. But I was still uncertain about my future. My apparent acceptance in the American churches and the increasing demand for a spiritual ministry were indications of my gifts. But I remained uneasy about the poverty that I associated with a long-term ministerial commitment.

Nettie and I continued to nurture our friendship. My affection and admiration for her grew. Shortly after Christmas I felt the liberty to suggest the possibility of marriage. She was noncommittal at first. She felt she had made a lifelong commitment to the nursing profession. Marriage was not something she had considered. I prayed earnestly that the Lord would lead her to a positive response, despite the uncertainty of my own plans.

In February of 1932 I faced a crisis that demanded decisive action. Two options, both attractive in their own way, suddenly opened up for me. One of these was in business. Sam Schneider, a member of the Buhler Mennonite Brethren Church and chairman of the Tabor College board, operated a chain of Shell service stations and had other high level involvements with the Shell Oil Company. He encouraged me to consider working for Shell, which at the time was entering the European market. He thought my European background, languages and personality would be assets for a successful business career.

The second invitation was to join the faculty of the Bethany Bible Institute in Hepburn, Saskatchewan. The first offer provided financial security, the second a more permanent involvement in Christian ministry. I knew a number of Mennonite Brethren ministers who were successful in business and who served in the ministry at the same time. Could I not be financially secure and still serve the Lord?

I wondered what Nettie would say. She came from a home that was considered wealthy. What would she choose if she became my life's partner? I decided to share my struggle with her. One evening as we walked together in the park near the Tabor College campus I told her about the two options I had to consider. She was quiet. Then finally she said in a subdued tone, "John, if you accept the position to become a teacher in the Bible school and a minister you will always be poor." We said little as we walked back to the Flaming home where she stayed. Then we parted. I didn't see her for another ten days.

I was at a crossroad. I knew God had gifted me for ministry. That part I had accepted. But could I not be active in ministry like William Dyck, the owner of a factory and a large flour mill in Russia? Other wealthy Mennonite Brethren ministers had served the Lord faithfully. Could I not go into the oil business with Shell and still be a minister? Other young men at Tabor, like Abram Nachtigal, Henry Rempel, B. J. Braun and Peter Klassen, were planning careers in medicine, business and teaching. Did I have to be an exception?

One afternoon I was on my way downtown to mail a letter to my parents when I met Nettie, who was on the way to the hospital. We stopped and chatted briefly. "John, you haven't come to see me for quite a while," Nettie said. "I need to talk to you." "When will you be off duty?" I asked. "This evening at nine," she replied. I agreed to meet her at the hospital at nine.

I couldn't study the rest of the day. I worried that she would lose interest in our relationship if I chose to go to Hepburn. At nine o'clock I met Nettie at the hospital. We walked together side by side, then stopped under a tree in the park. There was a moment of silence. I noticed she was crying. "What's the matter?" I asked. "It is all right," she answered. "What is all right?" I asked. Again she said, "It is all right." I repeated my question again. Then she said, "It is all right to be poor." I clasped her hand. With very little conversation we continued to walk together. God had given me the answer. That evening we pledged our relationship for the future. The struggles were not over, but I had made a major decision. I accepted the call to go to Hepburn in September of 1932.

The mutual commitment with Nettie marked a new chapter for both of us. We began to talk of our future together. Nettie was concerned how she would fit into a family environment so different than hers. She suggested that I go to Hepburn for a year while she stayed in Hillsboro. She needed time to process the decision. It was difficult for her to think of giving up her beloved profession as a nurse after all she had sacrificed to attain it.

She also wanted time to learn German so she could relate to my family, especially my parents. She had grown up in the Silver Lake church, where the services were in German, but she did not have a speaking knowledge of the language.

Nettie had not yet processed our decision with her own family. Her father, knowing of our emerging relationship, had warned her against marrying me. He sensed from the tent meetings of the previous summer that I was headed for the ministry. He had reminded Nettie of his brother, Henry Unruh, who had served in Mennonite Brethren churches in Kansas, California and South Dakota. He had pointed out that "those are people who always move around and are poor."

We agreed that I would go to Hepburn while she would continue nursing at the hospital in Hillsboro and study German. We would plan a wedding for the summer of 1933. Nettie went back to South Dakota to inform her family of our mutual commitment. I passed through South Dakota on my way to the scheduled meetings in the Central District churches so I could meet her family. I spent the last day of May 1932 in the Unruh home, dining with the family and then meeting with Nettie and her parents in the evening to request their approval of our relationship. Their response was very kind, and they gave their parental approval to our plans. Father Unruh graciously did not mention the concerns he had expressed earlier to Nettie.

A Conference Ministry

June and July were set aside for ministry in McClusky, Sawyer and Johannestal in North Dakota and Lustre, Wolf Point and Larslan in Montana. These were small rural churches led by lay preachers who farmed all week and preached on Sundays. As a young man from Russia and Tabor College, I was something of a novelty, so we had a good crowd of curious young people at the meetings. My father had said each service should have something for the children and young people. I followed his advice and taught them choruses followed by some dramatic story from my background in Russia. I told them about starvation, the revolutionary war, the loss of my horses and the poverty we experienced. The children and young people listened attentively and came back every evening. My ministry was something new to them. Visitors from the wider community came as well.

Our arrangement was that A. H. Unruh would precede me in each church with a week of Bible expositions before I followed with a week of evangelistic meetings. The grace of God abounded. We saw conversions in every church.

The concluding joint service of the McClusky and Johannestal churches was especially dramatic. Unruh gave a brief expository message as the introduction to the service. I followed with an evangelistic message and an appeal for decisions to accept Christ as Savior. While the small choir sang the invitation, "Come, Sinner Come," an emotional wave burst unexpectedly upon the audience. People flocked to the altar at the front of the church, fell on their faces and cried. Parents threw their arms around sons and daughters whose souls were in agony.

I stood behind the pulpit, taken aback. Finally I turned to A. H. Unruh with the question: "What shall I do now?" Gently he answered, "Just let them cry and weep over their sins. When they calm down we will show them the way to forgiveness." After about half an hour, when the emotions subsided somewhat, I asked Unruh to take charge. Calmly he read them the Scriptures and pointed out the way of salvation. The meeting ended with great rejoicing in many households.

I remembered similar scenes of sorrow and repentance from the renewal meetings in Russia during the post revolution years, but then I was only a teenage observer. This was my first such experience as a presiding minister.

The weeks of ministry with Unruh were enormously important for me. I learned much at the side of this patriarch. His instruction and example during those six weeks left an indelible impression on me.

These six weeks of ministry in the summer of 1932 were a strong affirmation of God's call to the ministry. I was overwhelmed by the persistence and patience of God as "the potter forming a vessel." I became completely at peace about my decision to go to the Hepburn Bible School. At twenty-six, my struggle for purpose in life seemed over.

While in Montana I received the first letter from Nettie since we parted in the home of her parents. The letter assured me of her support, but also raised the question, "How can I be sure that our decision of the past weeks is truly from the Lord?" Now that she was alone she was re-evaluating the long-range implications of our decision. Such struggles would be expressed frequently in her letters over the next year. It was not easy for her to think of exchanging her life's calling for a life of ministry at the side of a man whom she knew only superficially.

A Man Without a Country

It was a warm day in July. It had been three months short of two years since I had left Coaldale. As I drove my little Model T Ford towards the Canadian border, I mused over the church's parting words to me back in October 1930: "God resisteth the proud but gives grace to the humble."

I was going home to Coaldale. The whole family would be there: Father, Mother, Helen and David and their two children, Jacob, Henry, Lydia and even Liese, who worked in Calgary but was expected home for the family reunion.

I reached the border town of Sweetgrass, Montana, in late afternoon. From the border it was a hundred miles to Coaldale, so I would arrive home by late evening. The Model T had a top speed of only forty-five miles per hour, but I made good time. I expected to spend the night under the roof of the house which I had built. But then came a rude surprise!

The American immigration inspector informed me that I had overstayed my time in the United States. My visa had expired July 1 and it was now July 20. After some negotiations and a word of admonition he let me proceed across the border to Canada.

The Canadian immigration officer, at Coutts, Alberta, was more hostile. After examining my papers, he informed me that because I had overstayed my time in the U.S. I had lost my Canadian domicile and with it my status as an immigrant. With some harshness he said I could not re-enter Canada.

A Canadian border guard then escorted me back to the U.S side where an argument broke out between the Canadian and the U.S. officials. It seemed no country was open to me. In desperation I asked, "Well, what then can I do?" The answer was cruel: "You are a man without a country. We will deport you to Russia from where you came." A chill ran through me, despite the heat of the day.

The American officer questioned me about my stay in the U.S. Had I only studied or had I also worked? I forthrightly said I had served churches while in school and that they had helped me with financial donations. "Are you a preacher?" they asked. "No" I said, "but as a student I did preach."

At first they said that I would need to stay in jail at Sweetgrass until they could get a ruling from Washington on how to handle my case. But after further questioning they changed their mind. Instead they would impound my car and I could stay in a nearby hotel but report to immigration every three hours during the day, allowing six hours for the night. Leaving all my baggage in the car I checked into the hotel. The price was $2 per night.

Before leaving Coaldale nearly two years earlier I had visited Dr. Richards, a dentist in Lethbridge, a friend of the Toews and Janz clan. He knew us from the land purchase in which he was involved. I had shared with him my plans to go to the U.S. for study. His parting words to me were: "Be careful, John, so that you will not get into trouble. If you do, call me. I may be able to help you."

The hour of needing help had come. Uncle Benjamin in Coaldale had a phone. Although it was late at night I called him long distance. I told him of my dilemma and mentioned the last words of Dr. Richards.

The wheels began to turn. Uncle Benjamin would consult with Dr. Richards, whose brother, it turned out, was the Canadian minister of immigration in Ottawa. We agreed that I would call back in two days.

My case was referred personally to the Canadian minister of immigration. When I called two days later I was told that he had given assurance to review my case and instruct the local border official accordingly. In the meantime I maintained my schedule of reporting to the U.S. immigration officials every three hours. I told them Canada was reviewing my case and I expected a favorable reply.

On the third day in the afternoon I dropped by the immigration office at Coutts. When I asked if there were any new developments I received an angry rebuff. "Your case is not under consideration," I was told. "There's no way you can get entrance into Canada." I didn't tell the officer of my connections with Ottawa.

On the fourth day I again went to the Canadian border and asked the same question. The reply was even more harsh than before. "You need not come and inquire. Your case is closed. You have lost your Canadian domicile."

On the fifth day the response was different. Angrily the officer asked me, "What connection do you have in Ottawa?" Without answering I asked, "What is the message from Ottawa?" Finally the officer answered in an undertone: "You can go." "Will you hand me the needed document?" I asked. After a long silence he repeated his question: "Who do you know in Ottawa?" Here I became firm. "Officer, I don't owe you an answer. I want you to give me the documents to enter Canada." He handed me the papers. The wire from the minister of immigration said: "Give free passage to John Toews to enter Canada at once."

With the document in hand it was now my turn to speak. "You have treated me very unkindly," I said. "I want you to know that Ottawa will receive a full report of how you treat people at Coutts." The tables had turned. He apologized and pleaded that I not report the case any further. I left, insisting that a report would be sent.

It was late afternoon. My sense of relief was indescribable. That evening I called Uncle Benjamin to report that my long delay was over. I also wrote a long letter to Nettie in Hillsboro reporting the outcome of my ordeal.

My car had been impounded by U.S. immigration when my problems began. They released it to me upon presentation of my Canadian entry permit. But as far as the Canadian officials were concerned, my permit did not extend to the vehicle. "The car cannot be imported," they said. A used car dealer in Sweetgrass agreed to try to sell it and would send the money to me in Coaldale. I used the car one last time to take my baggage to the Canadian checkpoint, then returned the car to the dealer.

At ten o'clock the next morning David Pauls arrived at Coutts to pick me up. With him in his light delivery truck were my two brothers, Jake and Henry. "You will hear from Ottawa," were my last words to the immigration officer. Three hours later we arrived in Coaldale. The whole family was there to greet me. Mother had kept the *borscht* hot for our arrival. Before we sat down to eat, Father prayed thanksgiving to God for helping to reunite us.

In the family circle I reported in detail the story of Sweetgrass and Coutts. Father objected to reporting the border official to Ottawa. That would be revenge, he said, quoting Christ's command, "Love your enemies, bless them that curse you and persecute you" (Matt. 5:44). "John," he said, "you will not report that officer to the immigration authority in Ottawa." I heeded the admonition.

Three years later in spring of 1935 Nettie and I passed through Coutts on our way to meetings in Montana. The officer still on duty in Coutts, recognized me immediately. "You didn't report the incident of a few years ago to Ottawa?" he asked. "No, I did not," I said. The chapter was closed.

The car was sold in Montana for $50. The dealer charged $20 commission plus $2 for a money order. I received $28.

Back in Coaldale

The reunion with the family after two years of separation was joyous. Changes had occurred during my absence. Helen and her family had moved to Coaldale and occupied the house on the twenty acre farm. After Grandpa Janz's death in a car accident Grandmother had moved in with the Abram Toewses. Father had accepted a teaching position at the new Bible school in Coaldale so he could stay with the family.

The Central District Home Missions Committee paid me $125 for the weeks of meetings in North Dakota and Montana. In the eyes of my family I had come home a rich man.

Some things hadn't changed at all while I was gone. One was the cultural narrowness of some people in the Coaldale church. On my first Sunday the first person to greet me was Elder Franz Friesen. "You have come back," he said. "Yes, I am back," I answered. "Have you kept the faith?" he asked in Low German. "Yes, Uncle Friesen," I answered, "I have kept the faith." "But wasn't everything English where you were?" I couldn't help reacting. "Yes, Uncle Friesen, everything there was English, but there are more people who are Christians in the faith that speak English than there are who speak German," I replied. "That could not be," he said. "All English, and you say they were Christians?" Fortunately other people had came up to greet me so I did not respond further.

It was customary in Coaldale to have a brief children's feature as part of the morning worship. Heinrich Kornelson, who was to speak to the children that morning, asked if I would address them. Hesitantly I consented. I told the children briefly where I had been for the past two years and that I now had come home. Not having prepared anything, I asked if they would like to learn a little chorus. Their response was enthusiastic. So I sang the chorus, "Jesus loves me this I know, for the Bible tells me so." They enjoyed it. We sang the chorus two or three times.

Johann Dick, a very sincere veteran in the faith, put his hand on my shoulder after the service and said, "That was good, but should you not have taught that chorus in German? Why English?" These concerns were just the tip of the iceberg of a deep ethnic preoccupation that could not differentiate between "faith" and "culture." To them, language was the carrier and expression of faith.

This phenomenon was not unique to Coaldale. During four centuries of cultural isolation the Anabaptist movement had frequently allowed faith to be wrapped up in culture. Our forebears, mainly Dutch people who moved from Holland to the Vistula Delta south of Danzig, spoke Dutch for some two hundred years before finally adopting German. During 150 years of colony life in Russia, German language and traditions became virtually indistinguishable from faith.

In Coaldale the change from German to English was more difficult than in many churches. This was due largely to the strong personalities of people like B. B. Janz, Heinrich Cornelsen, Bernhard Dick and Jacob J. Siemens, all of whom clung to conservative ways.

The responses to my return were generally very kind. Young and old welcomed me back. Many of them already knew that I had accepted the call to teach at the Bible school in Hepburn where my father had taught for three winters.

My stay in Coaldale from July 26 to October 10, 1932 was very rewarding. In general I felt accepted. I had opportunities to speak to the young people's program (*Jugend-Verein*) and also shared in one morning worship of my experiences in the "English" world with a brief message from the Word.

Family and Farm

The family reunion was wonderful. After six years the circle was again complete. The various changes that had occurred testified of growth and maturity. Henry was a teenager. Jacob, eighteen, still did not feel the need to go to high school. I vividly recalled his fifteenth birthday in April 1929 when he had flatly refused to continue school. The school van, drawn by horses, came by that day but only Henry got on board. Half an hour later I found Jake sitting in the barn. Nothing I said could persuade him to go back to school. He had warned us the previous fall, before Father left for Hepburn: "I'll go to school only until I reach fifteen," the age up to which school in Canada was compulsory. "I don't like school. I want to be a farmer like Uncle Abe. I don't need high school." But Father, before he left, had instructed us to keep Jacob in school. A consultation with Mother confirmed the order. So as the older brother—nearly eight years his senior—it became my task to add the strap to the family's persuasive measures. "You are going back to school," I told him. His response was equally firm: "You can kill me, but I will not go back to school." Now, more than two years later, Jake still had not changed his mind, though he would later. He was home and did the farming under the supervision of Helen's husband, David Pauls.

The family had grown. Helen and David had two children, Helen and John, the latter named after his grandfather. Lydia, who worked as a maid in a wealthy home in Lethbridge, continued to contribute her monthly earnings for the support of the family farm operation. She had matured during the two years of my absence. Liese, even though she continued to do housework, was not well. She still suffered lingering effects of several surgeries on the forehead as a teenager.

The house had not changed much. It remained where I had left it. It had no external siding; the inside still consisted of bare boards nailed against two-by-fours.

After the experience at the Canadian border I made a point of visiting the Office of Immigration and Colonization. They recognized my time in the U.S.—because I had been attending college—as applicable to the five-year residence requirement for Canadian citizenship. In April 1933 I would become eligible to apply for citizenship.

Naturally the family was intensely curious about Nettie. Her photograph was passed around and studied carefully. The questions seemed endless. What was she like? What was her background? Would she be willing to come to Canada? Would she be able to adjust to the lifestyle of an immigrant family from Russia? How would my parents, who spoke only German, communicate with her?

Nettie and I exchanged letters weekly. She shared her relief that the border problems had been resolved. She continued work at the Hillsboro hospital.

While at Tabor I had missed only one threshing season. Uncle Abe had taken my place during the absence. My immediate task now was to arrange for the repair of the tractor. After four years of heavy use it required an overhaul. That was beyond my capabilities so I took it to a machine shop in town. The threshing machine also needed attention, but that was something I could handle. Every part of the separator was taken apart and replaced where necessary.

I also began preparing for the assignment in Hepburn. Dietrich Esau, who was principal of Bethany, provided the needed plans by mail.

From August to October 10 I worked on the harvesting crew, attending to the tractor and threshing machine. October 10 came too soon. The Bible school was to open on October 15.

A Bible School Teacher

My train trip required a stop in Saskatoon to connect with the train to Hepburn, which left every Tuesday. In Hepburn I would be lodged with a retired couple, the Jacob Priebs. My father had stayed in the Prieb home during his time in Hepburn. A small upstairs room became my bedroom and study, as well as a meeting room for consultation with students. The Priebs were a very interesting couple. Their marriage, the second for both of them, had brought together two large families. Their kitchen and dining room were in the basement. The upstairs room next to mine was occupied by two students of the Bible school, Peter Wiens and Peter Reimer. Room and board was only $20 per month.

Both of the Priebs were very sociable. They entertained many people. Mr. Prieb functioned as a bonesetter, or chiropractor. He also extracted teeth. All these services were administered in the main front room. There were very few dull moments in the Prieb home.

Teaching in the Bible school was an entirely new experience for me. Dietrich Esau, the principal, assigned me three areas: Bible doctrine, personal evangelism, and study of the Pentateuch, plus New Testament book studies. The students were mostly eighth grade graduates and had to be sixteen years old to be admitted. A number of students, however, were older men and women, workers in the church who felt the need for more Bible knowledge. In my classes I had three men and two women who were older than I was. The salary for teachers was $60 per month for the six-month school year. With no experience in teaching, other than a limited amount of student teaching while at the University in Russia, it was a very difficult beginning.

The Bethany library consisted of only a few dozen books. The library budget for that year was $45. My small salary, of which one third went for room and board, left very little to acquire personal library materials.

The curriculum of the first two years was designed to help young people acquire more Bible knowledge and relate it to life. The third year, designed for more mature students, covered doctrines of the Bible, theology, church history, and ministry in Sunday school, preaching and missions. A number of the early graduates from the upper classes—Daniel and David Wirsche, John Dick, Emma Lepp and others—went on to serve as missionaries. The available library materials were mostly books from Bible institutes—Moody in Chicago, Biola in Los Angles and Northwestern in Minneapolis. Authors like Reuben A. Torrey and Dwight L. Moody were the major resources in English. The German subjects were based on books known from Russia, mostly pietistic in content and very narrow in scope. I also used resources from my high school religious studies courses in Russia. To expand beyond these limitations I rooted my courses in the biblical text. Every class required hours of preparation.

The interaction with the students was a totally new experience for me. A spirit of deep piety and sincerity dominated the school. But many theological and philosophical issues of faith and life went unanswered. At that time the Mennonite Brethren churches and people of Saskatchewan were descendants of the Mennonite immigrants of the 1870s who came to Saskatchewan from Minnesota, South Dakota and Nebraska. In culture and practice they were similar to Mennonites I had learned to know while in Kansas. The churches in the Dakotas and Montana that I learned to know in my summer ministry before returning to Canada, were more open.

Before my arrival in Hepburn work had begun on building a third classroom, an addition to the old building left vacant when the Hepburn school moved into new facilities. The classroom addition, built at a cost of $426.22, was a spacious room with many windows.

Because I was the only faculty member who had mastered a degree of English, my major teaching assignments related to the third-year students. I was the first to teach in English. Dietrich Esau and Jacob Dueck were my colleagues.

Despite the difficulties of starting a new career, it was a good year, a time of personal reorientation. Because I could speak both German and English, I received many invitations to speak in the churches of northern Saskatchewan. The recognition I received far exceeded my maturity.

I spent June and part of July of 1933 ministering in the churches in Laird, Waldheim, Glenbush, Watrous, Mullingar and Saskatoon. In the middle of July I returned to Coaldale to resume my place on the threshing crew.

From Courtship to Marriage

My relationship to Nettie was generally known and accepted in the school and constituency. Our correspondence throughout the year was continuous. The mail, which then came to Hepburn only once a week, usually had a letter from Nettie. Some of these letters mentioned her inner turmoil over our mutual commitment. She read the reports of my experience in the Bible school and followed closely the expanding demand for my ministry in the churches. She struggled with her anticipated role in that context. "Can I fit into that frame of a public ministry?" she asked. In one letter she even implied that she should withdraw to make room for someone more suited to the role of a public ministry. I never questioned the commitment. Nettie's honesty and openness to question our mutual commitment only confirmed that she was a gift from God.

In April 1933, five years after we landed in Canada, I was eligible to apply for Canadian citizenship. Because I expected to spend the summer in Coaldale I sent the application to the office in Lethbridge. Their reply specified that I remain in Canada and not leave the country while the application was being processed. What a shock! Our wedding was planned for August in South Dakota!

The Coutts experience of a year ago was too fresh in our minds. I could not run the risk of violating the law. Nettie found this all very difficult. Should we postpone our wedding until after I received my citizenship? That could be too late to go to Hepburn for my second year of teaching. Was she to come alone to a to a strange community in a strange country where she knew no one? We had already been separated for a year, and now this? For some weeks the problem appeared insurmountable to her. Then, late in June, a letter came with her decision: she would come to Coaldale to be married.

Mother and Lydia were greatly troubled by this plan. Nettie was an American, professionally trained as a nurse, and came from a wealthy family. How could we bring her to our primitive house that had no plumbing, and didn't even have finished boards on the walls? Should we rent an apartment in Lethbridge for the time she would be in Coaldale?

I was committed to operate the threshing machine for August, September and the beginning of October—as school in Hepburn started October 15. Mother and Lydia thought this was too long for a newly-married woman to stay in a crowded house with a family she hardly knew.

The wedding date was set for August 27—in the middle of the threshing season. Threshing was to begin August 20. Uncle Abe would take responsibility to operate the machine. I would take off August 24 and meet Nettie in Medicine Hat, where she had to change trains. We would stop our threshing operation for Saturday and Sunday, August 26 and 27. Nettie and I would be married on Sunday afternoon.

With fear and trembling, Mother, Lydia and Helen, who lived just a mile away, began to make plans. Sunday afternoon was reserved. The customary *Polterabend* (wedding shower) the evening before the wedding would be held in a tent that was to be erected next to our house on the farm. The relatives—the Toews and the Janz clans—and some of the neighbors would bake *zwieback*, cookies and bread. They would also cook *borscht* and *plumamoos*. A year-old ox calf would be slaughtered to provide meat.

Various events were planned, though not without some tension and questions. A rich program was prepared for the *Polterabend*. Father wrote a play to be presented by Lydia, Jake and Henry. Songs were selected and the music organized. The church choir and the extended family would be invited for the evening. Nettie was kept informed as preparations were made.

Nettie packed her trunk, two suitcases and the wedding dress she had purchased together with her sister Grace. Our last letters were exchanged.

The day came. On August 22 Mr. Unruh took his daughter to Sioux Falls in his new Buick. She boarded the train. It was a line from Kansas City that stopped in Sioux Falls and went into Canada and across the Prairies to Vancouver. She did not need to change trains until Medicine Hat, about two hours from Coaldale. No one from her family accompanied her. She was alone on the train for two days and one night. She was to arrive in Medicine Hat the second night at 3:00 a.m.

On Wednesday, August 24 I took the evening train to Medicine Hat, arriving there at 9:30 p.m. It would be a long wait until 3:00 a.m.! I spent the five-and-a-half hours in the railroad station reviewing the more than two-and-a-half years since Nettie had appeared on the stage of Tabor College and recited "The Picture on the Wall." It had not been an easy time for Nettie. I had not seen her for more than a year.

The train arrived on time. It was a long train. From which car would she emerge? I spotted her as she appeared in the door of a car in the center of the train. I was immediately at her side. At last she was here!

We placed her luggage in a locker and spent the next hours in a small park next to the station. Here we could be alone as we awaited the 7:00 a.m. train to Coaldale.

These were precious hours for both of us. After a year and three months we were again together. We reviewed all that had happened since our separation. She did not hesitate to share with me the depths of her past struggles. There were tears. There were also prayers of thanksgiving as we recounted the leading of God in both of our lives up to this point. We reviewed the wedding plans. She asked if I had any suggestions for how to meet my family, whom she had never seen before.

A few minutes after 9:00 a.m. the train pulled into Coaldale. My brother Jacob met us at the station with David's old truck. Nettie seemed not to notice the contrast between the new Buick that had taken her to Sioux Falls and the old truck that met her at the end of her long journey.

When we arrived at the farm the whole family was gathered to meet Nettie. She addressed them in German. Mother embraced her with tears in her eyes. Father's greeting was more formal. Lydia and Helen followed mother, embracing Nettie with tears flowing over their cheeks.

Nettie was not emotional by nature, but the reception overwhelmed her. Such outpouring of emotion was not known in the Unruh family. She could not withhold her tears.

Moisture of a different kind came upon us most unexpectedly. A deluge of rain during the night soaked the grain and postponed any further threshing for at least three to four days. The family and everyone involved in the wedding celebration was now free. Father affirmed that this was a special provision of God.

Six decades later I still remember Nettie's gracious reaction to the primitive environment she now faced. She made no comparisons between our poverty and the circumstances from which she came. My family's outpouring of love helped her relax. Her German, used to converse with my parents and also Helen and David, who did not speak any English, was remarkably fluent. She appeared relaxed and comfortable when on Friday she met my sister Liese, who came home from Calgary where she worked at the time.

Lydia assigned Nettie a corner room upstairs. She unpacked the most necessary things. There were no closets for her clothes, just a few hangers and nails on protruding two-by-fours. On Friday morning, Nettie joined the planning and preparations. Lydia, always ahead of everybody, provided leadership.

More rain came Friday and Saturday. The family and people in general were relaxed. We were the talk of the community. John B. Toews was going to marry an American nurse!

Rain in Coaldale changed the landscape considerably. The roads then were not paved or graveled. The soil, when wet, was sticky. David's old truck got stuck in the mud. Horses and trailer were more practical.

On Saturday a tent was erected beside the house to entertain guests and to serve meals on long tables that had been improvised with boards borrowed from the lumberyard and placed across sawhorses. A table cloth was spread over the boards. The extended family all participated. Some of the food was cooked in a large kettle outside.

The *Polterabend* on Saturday night brought together the extended family, the church choir and friends. Many of them came in rubber boots because of the continued rain. Those from some distance away came with horses and buggies. My uncle Aron Toews and his family from Namaka, Alberta, came by car. The 1928 Chevrolet was to take us, the bridal couple, to the church, a distance of four miles. This cultural environment and the unusual methods of celebration were new and very strange to Nettie, but she took it all in stride.

Sunday, August 27, brought sunshine after the heavy rains. It was a beautiful day. John A. Toews, my cousin, was our chauffeur with his '28 Chevy. The roads were slick and the car slid from side to side, but we reached the church.

The choir sang. My uncle, B. B. Janz gave the first message based on Psalm 27:1: "The Lord is my light and my salvation; whom shall I fear? The Lord is the strength of my life; of whom shall I be afraid?" My father followed with a message based on Ephesians 5:25: "Husbands, love your wives as Christ loved the church and gave himself for it." My father also performed the ceremony. A coffee hour with refreshments followed at the reception.

Monday and Tuesday were days of family gatherings. We still could not thresh because the grain was moist. They were perfect days to introduce Nettie to the extended family: the Abram Toewses, the B. B. Janzes and the Jacob Janzens, as well as uncles and aunts, cousins and close friends. On Tuesday Nettie and I went to Lethbridge. We travelled by horse and buggy, something Nettie hadn't done since childhood. We had lunch together in Lethbridge and shopped at Eaton's.

By Wednesday the grain was dry and we began threshing at noon. I took my usual place and was responsible for the operation. Nettie brought mid-afternoon coffee and snacks to the threshing crew. How well I remember that event and all the attention focused on her. Here was a nurse from South Dakota, a member of a wealthy family (by the standards of the 1930s), and still a very common person who could fit right in with our immigrant social structure. She had won the admiration and respect of the total community.

The month of September sped by. The weather was dry and the threshing went well. Nettie continued to bring mid-day refreshments to the threshing crew. Lydia returned to her job in Lethbridge. Nettie spent time with my mother, and a very close relationship developed. She had become part of the family.

Bethany Bible Institute

The good time in Coaldale after our wedding ended too soon. It was time to move on. We prepared to relocate to Hepburn. A teacher from the Herbert (Saskatchewan) Bible School, Nick Janz, who was visiting in Coaldale, offered to take us to Hepburn in his 1930 Chevrolet. Nettie's trunk fit into the back seat and the suitcases went into the car trunk. With the three of us in the front seat we left for Hepburn, stopping overnight in Herbert. On October 11 we arrived in Hepburn.

There was no house available for us. We moved in with the Priebs, who had an extra bedroom and a heated porch on the south end of the house. We had all our meals at the Priebs' table. They were wonderful people, but as a married couple we found the adjustment difficult. It was too crowded and there wasn't enough privacy.

It wasn't until February of 1934 that a small house—a shed with a slanting roof—became available. It had two rooms. One large room served as living room, kitchen, pantry and study. The bedroom was large enough for a double bed, with no clothes closet. To store our clothes we improvised a shelf with boxes on top and hangers underneath. A wood stove in the big room served for cooking as well as for heat. During the coldest winter months, November to February, the water in the house froze during the night if the fire in the stove went out. Water had to be fetched from the town well a block away.

Our lifestyle was very primitive, but at least we had a place to call home. It would remain our home until January 1936 when a larger house became available to rent. What a contrast to the comfortable Unruh home in South Dakota with several bedrooms, spacious living and dining rooms, a large kitchen, a full basement, inside plumbing and bathrooms, and electricity. But Nettie appeared content. "It is all right to be poor" was part of our commitment.

The school year of fall 1933 marked the sixth anniversary of Bethany. George W. Peters joined the faculty to replace the ailing Jacob Dueck, one of the three teachers. The enrollment was growing. Plans were made to purchase a house to serve as a student dormitory with a kitchen and din-

ing hall. Consideration was given to adding a fourth year to the program.
A course in practical nursing for women students was introduced.

Bible Institute Administration

Bethany, with an expanding program, needed to interrelate with other
Bible schools such as Briercrest and Prairie Bible Institute where some of
our Mennonite Brethren young people attended. Dietrich Esau, our principal, did not command enough English to negotiate such relationships.
As a farmer, he could not provide the necessary leadership and attention
during the six months when school was not in session. On July 27, 1934
the Bethany association invited me to become the principal.

I had planned to give a good portion of the summer months to the
churches in the northern states—the Central District Conference—where I
had found wide acceptance. To accept new responsibility at school did
not fit into these plans. The prospect of my assuming the leadership had
also come up in fall of 1933 but I had declined because I felt I was not
ready. The association kept up the pressure, and after prayer and consultation with Nettie I finally accepted.

In the summer of 1934 a building from Main Street was moved to the
Bethany campus. A full basement provided the kitchen and dining room
plus a large pantry. The upstairs had room for a small classroom for fourth-
year students, a one-room apartment for the houseparents of the girls dormitory, and rooms for eighteen women students.

All work on the moving and construction was done by volunteers.
My full time was needed to recruit volunteers, collect the finances and
organize the school program for 1934-1935. The first catalog was printed,
the first official letterhead designed and a broader public relations effort
launched.

My father returned to Hepburn to fill the position of a fourth teacher.
This time Mother came with him. They became the first houseparents in
the new dormitory. Now in his sixties, he was a major influence in the life
of Bethany. To the student body, the faculty and constituency he became
known as *Vaeterchen Toews*, (roughly translated as "Beloved Daddy
Toews"). His unquestioning confidence in God's providential control of
human history and the life of the individual provided a healthy balance
during this time of expansion.

I deeply valued my father's stabilizing presence and influence, though our spiritual and theological orientations were not identical. Though only twenty-eight, I was now principal of a Bible school. My background was one of Pietism buffeted by exposure to atheism in Russia, rationalism in the Netherlands, narrowness in Coaldale, and the influence of Tabor College. Though in principle I had committed my life to the ministry, I continued to struggle with the naivete of faith and the implicit theology that characterized the early Mennonite Brethren Church and the Bible school movement in North America.

The Bible schools in the 1930s sought to meet a twofold need. First, they offered young people a basic grounding in Scripture. The age of sixteen was the criterion for accepting a student, with no consideration of previous education. The second purpose was to offer advanced courses to older students who showed promise for Christian service, either in the church or missions. The third and fourth years were added for that purpose.

I was responsible for most of the instruction in doctrine and theology. This was really beyond my qualifications, as I had no advanced theological training. My biblical training in Russia was enough for the first two years, but I was not prepared for the advanced courses such as biblical exegesis and theology. Even the courses I took at Tabor did not properly equip me for the task.

I embarked on a rigorous course of self-study. Abraham H. Unruh, then at Winkler, Manitoba, suggested materials: Decksel's *Bibel Werk;* Osterzee's *New Testament Theology;* Ohlinger's *Old Testament Theology* and the works of Adolf Schlatter. Hepburn thus became the place where I was introduced to theological studies. Kept busy with administration by day, the evenings often stretched into the early morning as I searched and studied what I needed for the upper-level students. Looking back now I wonder if my overwork then didn't eventually lead to illness. The benefit of these studies, however, became obvious later at seminary where I was able to "challenge" a number of courses in theology by writing exams covering these areas.

In time I came to view the Hepburn years with great fondness. The commitment of the faculty to the cause of Bible training, the support of the constituency and the enthusiasm of the student body, provided a dynamic setting.

The tuition was $15 per student for the six-month school term. All meals were served at the dining hall for $6 per month. Staple foods—potatoes, vegetables, meat and flour—were donated by farmers. A regular item in the diet was frozen fish shipped in from the northern lakes for seven to nine cents per pound. Wood for the large stoves in each classroom was donated by the farmers, who cut it from the poplar forests that still existed in the area. These were the depressed 1930s. Prosperity was a stranger. Students and faculty alike were devoted to spiritual values, not material success. That commitment continues to characterize many of that generation, now in their seventies and eighties.

Bethany's Faculty

The years with my father as a colleague at Bethany were very important. Dietrich Esau left the school in the spring of 1936 to accept a position at the Mennonite Collegiate Institute in Gretna, Manitoba. Henry G. Wiens, a graduate of Prairie Bible Institute who had also done some work at the University of Alberta, was appointed to fill the vacancy. He and G. W. Peters, another faculty member, both had strong personalities and frequently rocked the boat. I had severe confrontations with both of them. During that time my father's wise way of dealing with tensions, which he had experienced often in his many years in leadership, was a source of guidance.

Nettie particularly remembered one of those confrontations. Several times I had mentioned to her that I was experiencing tension with G. W. Peters, who stayed at the home of Aron Peters, a store owner whose house was across the street from Bethany. One day at the supper table, after a typical depression meal of fish and potatoes, I had been very quiet. Finally I told her, "I must go to see my father." An hour later I came back and said now I needed to go and see G. W. Peters. He was a very gifted man, but very single-minded about some things and insubordinate to the decisions of his colleagues. He had defied some decisions of the faculty in matters of school policies and curriculum. Nettie sensed tension in my voice. I left the house about 7:45 in the evening. When I did not return by ten she became concerned. The temperature, typical for January in Saskatchewan, was nearly thirty below zero. She waited until eleven, then eleven-thirty. What could have happened to me? Had I fallen on the icy road? By midnight she decided to go looking for me. As she neared the Peters' home she saw light in the window of George's room and concluded that the discussion was continuing. She turned around and went back to our little shack. About one in the morning I finally came home. She had waited up for me. I briefly summarized our long discussion and said, "What a stubborn man."

The next day Peters' classes had no teacher. I had left him with the words: "If you are ready to cooperate so we can work in harmony, then I will expect you to meet your classes tomorrow as usual. If you will not be there, I will conclude that you are not accepting the conditions for our work together." The executive members of the board had been informed of the approaching crisis and had assured me of their support. From his absence I concluded that he would leave the school. But on the second day he was back teaching his classes. Nothing more was said of our clash, and Peters continued on the faculty.

A most significant event in Peters' life was his marriage to Susie Lepp in summer of 1935. God provided a balancing influence to his driving, sometimes impetuous, temperament in the person of a woman who also had a strong personality but was controlled by a tender, wise and gracious spirit.

My relationship with Peters later developed into a lifelong and very cherished, friendship. We continued to debate various issues over the years but we never let it affect our relationship as very close friends.

The problem with Henry G. Wiens began when he, a member of the faculty, began to date one of the women students, Margaretha Niesen. Today that would not be as severe a problem as it was in 1935. The Bible institute rules forbade any courtship while school was in session. For a faculty member to violate the policy was especially problematic. Wiens ignored all admonitions. In the summer of 1936 they married and the immediate problem was solved.

The story of Henry G. Wiens, however, did not have a positive end. He left Bethany in 1937 to enter Dallas Theological Seminary and later completed a doctorate at the Baptist seminary in Fort Worth, Texas. Against my warning, the Reedley Mennonite Brethren Church called him as an associate pastor in 1946. He created problems that brought about a crisis in the Reedley congregation (to be reported later). Following this crisis, Wiens became one of the casualties of the ministry of the Mennonite Brethren Conference.

The Hepburn Farm

In March 1934, while in Hepburn, we received a letter from Nettie's father mentioning some land he had bought some years ago in the Waldheim municipality. He asked if we would be in a position to investigate the location of the 480-acre farm that he was renting to a family by the name of Loewen.

Nettie had not known that her father owned land in Canada. At the first opportunity I made my way to the municipal office in Waldheim to investigate the location. The farm was only three miles northwest of Hepburn. That fall Father Unruh sent us the deed for 160 acres of the farm, containing some old dilapidated buildings, a house and a large barn. We became the owners of a quarter section of land. It was a special day when we announced to the renter that we were the owners of the land and that upon Father Unruh's request we would negotiate new rent conditions and look after Father's interest related to the farm.

In June of 1935 Nettie's parents and her brother Isaac came to Hepburn to visit us and to look over their investment in the farm. A large part of the land was pasture, eighty acres were still virgin soil with poplar trees, and the rest was in grain: barley, oats and wheat. As a result of this visit Father Unruh sent us the deed for the remaining acres and the money to tear down the old barn and build a new one. Now we were the owners of a 480-acre farm only three miles from Hepburn!

As it turned out, our new renter was no stranger. He was George Braun, a playmate from my childhood in Russia. He had been a neighbor of my grandparents in Alexanderkrone. Now he and his family moved onto our farm for the next two years.

Nettie and I could no longer consider ourselves poor. We wondered if this provision for additional income was intended so we could be independent in our future ministry.

I had committed July and August of 1935 to a ministry in the Central District churches in Minnesota, North Dakota and Montana. We bought a 1929 Model T Ford to make the trip. Since I had received my Canadian citizenship in 1933, we could now cross the border with confidence. Nettie travelled with me for the six-week tour, the only time she did so, for such an extended time, in the fifty-three years of our very happy marriage.

A Family Tragedy

In November of 1935 Father Unruh, with four other men from the community, went to a public auction sale in Sioux Falls. On the way back they were in a head-on collision with a drunk driver. Nettie's father and two others in the car were killed. Our shock was indescribable. We boarded a train in Saskatoon and travelled via Regina and Minneapolis to Sioux Falls to be with our family. The Freeman-Marion communities were also in shock. The men, Isaak Schmidt, Henry Buller and our father, Cornelius Unruh, were all prominent people of the community. Because the Bible school was already in session we could only stay a week to share the family's deep grief.

We wondered if some premonition had led Father to transfer owner-ship of his Hepburn land to us, so shortly before his death.

Our Ordination

In 1936, after three years in Hepburn, the North Saskatchewan Dis-trict pressed me to accept formal confirmation of my call to the ministry. As principal of the Bible institute, they felt, I needed to be ordained. Such a distinction was very important in the earlier history of the Mennonite Brethren Church. I declined their request because I was waiting for my home church in Coaldale to extend this confidence to me. Without my knowledge, the Bethany board secretary, Frank J. Baerg, wrote to the Coaldale church to inquire about their plans for my ordination. He ex-plained that my extensive ministry, in their opinion, required the affirma-tion of ordination. The Coaldale leadership responded as follows: "For the present we have no intention to recognize the ministry of J. B. Toews in an ordination. We are not certain about the future direction of the brother." The statement no doubt had something to do with their earlier doubts about my studies, but it also reflected the deep and even fearful conservatism of Coaldale.

When the Bethany board shared the reply with me I felt greatly re-jected by my home church. The North Saskatchewan Conference then renewed the invitation to be ordained, and I consented. The recognition of my ministry was important to me.

Jacob Lepp, a veteran in the faith, brought the message based on Isaiah 53:1-3. He described the humility of Christ as a tender plant and as a root out of dry ground, one who "is despised and rejected of men; a man of sorrows and acquainted with grief." He ended his discourse with the statement, "The ministry is a service of deep humility; it promises very little recognition. You may be used as a floor mat for people to step on and clean their shoes. If you are prepared to be a servant after the example of Jesus, express your commitment by rising to your feet."

For a moment I was petrified. I looked at Nettie who sat next to me. She took my hand and we both stood. Lepp, Jacob Dyck and Peter Nickel laid hands on us and prayed, dedicating us to God for such a ministry.

We had taken another crucial step. Earlier we had said yes to "It is all right to be poor." Now we were making a commitment to humility and possible rejection.

The Farming Experiment

In the fall of 1936 we bought four horses and the necessary implements to operate the farm the following spring. Jacob Neufeld, a Bethany student, lived on the farm and tended to the horses. The school year closed at the beginning of April. Nettie and I moved for the summer, into the old house on the farm. We bought a milk cow and a few calves to take advantage of the large pasture.

With four beautiful horses and a one-way seeder disc, I personally put in the spring crop. What an opportunity! We had a farm, a good team of horses, a large pasture, and a happy marriage. In winter I would teach at the Bible school and in summer I would be a farmer.

One evening I had just finished seeding a field close to the road when Jacob Schellenberg, a prosperous farmer a mile and a half to the north, stopped and reviewed my work. As I unhitched the horses he came to me and said: "If that field will bring a crop, that will be more luck than brains." "Why do you say that, Mr. Schellenberg?" I asked. "You just are not a farmer," he answered. He drove off and I took the horses into the barn, fed them and went in for dinner.

I was very quiet during the meal. After dark I decided to go for a walk. Returning to the field I had seeded, I pondered what Schellenberg had said: "You just are not a farmer." I knelt down on the open field and prayed. Had we made a mistake, moving to the farm? Nettie had expressed her own concerns about this venture. "Do you think that you will be a farmer?" she had asked. Inwardly I struggled.

At the end of August I bought a New Harvest binder to cut the crop. The Schellenbergs looked after the threshing. The crop was only fair because of drought. The issue of the farm was a critical factor in my struggles over the future ministry to which we were committed. A good farm operation had the potential to provide economic security. Was this to replace the medical profession to which I had aspired since the death of my older brother, Aron?

We tried again in 1937. Jacob Neufeld took care of the horses and the few cattle in fall and winter. I took over the supervision of the farm in spring of 1938, the year when Saskatchewan experienced a complete crop failure because of drought and a grasshopper plague.

The Birth of John Eldon

Both Nettie and I were mature when we married, thirty and twenty-eight. We both wanted to have children. For three years we hoped in vain. In early spring of 1936 a medical specialist in Saskatoon said Nettie's condition would permanently disqualify her from bearing children.

At the same time a mother in Laird, some twenty-five miles from Hepburn, died, leaving eight children behind. An opportunity arose to adopt the two youngest children, one eight months old and the other two years. Their father could not provide for them all and sought parents for the two children. We entered into discussions with him.

One night when Nettie could not sleep she awoke me and said, "Tomorrow we will notify the family in Laird that we will not continue further consideration of adoption." When I asked why, she answered, "I believe we will have our own." More than one year later, on July 27, 1937 our first son Eldon John was born (later, when grown, he would change his name to John Eldon). We accepted him as a special gift from God.

The joyous prospect of a child forced the issue of our living conditions. Our shack had been adequate for us but was not suitable for a child. In late fall of 1936 a house on the north edge of Hepburn became available for rent. We moved during Christmas vacation. In the spring of 1938 a house close to the railroad on the south edge of town became available. We purchased the house with a half acre of land for $750 and moved in. Our plan was to settle down. We had no idea it would be just for a few months.

A Brief Pastorate

Before my coming to Hepburn, Peter Friesen, an ordained minister, had resigned from the leadership of the Hepburn Mennonite Brethren Church. For some years the leadership was in the hands of a deacon, David Schmor, with teachers from the Bible school providing the teaching and preaching ministry. Brother Schmor was a very kind person but his leadership gifts were limited. The Bible school teachers, whose first priority was the school, could not give the time for the spiritual nurture of individuals and families. The congregation was suffering spiritually. The Bible school, an integral part of the church's life, was also affected.

In January of 1937 the church appealed to me to become their leader. Considering the unanimous vote of the church, the faculty encouraged me to accept the pastorate for a year or two to help bring stability, while continuing to teach part-time. After some struggle, Nettie and I accepted the invitation of the church. With the close of the 1936-1937 academic year, G. W. Peters was appointed principal of the school.

The Hepburn congregation, then the largest Mennonite Brethren church in Saskatchewan, was a wounded fellowship. The resignation of Peter Friesen had precipitated a crisis that divided the church. Some large family groups had taken different sides regarding Friesen's leadership and had never found healing. To shepherd a flock with so many wounds was difficult for us. The church badly needed renewal and reconciliation.

I had served on the church council for the past three years. In rereading the minutes of that time, it amazed me how much intense conflict can be generated in a congregation that lacks strong leadership.

During the winter of 1937 and 1938 I devoted much of my time to house visitation. With a small sleigh and two horses I travelled from farm to farm to visit individual families and groups of people. A midweek prayer meeting was instituted. Concern for the condition of the church spread. The response to our ministry was very positive. People began to rally. There were some conversions. In June of 1938 we had a baptism.

As a church we had invited J. N. C. Hiebert, a missionary to India who was home on furlough, to come to Hepburn for a week of services at the end of July 1938. The church was ready. God brought deep repentance to the congregation, and many individuals were reconciled. The meetings were extended. There were also first-time conversions. It was a blessed time. In August we had a second baptism with fifteen people following Christ in obedience.

When I was three: A school picture; the teacher in the middle, my father. To his left, the boy with the cap, "Hans" as I was called in my early childhood. To fathers right my sisters Helen and Liese. Aron, my older brother standing in the last row, the fourth from the left.

1914-1917, My father in the Red Cross service in Moscow, as a chaplain for the Mennonite men.

A group of college university students, 1925. I am the second from the left in the second row.

A photo taken a few hours before we smuggled out my uncle B. B. Janz to escape the secret police in Charkow, spring 1926. From left to right, Helen my sister, David Reimer, who planned the escape, my uncle B. B. Janz and myself.

A farewell picture with my close friend Daniel Reimer a few hours before we left our native village, Alexandertal. The scene, a big rock on the meadow across the creek Chekrak behind our farmstead.

A family picture taken in the morning of our departure in the backyard of our house. From left to right sitting, Father and Mother. Standing, John, Helen, Eliesabeth, Lydia, Jacob, Henry and Jacob Dahl, who travelled with us because his family had preceded two years earlier and left him behind because he did not pass the health inspection.

The family van Tigohelhoven who provided a home for me for the time that I was in Holland.

The tractor that provided the first job for me. I am at the steering wheel. On the tractor, my brother Henry. To the right the house I built.

Our farmstead in 1930 when I left Coaldale to go to Tabor College.

The Coaldale Church choir, a farewell gift from the choir members on the occasion of my farewell. Members of the extended family: sitting in the front row from left to right, Peter Dick, Helen Janz, my first cousin, myself as the choir director, Mary Janz, later Mrs. Jacob Neuman. In the last row second from the right my sister Lydia who later married Peter Dick.

My first car given to me by the church in Lehigh, in appreciation for my ministry while serving them as their pastor — preaching on Sundays. To my left Lando Hiebert, who later became a professor at Tabor College.

Nettie Unruh, as I learned to know her while at Tabor College.

One hour before we said yes to "until death shall part you."

The extended family and guests on the day of our wedding.

A family picture taken the day after our wedding. Left to right, front row: myself, Mother, Helen Pauls, daughter of my sister Helen, Father, John Pauls, son of my sister Helen, Helen my sister. Second row: Nettie, sister Lydia, brother Henry, brother Jacob, sister Elisabeth, David Pauls, husband of sister Helen.

Our transportation for deputation in the churches for students and faculty, 1932-1938 (courtesy Henry and Margaretha Thiessen, Hepburn, Sask.).

Our farmstead near Hepburn, circa 1952.

Rest and Redirection

By the third year of our marriage I was beginning to experience times of extreme exhaustion. I would come home from school and have to lie down to rest. When this condition persisted, we consulted Dr. Neufeld, a physician in Saskatoon. He did not find any organic misfunctions. With some prescribed vitamins we continued our schedule, spending the summer ministering in churches and returning to school for fall and winter.

A Critical Diagnosis

When we began to operate the farm we assumed it would bring relaxation. When my exhaustion continued we again consulted Dr. Neufeld. Still not finding anything abnormal he referred us to a group of doctors specializing in diagnostic investigations. Several visits and many tests later I was diagnosed as having a malfunction of the adrenal glands. For two years I was sustained by daily injections, which Nettie, as a professional nurse, could administer. Still, the exhaustion got worse. I withdrew from part-time teaching during the final quarter of 1938 to save my strength to cope with the demands of the pastorate. In June I had a battery of tests by another specialist. He told me, "Mr. Toews, you are a very sick man. Your adrenal glands have stopped functioning. You are only being sustained by daily injections. You are a young man. Maybe you can be helped if you withdraw from all responsibilities and possibly move to a warmer climate."

Somewhat dazed, we drove back to Hepburn. "What does this mean for us?" we asked. I was only thirty-two years old. We had the school, the church, and now also the farm. How could we detach ourselves from all this and face an unknown future?

We shared the diagnosis in confidence with only a few close friends, the Frank Baergs, who had become like parents to us during our six years in Hepburn, and G. W. Peters as the school principal. While we struggled for an answer we continued our work. The farm operation, which we had continued with some hired help, was a complete fiasco. Grasshoppers and the drought had destroyed our crop. Provision had to be made for the farm's future.

The church had just begun to respond to our ministry. Could we resign and leave it again without leadership? Where could we go to find a suitable climate? Our financial resources, after the heavy investments in the farm, were limited. We felt helpless and perplexed. We had invited J. N. C. Hiebert to lead meetings in July. The church should not be in uncertainty. For now we would press on, and wait.

Hiebert had spent part of his furlough in Salem, Oregon, and attended the Western Baptist Theological Seminary. As we told him in confidence about our situation he made a suggestion. Oregon provided the mild climate our doctor had recommended. I could audit classes there to enrich myself while we waited for my health to improve. This sounded to us like a direction from God.

After consulting with the F. J. Baergs and G. W. Peters, the following plan emerged. We would inform the church of our situation and the doctor's urgent advice, and request a leave of absence. My father, who was in Hepburn, would assume the pastoral responsibilities of house visitation and individual nurture. The Bible school faculty would again take charge of the teaching and preaching ministry.

On September 12 we followed through with this plan and shared our situation with the church. A small minority of the congregation was by this time aware of our crisis. We found understanding. They granted us a leave of absence without stipulating a date of return.

A Change of Climate

My parents moved into the house we had purchased less than a year ago. We turned the farm over to John H. Toews, no relative of ours, and in mid-October took the train to Portland without making advance contacts or arrangements for our stay.

My spirits were at a low ebb as we arrived in Portland early on an October morning and checked into a hotel close to the railroad station. The struggle of that morning is deeply ingrained in my memory. Here I was, sick, with a wife and child, and no plans for the future. While Eldon, a babe of a year and three months, slept, Nettie and I sank to our knees to ask God for guidance.

We had breakfast. We had marked the location of the seminary on the city map. What we needed was an affordable apartment close to the seminary so that I could use the library and possibly audit some classes as health would permit.

I took the streetcar to the location of the seminary. I walked through the streets of the surrounding area, looking for a sign, "Apartment for Rent." Four blocks from the seminary, on Salmon Street, I saw such a sign. Upon inquiry I learned the facility was still vacant. It was a two-bedroom apartment with a small living room and a kitchen. The rent was $22 per month. I accepted this as a provision of God, paid the first month's rent and returned to the hotel.

That afternoon we packed our few belongings into a taxi and went to the apartment. By evening we were settled. The location was very favorable. Some grocery stores were only a block away on Hawthorne Avenue. Only two blocks away was an open market. Our resources were limited. We had a little money saved from the meager wages at school plus $750 that Nettie's father had given us. We thought we could make it last a year.

Our lifestyle was very frugal. We bought milk for Eldon at the store on Hawthorne. A few blocks away we discovered a bakery where we could buy day-old bread for twelve cents a loaf. The open market had plenty of fruit and vegetables. Nettie found that if she waited until the end of the day, about four o'clock, she could buy fruit and vegetables at a discount. The wood for the stove was also reasonable. We often thanked God for the provisions we found for a time like this.

The sudden and dramatic changes left many questions for us. We struggled with indecision. We had consented to come to Hepburn. The provision of a farm that could provide the economic independence I had struggled about, had seemed to confirm our direction. But now my broken health shattered my interpretation of the past. The physician had said my health might restored; he did not say, "it will be restored." Everything seemed out of focus. Nettie, always quiet in times of pressure and difficulty, showed little alarm. Eldon John, an active child, provided the diversion we needed.

Looking back now I recognize the hand of God in our crisis. The Potter was at work, teaching us to trust. We had to accept an unknown future.

Seminary Studies

The change of climate and the freedom from stressful responsibilities produced an immediate change in my health. In November and December we took many walks. Nettie, Eldon and I enjoyed the mild rainy weather together. With no demands, I was able to sleep. I spent many afternoons at the seminary library. Soon after our arrival I asked the seminary to process my academic standing. The certified affidavit from Gerhard Duerksen, a former member of the Ukraine university senate, describing the work I had done, was recognized. The work in the Netherlands, the elementary Greek that I began under the tutorship of Dr. Benjamin H. Unruh in England and continued at Tabor College with Dr. H. W. Lohrenz, was also recognized. My courses in philosophy, theology and public speaking were also accepted and applied toward seminary requirements. I was classified as a second-year student in the bachelor of divinity program.

In the middle of January, the beginning of the second semester, I enrolled for twelve hours. My health continued to improve. The injections on which I had depended for the last two years were discontinued. By spring of 1939 I felt like my old self. The change recommended by the physician, and the healing grace of God, had restored my health. Altogether we spent two years in Portland, until the fall of 1940.

I enjoyed the academic program at the seminary. Professor W. Milligan was particularly helpful to me. He had a Ph.D. in science and philosophy and a Dr.Th. in New Testament. My unique Russian background, my Anabaptist tradition and my maturity in contrast to the younger students earned me his special friendship.

Commitment to An Anabaptist Theology

The Western Baptist Theological Seminary had been pioneered by the Oregon Baptist Convention, which for years was in tension with a perceived liberal tendency in the Northern Baptist Convention, especially in the area of higher biblical criticism. The Seminary faculty placed major emphasis on the early history of the Baptist movement, which had its roots in the left wing of the Reformation, namely Anabaptism. They spoke openly of Anabaptism as the womb of the Baptist movement, and called for a return to the roots of their faith.

This focus provided many occasions to speak with Dr. Milligan, the New Testament scholar, and Dr. Collin Cline, professor of theology, about the Mennonite understanding of biblical soteriology and ecclesiology. Unforgettable for me was a class discussion where Dr. Milligan singled me out by name and said, "He is a Mennonite Brethren; they are people who have stayed true to the Scriptures."

Here was where my spiritual consciousness took another decisive turn. I made a third ministry commitment that would shape my pilgrimage for the rest of my days. The first had been in the park in Hillsboro when Nettie said, "It is all right to be poor." That commitment gained further definition during my ordination in Hepburn when I made a second commitment to be open to the prospect of humility and rejection.

Now I made a third major commitment to be not only evangelical but Anabaptist. I had been born into a Mennonite Brethren family. I had the benefit of a father who was a biblicist not only in profession but in actual life. But now, at the age of thirty-four, in a Baptist seminary, I made a conscious decision that what I professed to believe must also be expressed in daily lifestyle and relationships. As the Anabaptist Hans Denck had said, "To believe in Jesus means to follow him in life."

In the more than half century since, I have never questioned that commitment, though I have deep regrets for those occasions when my humanity stood in the way of its full realization. Jesus said, "If any one wants to follow me, let him deny himself, take up the cross and follow me" (Luke 9:23).

The years in Portland were good for us. Nettie and Eldon spent much leisure time together. They frequently took the streetcar to a park with some lakes where Eldon frolicked in the grass under the shady trees and fed the ducks.

Our financial support came from several sources. The tuition at the seminary was paid through a scholarship furnished by the industrialist R. G. LeTourneau, a builder of earthmoving machinery and a member of the seminary board. Dr. Milligan's wide contacts generated many opportunities to minister in the Oregon Baptist churches. Each Sunday provided some financial stipend.

For the summer of 1939 we were invited to come to the church in Dallas, Oregon. Brother F. F. Wall, their pastor, did not preach English, so I had an opportunity to share the ministry. The church paid our rent. Being close to the city park with flowing water and many ducks was again a paradise for Eldon.

I had an opportunity to earn some money during the week through the kindness of Immanuel Nazarenus, a builder. I started out helping the carpenters, but within two days discovered that carpentry was not one of my skills. (I did not tell him of my building the farm house in Coaldale where, as my sister Lydia put it, "not a single corner has a right angle.") He assigned me to saw a group of two-by-fours to a specific length, but the sixteen pieces I cut did not fit. He reassigned me to paint house exteriors. Immanuel, out of the goodness of his heart paid me good wages, which I perhaps never earned.

In fall of 1939 I was invited to be the special speaker at the Pacific District Conference in Dinuba, California, and at a Bible conference to follow the business sessions. Immanuel offered to drive us there. The wife of my brother Jacob, who had come to Portland that fall, offered to take care of Eldon so Nettie could go with me on her first trip to California. God blessed our ministry at the conference. A second invitation followed to come to Los Angeles in January of 1940 for the dedication of the Mennonite Brethren church there.

On the morning that we left Dinuba to return to Portland, Nettie said, "I'm so glad I don't need to live here. I would never want to live in California." How little did we know that the largest part of our life's ministry would be in California. In January 1940 I received my first invitation to minister in British Columbia. Again we sensed the blessing of God. A revival broke out in the churches of the Abbotsford area that is still remembered by people who found new life there more than fifty years ago.

The years in Portland served as our introduction to churches all along the West Coast: British Columbia, Washington, Oregon and California. For the last ten months of our stay in Portland it was our privilege to serve the Powelhurst Baptist Church, which was just getting started.

With the credit I was given at the seminary for my previous academic work, I completed the requirements for the bachelor of divinity degree the first semester of 1939, one year after I entered as a full-time student. The second semester, in the spring of 1940, plus additional classes in the summer, enabled me to complete the residence requirement for the master of theology degree.

Two invitations came to us in February of 1940. The church in Hepburn, which had made only provisional arrangements for the pastorate, hoped we would return. Bethany Bible School, too, was asking for our return. The other door open to us was an invitation to teach Bible at Freeman (South Dakota) College, Nettie's alma mater. Freeman offered the chance to devote one quarter per year plus the summer to continue my studies. We chose to go to Freeman. In late summer of 1940 we were ready to return to Saskatchewan, liquidate our household, make future arrangements for the farm and move to Freeman College for the new school year in September.

The Freeman College Experience

We recall our two years in Freeman with deep affection. Mother Unruh had been a widow since 1935. The move gave us our first opportunity to relate to Nettie's family. We rented a very small apartment in town, though Mother's large house on the farm was also open to us and we spent much time there. Eldon, then three years old, delighted to follow his Uncle Isaac, the youngest of Nettie's brothers, who operated the family farm.

Freeman College, though owned and operated by the General Conference Mennonite Church, was truly an inter-Mennonite institution. The communities of Freeman, Marion and Bridgewater had a cluster of churches representing various ethnic and conference affiliations. In addition to several General Conference churches there were also Krimmer Mennonite Brethren, Evangelical Mennonite Brethren, Hutterites and Mennonite Brethren. The students from these churches represented an ecumenical Mennonite stew. Faculty members also represented several Mennonite varieties. Despite their own uniqueness of character, these church traditions were open in relationship and functioned well together.

The Bible department, which served both the junior college and the academy (high school), concentrated on a historical approach to Scripture. With my experience at Bethany and my recent seminary training, I found the assignment very elementary. During the 1940-1941 academic year I found time to write my thesis for the completion of the master of theology degree on the subject, "The Christ of the Johannine Theology," I went back to Portland for graduation in the spring.

The Freeman sojourn, though short, broadened my experience with the various Mennonite groups. For a few months I served as an interim pastor in the Salem Mennonite Church and also taught their catechism class to baptismal candidates. The pulpit committee, seeking a permanent replacement for Dr. Peter R. Schroeder, their pastor for many years, even invited me to consider the position on a long-term basis. I had the opportunity to minister widely among General Conference churches in South Dakota, Minnesota and Nebraska, as well as the Krimmer and Evangelical Mennonite Brethren of the Midwest. With my own spiritual and theological commitment settled, I experienced great liberty in my ministry. The struggle for self-identity, which had been so much a part of me during the years before Portland, were in the past.

Freeman was also the place where our second son, Paul, was born. November 27 has been a very special day ever since. We enjoyed the benefit of being close to the larger family during this time. Nettie's mother was there to care for Eldon and to help with the new-born. For a time we even moved in with her. Mother Unruh was a very gracious person. She did not carry an ounce of selfishness. Her life was devoted to her husband, which was not always easy, and to her family.

Nettie's sister Grace taught in one of the local schools. Emma, the youngest of the family, worked in a department store in Minneapolis. August Unruh, an older brother, and his family lived on a farm only a mile or two from the parental farm. Nettie's sister, Martha Ratzlaff and her family, also lived only a few miles away. All in all, our time in Freeman was a great period of our life, and the only time in our fifty-three years of our marriage that we could enjoy firsthand all the love of the Unruh family circle.

Fort Worth, Texas

In the summer of 1941 I left Nettie and the boys with Mother on the farm and went to Southwestern Baptist Theological Seminary in Fort Worth, Texas, to begin studies toward a doctor of theology degree. Nettie, Eldon and baby Paul were happy in the caring environment of family and community in Freeman.

The experiences in Fort Worth were academically encouraging. By spending a few summers there I could complete the residence requirements. There was also a possibility of spending the spring quarter of 1942 to work in Fort Worth.

One experience in Fort Worth that first summer has remained indelibly in my memory. One day I received a note in a closed envelope telling me to stop by the office of the student dean. When I arrived he invited me to sit down. Noting my Russian background he explained that I needed to conform to the social rules of the institution. Two violations were called to my attention.

In the dining hall we were served by American black stewards. I felt free to speak to these young men and after the meal would converse with them. This, I was told, violated the social distance that was observed by other white students.

I had committed the same "offense" with a group of black women who sat under a large tree behind the dining hall peeling potatoes and cleaning vegetables. I had accepted their invitation to sit down on an empty chair and chat with them. They were very friendly and appeared delighted that I noticed them.

These incidents, the dean said kindly but firmly, violated the institution's standards of social conduct. He wanted me, as a foreigner, to know the local customs. Whites were to have no contact with blacks.

I found this very difficult to accept. I left the office without responding. I was outraged that a theological institution known for its emphasis on evangelism and scholarship would have such a blatant policy of segregation. I had chosen Southwestern on the suggestion of Drs. Milligan and Cline. How could the seminary in which Harvey E. Dana, a great New Testament scholar and president from 1919 through 1938, or his successor, Dr. Lee Rutland Scarborough, known for his evangelism and author of the book *With Christ After the Lost*, be so inconsistent in their understanding of the New Testament? It became a severe test for my biblical Anabaptism, which had come into focus while in Portland.

A Fork in the Road

In spring of 1941 two invitations came to us; one from Tabor College, our own Mennonite Brethren school, and one from the Mennonite Brethren church in Buhler, Kansas. The Buhler congregation had a significant historic background. Abraham Schellenberg, one of the leaders of the 1870s immigration, had spent the largest part of his life ministering there. For the last fourteen years the church had been served by Peter R. Lange, known in his day as the "Prince of Preachers." We were not ready to respond to these invitations, as we were comfortable in Freeman in the circle of our family.

While in Fort Worth, a request came from Buhler to stop in for a Sunday on my way back to Freeman. I consented. It was an uplifting experience. After the evening service the church committee renewed the request to consider their invitation. A significant plus for Buhler was the overnight train from nearby Newton to Fort Worth. Being located in Buhler would make it easier to complete my studies for the doctorate.

Rejoining the family after a long summer in Texas was a joyous occasion. Awaiting me was a letter from Tabor College, outlining the importance of considering it as a place for my future ministry. We were not ready to respond to either invitation but eventually I informally told Tabor I would come there after another year at Freeman.

My second year's schedule at Freeman College included a number of invitations for Bible conferences. One was for a four-day ministry with the large General Conference church in Henderson, Nebraska. While delivering the message on Friday night I noticed four men from the Buhler church. One of them was Peter Reimer, whom I knew so well from my ministry in Jansen, Nebraska. The Reimers had moved to Buhler and had joined the Mennonite Brethren church there. They requested a brief meeting.

They said they had been sent to personally convey the continued prayers of the church that the Lord would direct us to consider the Buhler pastorate. They knew also that Tabor College had extended us an urgent invitation. Peter R. Lange, their former pastor, had joined the Tabor faculty. My thoughts raced. Should I also go to Tabor College?

Back in Freeman, Nettie and I considered these invitations together. The plea from the Buhler congregation through their delegation lingered with us and caused us to reevaluate our decision to go to Hillsboro.

Tabor was in crisis. William Bestvater, one of the most gifted Bible teachers, a former principal of the Herbert Bible School, and for years a pastor of the church in Shafter, California, had been released from the faculty because of moral indiscretions while in Shafter.

Two major considerations helped us decide which invitation to accept. First, I realized that if I went to Tabor I would inevitably become embroiled in various institutional crises. Second, the Bible department at Tabor did not reflect a clear commitment to the Anabaptist faith that I had recently made a priority. Peter R. Lange, the new head of the Bible department, had described its focus as follows:

(a) It was to be central to the life of the college.

(b) It was to be evangelistic, instilling a passion for the lost.

(c) It should train future missionaries for the conference.

(d) It should magnify the prayer life of the individual student as well as the church.

With my recent commitment to an Anabaptist theology, I considered Lange's emphasis for the school pietistic and limiting. It aimed to be broadly evangelical but seemed to lack clear direction or theological character.

In reflecting on our decision to accept the Buhler invitation I can see a desire to become more firmly rooted in the life of the church. It was in the pastorate that I recognized the implications of a consistent Anabaptist commitment. In the interest of my development, I needed to be immersed in the church community. Buhler was in the plan of the Potter as he formed the vessel.

The General Conference of the Mennonite Brethren Churches of North America was scheduled to convene in Buhler in summer of 1942. The church urgently hoped that the Lord would furnish a pastor to provide leadership for this important event. For me to fulfill this role would require going there at the end of Freeman's second quarter. That was the time I had planned to return to Fort Worth, since the one quarter and the summer would enable me to complete the residence requirements for the doctorate. Another consideration was the need to stay close to Nettie's mother, whose health was failing.

The decision was difficult. We finally concluded that our long-range future required further pastoral ministry, an area where we I had the least experience. We could always return to teaching later. Since the spring quarter of 1942 was provided for, Freeman could spare me. In October 1941 we committed ourselves to move to Buhler. The next year's General Conference made it urgent to be there for spring and summer. We made the move at the beginning of March.

CHAPTER 13

The Buhler Ministry

O ur new home in Buhler was the parsonage across the street from the church. It was the first comfortable house we had lived in since our marriage. Not everything else in Buhler would match that degree of comfort, however. We found a church in transition. I would learn some critical lessons about what it means to be a pastor.

One of these lessons was that congregations need more than a pulpit ministry. Under P. R. Lange, the Buhler church had been blessed with great preaching. He read widely in the devotional literature of his day. His sermons tended to be more topical than deeply exegetical. He would read the text, close the Bible and in an oratorical style present the message. From the perspective of polished delivery, Buhler had experienced great preaching.

The Role of a Shepherd

In Lange's years, however, the relational dimension had received less emphasis. The church annual report dated December 27, 1942 notes that membership was 502, of which 103 were non-resident. In some of these cases years had gone by with no contact with the church. A clear lesson to me was that building the body takes more than preaching, it also takes a strong relational dimension. Jesus said, "I am the good shepherd; I know my sheep and my sheep know me" (John 10:14). It was in Buhler where the Lord taught me what it means to be a shepherd of the flock.

I made it my first priority to get to know my people and to be available so they could know me. Church records show that within the first ten months of 1942 I made 124 house visits, 41 consultations with members in spiritual need, plus 61 hospital calls and 49 sick visits in homes. I also preached 122 sermons, 66 in morning and evening worship services, and the rest at weddings, funerals, family events and special meetings.

Nettie accompanied me on many visits, especially those in homes. God gave us reliable people to serve as babysitters for our boys. Ably assisting in the leadership of the church were Ministers John Hildebrandt and A. R. Epp, plus the four deacons who served at the time. All were very solid people and offered every support I needed.

There were tensions below the surface that needed to be addressed. One prominent member had borrowed money from many others in the church, and when his business failed he could not pay it back. This created much pain in the congregation. There were also cases of family disunity. Some families were so stricken that parents and children sat on opposite sides during church services. There were wayward young people who needed care and guidance.

Unified leadership and a faithful ministry of intercessory prayer became the keys to addressing these tensions. Within the first eighteen months we began to see victories from God. Some divisions were finally settled through God's providence as certain people were removed through death. Our struggle toward
purification resulted in a great renewal that God brought to us through the special ministry of Theodore Epp from Back to the Bible Broadcast.

Through all this, we as a family experienced much love and care. We were the first pastoral family to come to the church from the outside. Up to that point all leadership had come from within the community fellowship.

The Test of Impartiality

One of the early tests at Buhler was that of impartiality in relationships. My predecessor for the past fourteen years had come from within the community and had long ties to certain families. A circle of close friends had supplemented his meager income as the first paid pastor of the church. Business people, friends from his youth, had regularly provided him with new cars that he would otherwise not have been able to afford. Now I came along with an old car, a 1934 Chevrolet, which had been given to us by Nettie's mother.

The Buhler church was somewhat sophisticated. It had a strong group of wealthy and talented people. The local bank and flour mill were owned and staffed by members of the church. Other establishments, too, including stores, machine shops, garages, filling stations, city government and the post office, were all staffed by members of the church.

Without ulterior motive, some men from the business community became concerned about the old car their new pastor was driving. Being wartime, new cars were unavailable, so they purchased a good quality used car and came to present it to us. It was an awkward moment. I had already learned of the lifelong friendship between the former pastor and certain people in the church. I did not want to question their motive, nor could I accept their well-intentioned gift. I told them gently that in my position as pastor I could not accept such a gift from a particular group within the church. They seemed to understand.

One Sunday morning several months later, John Hildebrandt, chair of the church council, came up to the platform and asked for the opportunity to speak. On behalf of the church he read a statement expressing appreciation for our ministry and said that the whole congregation, including every Sunday school class, had participated in the purchase of a car for their pastor. Then he handed me the keys to a 1941 Ford. Now I could accept the gift, for everyone had had a share in it. The gift was a project that unified rather than divided the church.

This was a lesson for all of us. The service of the pastorate demanded that I be known not as a hireling, not one who served because I was paid, but as a servant irrespective of any economic returns. This became a lifelong principle of ministry for me. It remained consistent with our covenant in the park in Hillsboro: "It is all right to be poor."

The Painful 1943 Conference

The conditions of wartime had necessitated postponing the General Conference, giving the Buhler church more time to prepare. Planned for 1942, the conference assembled May 26-30, 1943. Being host pastor gave me a new level of General Conference participation. At the 1933 conference in Reedley, California, I had been appointed to the General Conference youth committee along with J. W. Vogt of Hillsboro and Leslie Wiebe of Corn, Oklahoma. In 1936 this committee was enlarged to five members. A youth committee meeting in 1934 marked my first active participation in a General Conference assignment. In 1937 *The Christian Leader* was launched as the first English publication of the General Conference. I, with J. W. Vogt and Leslie Wiebe, served as the editorial committee.

The Buhler conference dealt with several crucial issues. One was a conference policy on how to handle moral lapses of ministers. It concerned one of the most popular and esteemed Bible teachers of the conference. A second very painful experience of historic proportions was the censure of the Tabor College president, Dr. P. E. Schellenberg, over questions of the orthodoxy of his faith. I found it devastating to see students from the college publicly question the spiritual integrity of their teacher and president.

The crisis of Tabor College in the 1940s was partly a consequence of its own history. The motive for establishing the institution in 1908 had been to lead Mennonite Brethren beyond their spiritual and cultural isolation as a rural agricultural people. It was to draw them, as the college song said, "To a higher plane of vision."

The initial response of the young people to the opportunity of a Christian liberal arts education was phenomenal. Seventy-five percent of the graduates of the first eight years went to graduate schools. Ninety-four percent of the graduates of the second decade went on in their search for knowledge. By 1920 Tabor graduates attended such prestigious schools as the University of California at Berkeley, Yale Divinity School and the University of Chicago.[7] The churches, however, were not prepared to absorb such a wave of talented men and women. As a result some of the most gifted potential leaders were lost to other denominations and institutions.[8]

This phenomenon was not unique to the Mennonite Brethren, however. The early history of Tabor was strongly affected by a seismic clash that affected American Christianity generally. This was the struggle of fundamentalism versus modernism, with the battle between creationism and evolution at its center.[9]

As the only Mennonite Brethren institution of higher learning, Tabor quickly became enmeshed in the spiritual struggle on the larger American religious scene. The extent of this involvement is reflected in the annual Bible Normal (Bible conferences) that provided the focus for Tabor's religious emphasis. The roster of conference speakers in the 1920s and 1930s included such fundamentalist luminaries as R. A. Torrey, James Oliver Buswell, J. W. Riley, William Evans, Paul Ruth, J. D. Drowell and Gerald Winrod.

The narrow fundamentalism that dominated Tabor College during this time was a reflection of the larger Mennonite Brethren Church. Before the 1950s and 1960s the United States Mennonite Brethren had no scholars in theology who could articulate the fundamentals of their own Anabaptist heritage. Thus it was not surprising that Mennonite Brethren would be drawn to the side of fundamentalists who shared several emphases with Anabaptism: the emphasis on Scripture as inspired, absolute truth, repentance, conversion and sanctification, as well as a strong eschatological thrust. My own spiritual pilgrimage reflects a strong fundamentalism because that was the major emphasis to which I was exposed in North America. At the time, all literature available to me came from fundamentalist sources.

The leadership of P. E. Schellenberg had promised a new era. Not a trusted churchman like his predecessors H. W. Lohrenz, P. C. Hiebert and A. E. Janzen, he was nonetheless ready to chart a way out of the religious controversy of the 1920s and 1930s. A grandson of Abraham Schellenberg, he was deeply committed to the Mennonite Brethren Anabaptist heritage. The opposition to his leadership came from the ranks of the fundamentalists in the Mennonite Brethren churches, some trained in Bible institutes like Northwestern, Moody and Biola. Some of my friends, Tabor alumni and graduates of Central Baptist Seminary, were among the leaders who could not reconcile themselves with P. E. Schellenberg's leadership.

During the elections at the 1943 conference I was nominated from the floor and subsequently elected to become secretary of the Board of Education. Our committee subsequently released several articles defending the Tabor administration and signed by Dr. A. H. Unruh as chairman and me as the secretary. But the discontent persisted. The birth of the Pacific Bible Institute in Fresno, California, in 1944, was in part a protest against the assumed "liberalism" in Tabor College.

My involvement in this struggle was very difficult. Coming from an educational background that included exposure to Pietism, atheism and rationalism, I had surrendered to a faith in Christ that was rooted not in intellectual understanding but rather in obedience. Paul's word in 2 Corinthians 10:5—"Casting down imaginations and every high thing that exalteth itself against the knowledge of God, and bringing into captivity every thought to the obedience of Christ"—seemed so contrary to fundamentalism's struggle for proof and its rejection of all that did not fit into a narrow and simplistic frame of scriptural interpretation.

Throughout my ministry I have been troubled by the absence of historical perspective among Mennonite Brethren. Esteemed leaders and colleagues, though deeply committed to the Scriptures, do not connect our theological heritage to the Anabaptist origins in the sixteenth century. Even a pamphlet on "Mennonite Brethren Distinctives," published in 1966, made no reference to our historic origin so distinctly focused in the 1860 founding documents of the Mennonite Brethren.

Into Africa

Another historic decision at the 1943 conference was to accept the mission work of the Africa Mission Association (*Afrika Missions Verein*), formed by the Mennonite Brethren churches in Canada. The background to this was that for twenty years the Board of Foreign Missions had not responded to the mission interests of the seven to eight thousand Mennonite Brethren who had immigrated to Canada from Russia in the years 1923-1932. To provide an outlet for their mission interest, these immigrants had organized a separate mission society and sent some of their own young people to Africa. The operation of two separate mission boards within the conference caused tension and endangered future unity. The 1943 conference sought to find a basis to incorporate the work and personnel of the Africa Mission Association into the larger General Conference effort and thus remove the threat of eventual division. Unfortunately the tension was not so easily resolved.

The original 1870s immigrants from Russia were by and large from the less prosperous class of Mennonites. In addition, they had not been part of the rapid economic and cultural development among the Russian Mennonites in the second half of the nineteenth and the first part of the twentieth century. It was during those fifty years that the Mennonites in Russia emerged from their isolation. Many young Mennonites went to Europe for advanced education in architecture, engineering and theology. The industrial development and the growth of Mennonite institutions of higher learning were also products of this period. Thus the immigrants of the 1920s and 1930s reflected a degree of economic and intellectual sophistication that the previous immigrants did not have. The differences between the "Russlander" (new immigrants) and the American-Canadian Mennonite Brethren were quite distinct, and both groups felt them keenly.

One example will illustrate the tension. In the spring of 1946, my first year at the Mennonite Brethren Bible College in Winnipeg, P. R. Lange of Hillsboro and Heinrich S. Voth of Winkler, Manitoba, both members of the Board of Missions for many years, came to the college to interview two women students who had applied to be missionaries to India. Both women were "Kanadier" (1870s immigrants to Canada).

The college faculty had already reviewed these women's suitability for such an assignment in anticipation of the pending visit from members of the board. The review raised concerns about their suitability in terms of gifts and social relationships. I, as president, was delegated to convey our evaluation to the board representatives. My report elicited the following response: "The time has not yet come that the Russlander will tell us whom we send to India as a missionary." Both of the candidates were sent to India despite our objections. One of them had to be recalled from the field during her first term because of relational tensions she created with the nationals as well as in the mission fellowship. The second one married a missionary in India whose wife had died, and found a place as a mother and helpmate in a family.

This tension in the leadership of the mission program continued for more than twenty years before it finally dissipated.

Citizenship Crisis

It was during our Buhler ministry that we again faced a potential citizenship problem. We had left Canada to go to Freeman in 1940. In August of 1944 I visited the Canadian Consulate in Chicago to clarify my immigration status and discovered something I had not known about Canada's immigration regulations: naturalized citizens of Canada could not reside outside the country beyond five years.

Recognizing the implications for us and the Buhler ministry, we tested a twofold approach. First, I applied to Canadian immigration authorities to extend my citizenship status beyond the five years. Second, in case my request would be denied, I explored the possibility of obtaining U.S. citizenship. This had been suggested by C. N. Hiebert, co-owner of a large flour mill in Buhler and a close friend to U.S. Representative Clifford R. Hope from the Wichita district.

Complicating my desire for U.S. citizenship was American involvement in World War II. Would they grant citizenship to a conscientious objector? As a pastor I had gone to court to represent some of our young men who were drafted into the army but refused to bear arms. One man from the Buhler church had been imprisoned. I had intervened in an effort to get the imprisoned brother re-assigned to a noncombatant classification. We succeeded in the attempt. I discussed the dilemma with

Representative Hope and he assured me that he was in a position to represent me and get my application approved.

Months of uncertainty followed. In December C. N. Hiebert received a letter from Representative Hope. He had tested my application with members of the Supreme Court. After some weeks they wrote Representative Hope as follows: "The request for U.S. citizenship of the Rev. J. B. Toews would be ruled upon according to the McKintosh and Warkentin applications which both were rejected." (Dr. Warkentin was also an immigrant from Russia and at the time professor at Bethel College, North Newton, Kansas.)

With that option now closed I had to decide whether to risk my Canadian citizenship status a second time. The 1932 border-crossing crisis was still too vivid in our memory.

The Call to Winnipeg

In November 1944 I had received a letter from the board of the new Mennonite Brethren Bible College in Winnipeg, inviting me to consider accepting the presidency. Dr. A. H. Unruh, with the help of two part-time teachers, had opened the college that year with a student body of twelve. It was felt he did not know sufficient English to develop the institution and attract students during wartime. My initial response to this inquiry was somewhat cynical.

Exactly a year earlier my uncle B. B. Janz had come to Buhler to visit us after a meeting in Hillsboro. He expressed concern about my ongoing work toward a doctoral degree (I had continued my studies in 1943 by attending summer school). "Hans," he admonished, addressing me by my nickname in the extended family, "you are going too far." He said Mennonite Brethren had only one example of a man who acquired a doctorate in theology. That was Dr. Benjamin Unruh in Europe, and he had estranged himself from the brotherhood (Janz was in continuous correspondence with Unruh in matters of immigration). Dr. A. H. Unruh, meanwhile, had received an honorary D.D. from Bethel College in Kansas.

Uncle Ben reviewed my educational pursuits in Russia, the Netherlands, Tabor College and Western Baptist Theological Seminary, pointing out the degrees I had already earned. He noted that I was the first Mennonite Brethren to get so much theological education.

"Hans, now that is enough," he warned. "You will not be accepted in the brotherhood if you continue to pursue a doctoral degree in theology. You will lose your simple faith in the gospel."

These were strong words, and in those days B. B. Janz's words carried much weight in the Mennonite Brethren Church. Now, only a year later, he was writing to me as a member of the Winnipeg college board to invite me to accept the presidency. It all seemed very manipulative. I was ready to decline. I felt hurt. I could not forget the conversation of a year ago. But the uncertainty of my citizenship called for caution. Could this be a providential opportunity in case the Canadian authorities declined my request for an extension?

We shared the matter with the church. Special prayer meetings were held to lead the Canadian immigration authorities to extend my permit to stay in the U.S. without penalty. But in early March 1945 the Canadian Consulate sent us a negative reply.

Days of severe struggle followed. Our ministry in Buhler had just begun. Should we risk losing citizenship and face the possibility of expulsion? The reality of war made the situation all the more tenuous. On March 21, 1945 I announced my resignation to the church and accepted the call to the college in Winnipeg. The following three months in Buhler were very trying.

Nettie's sister Grace had accepted a teaching position in Buhler to be near us. Nettie's mother, who needed help from her daughters, had moved in with Grace and lived only a block away from us. The plan had been that Grace and Nettie would care for her together, as we had visualized a long stay in Buhler. July 1945 came too soon, not only for us but also for Mother Unruh, for Grace and for the church.

Now we had an entire household of goods to dispose of. The people of the church had helped us to furnish the house, the first parsonage the church owned. They had equipped the kitchen with a range and a refrigerator, a luxury during the war years. The church leadership suggested a public sale. I found the process too difficult to handle. On the day of the sale we turned the entire house and contents over to the brethren of the church. We couldn't face the pain if seeing the first real household we had acquired in twelve years of marriage being turned over to a public auction. So on the day of the sale Nettie went to be with her mother. I took the two boys, Eldon, eight, and Paul, four, to Hutchinson to play in the city park.

I preached my last sermon as Buhler's pastor. I managed to contain my emotions during the farewell service. The last night in Buhler was most difficult for Nettie and me. We slept little. Our departure was scheduled for early morning. We had been asked to stop at the church before leaving. To our amazement we found a large group of people assembled there at 6:00 a.m. to give us a last expression of their love.

On the Road Again

The first day of our trip, Nettie and I were very quiet. Inwardly we both pondered the question, "Why?" Our sons in the back seat took the change as an adventure and had many questions. Where would we live? Would there be a park to play in? Eldon was concerned who his teacher would be. They had their apprehensions. Freeman and Buhler were only small towns, and Winnipeg was a big city.

I had been in Winnipeg in April to find a place to live. Since it was wartime, housing was scarce. With the help of Cornelius A. DeFehr, a prominent Mennonite Brethren business man, I had bought a house, only one year old. It was on Henderson Highway, a very busy street, but in 1945 there was not much choice in Winnipeg. "The street we will live on in Winnipeg has much traffic," I warned the boys. "Streetcars, trucks and cars travel on the street passing our house."

"Are the streetcars bigger than our car?" was Eldon's question. Would we have a sandbox? Were there other children to play with? These were all questions of importance.

The second day of our travel was the fourth of July. Our progress was slow. We had to make frequent stops for the boys who became very restless penned up in the back seat of the car. Toward evening we began to look for a motel to provide some freedom for the boys. But in 1945 motels were less common than today, and we found nothing. We had to drive on.

It was 8:00 in the evening when we reached the border. Wartime inspections were more thorough than usual, and we faced many questions. Nettie and Paul had been born in the U.S. I had been out of the country for five years. The official wanted to know why we wanted to live in Canada.

Finally we were allowed to cross. By now the boys in the back seat had fallen asleep. We looked for motel accommodations at the border, but it was the fourth of July and "No vacancy" stared us in the face at the few places we found. We had no choice but to drive on to Winnipeg, another two hours.

It was after midnight when we arrived in Winnipeg. We were complete strangers. At every hotel we stopped there was no vacancy. We wondered if we would have to spend the night in the car. Then we reached the large Canadian Pacific Railway depot. Beside it was the luxurious CPR Hotel, perhaps the highest-priced hotel in Winnipeg. It was 1:30 a.m.

"John, we cannot stay on the street," said Nettie. "We don't know where to go even in the morning. The boys need to be cared for. We can't go to people without cleaning up and changing clothes."

And so we spent our first night in Winnipeg in the most luxurious hotel in the city. It was past two o'clock when we finally retired. What an introduction to Winnipeg.

The next morning we took our time and ate a leisurely breakfast. Nettie stayed with the boys while I studied the map and went to locate the residence of C. A. DeFehr, who had the key for our new home. I picked up the key and went back to the hotel. Nettie and the boys had been on a walk, investigating the area around the hotel. A beautiful flower garden in the back of the hotel offered the needed diversion for the boys while they waited for my return. By noon we were in our house on Henderson Highway.

We had shipped our personal belongings from Hutchinson by train and had to wait ten days for their arrival. The stove had been bought with the house, and we had brought along basic cooking utensils, dishes and bedding. So for the first week or so we camped in the house and slept on the floor.

The DeFehrs helped us to get settled temporarily. They provided a table and some chairs. They owned a furniture and appliance store, and let us select the items we needed most without a down payment.

On the third day, having made the most urgent preliminary provisions for Nettie and the boys, I decided to visit the college, which was a mile and a half from our house on the same street. No one was there. I had failed to ask Mr. DeFehr for a key before he left for his cottage on Lake Winnipeg. The college building was a former public school bought by Mr. DeFehr in foresight that it might be suitable for the beginning of a college. In the churches it was referred to as *Eine Hohere Bibelschule*, a "higher

Bible school" in distinction to local Bible schools like Winkler, Hepburn, Herbert, Coaldale and Yarrow. No one was around the school. The backyard was overgrown with high weeds. I checked around to see if I could find a window that wasn't bolted. I found one next to the back door and crawled through. Now I was inside what was to be the Mennonite Brethren Bible College.

I found a spacious hall, four classrooms, a very small office and a furnace room with an old furnace that turned out not to work. The one room that had been used during the 1944-1945 school year had a wood stove in the back with the stove pipes going through a window. It also had school desks, a teacher's desk and long blackboards. The office had one bookshelf, a desk and a few chairs. The other three classrooms had school furniture, some desks, tables and chairs. The rooms were thick with dust.

My spirits sank. Here I was in Winnipeg to be president of a school that in reality had not yet begun. Amid the dismal surroundings I remembered the fulfillment and joy of the ministry in Buhler. In contrast the task before us here in Winnipeg appeared totally impossible. Was there no other alternative?

That July afternoon has remained indelible in my memory. I fell to my knees in the empty building that had stood vacant for a number of years before C. A. DeFehr bought it. Amid the locked doors and the high weeds I asked first to understand the implications for me and my family, and then pleaded for God to show how the impossible could be achieved. I crawled back out through the same window and walked the mile and a half home to join Nettie and the boys. I did not share with her my utter frustration.

The belongings sent by train from Hutchinson, Kansas, arrived after ten days. The household began to take shape. As there was only one bedroom downstairs, the boys had to sleep upstairs. Gradually the family settled down.

Very soon the busy street became a problem. On several occasions the boys' ball rolled out on the street and Eldon or Paul ran after it. Nettie soon decided this was not the house for us. "The danger for the boys is too great," she said.

On the world scene, the German armies in Europe had capitulated in May of 1945. The war in the Pacific continued to rage, but atomic bombs on Hiroshima and Nagasaki soon sealed the outcome of that struggle. Politically there was the prospect of peace.

CHAPTER 14

The Winnipeg Chapter

The birth of a Bible college in Canada near the midpoint of the twentieth century was a logical, but controversial, next step in a long history of Mennonite Brethren Bible teaching.

It must be remembered that the Mennonites, throughout their four hundred-year history in Prussia and Russia, had operated their own programs of education. Mennonites who came to North America, first in the 1870s and then later following the Russian Revolution, surrendered this privilege. As their isolated, tightly knit rural communities began to feel the pressure of urbanization from the larger society, it became clear that they would have to regain control of religious education in order to nurture their faith as they had in the past.

Small, local bible schools sprouted in numerous communities across Canada. The first one opened in 1913 in Herbert, Saskatchewan, led by Johann F. Harms, the legendary Mennonite Brethren editor and educator. It closed from 1918 to 1920 and then reopened in 1921 under the leadership of William Bestvater. More schools opened as the second wave of Mennonite immigration to Canada began in the 1920s and continued for several decades. Twenty Mennonite Brethren Bible schools emerged in Canada in the years 1924 to 1955. Following the Second World War Mennonite Brethren high schools also emerged in Ontario, Manitoba, Alberta and British Columbia.

The Bible schools provided courses not offered in public schools: religious instruction and German. The purpose was to train young people for work in the church as Sunday school teachers and lay ministers.

By the early 1940s conference records show a growing desire to unify the various Bible school programs. In 1943 the conference expresses the need for a "*Hoehere Bibelschule*" (a higher Bible school) to prepare workers for the ministry in the churches and teachers for the Bible schools.

The July conference of 1944 received a report from a committee led by B. B. Janz that contained a complete plan for the higher Bible school, or college, to be opened in the fall of the same year. The conference records reflect a lengthy debate. What would the establishment of such a college do for the many Bible schools scattered across Canada? Should it be a Bible college or a school that could be affiliated with a university with a broader program of higher education?

There were some strong voices in opposition to the idea of a new college. Some came from places like Winkler, where supporters of the existing Bible school (in which A. H. Unruh had been a leading figure) felt threatened by the new developments. A letter from a Winkler man to a number of the Coaldale delegates focused the issue sharply and implied that proper conference procedures had been violated.

Nonetheless, the decision was made to proceed, and A. H. Unruh left his post at Winkler to launch the new school in Winnipeg. Unruh, then sixty-five and not fluent in English, had no intention of assuming the responsibility to build a college, but as a leader who had earned the trust of the conference he was willing to do what he could to help make a start. The task of actually developing the new institution would be mine. When I accepted the position I was not fully aware of the depth of the tension in some quarters.

The momentum of the new development and the response from students silenced most critics in the constituency. The evidence of need was beyond dispute. The rallying of the churches behind the college was also due in no small measure to the strength of the college board. Men like Johannes Harder of British Columbia, B. B. Janz of Alberta, John M. Neufeld of Saskatchewan, C. A. DeFehr, Cornelius C. Warkentin and Heinrich Toews of Manitoba, and Henry H. Janzen of Ontario, were very much "the conference" of the 1940s.

Pioneering A Bible College

It was in early July when we arrived in Winnipeg. The college was to open on September 15, giving us two months to prepare. C. A. DeFehr provided some additional furniture for the office. Physically, things began to take shape.

We still had no catalog outlining the planned three-year program of the college, with the second year to be added in 1945-1946 and a third year in 1946-1947. I spent all my time the last two weeks of July writing a draft for a catalog, outlining a preliminary study program that would take the students beyond the local Bible schools. Principles and policies for the college also needed to be formulated.

The executive committee of the board met quite frequently. Dr. Unruh, the founding president for the first year, was not available for consultation. He was busy in the western provinces serving in Bible conferences and promoting the new college without an official catalog. A small pamphlet outlining the projected courses was made available for distribution. We also had a preliminary list of students who had expressed interest in coming.

My next task was to project a study curriculum. In the year 1944-1945 A. H. Unruh had been the only full-time faculty member with three adjunct faculty: Heinrich Wall for German, and Isaak Friesen and Abraham J. Voth for Old and New Testament. No further faculty had been appointed, yet we were to begin a college in two months!

A pamphlet titled *"Auskunft uber das Bibel-College"* (Information About the Bible College) (translation) was quickly prepared with a preliminary course designation for a three-year curriculum, much of it borrowed from other school programs.

Two new faculty members, with whom I had corresponded while in Buhler, were recruited: Rueben M. Baerg, Hepburn, a graduate of Bethany and the University of Saskatchewan in Saskatoon, and Jacob H. Quiring, who had just completed his work in the college of theology at Tabor. Adjunct faculty members available in Winnipeg were Ben Horch in music and his wife Esther Horch in English.

With this skeleton faculty and a curriculum that was projected but not yet backed up with academic resources, we prepared to begin school on October 1, 1945. There was no library. My personal library of some one thousand books served as the nucleus.

Students were billeted in private homes. We had no facilities for meals on campus. A two-story house next to the college was for sale. Cornelius A. DeFehr, who had bought the school building for the college and then offered it to the conference, also purchased this house for our purposes. A kitchen and dining hall were established downstairs.

We managed to recruit Margaret Peters to establish a kitchen service to feed the students. She had come by train from Vancouver, accompanying a newly-widowed woman and her two small children. (One of those children, Alvin Dueck, would later attend the Bible college and eventually become my colleague at the Mennonite Brethren Biblical Seminary in Fresno.) She agreed to stay on with us and become part of our new team.

The upstairs of the house, with four rooms and a bath, provided housing for eight students. Another residence, a three-story structure on Glenwood Crescent, was rented to house an additional twelve students.

The school heating system, an old steam boiler that had not been used the first school year, proved to be non-functional. In October, while a new boiler was installed, we met in cold classrooms. Students and teachers wore extra clothing.

How, under these circumstances, we began the school year with seventy-five day students and twenty-three evening students remains a mystery to me even now, half a century later. In the providence of God, this was the right time to meet a need for higher education that had been felt by the Canadian Conference. The close of the Second World War that year was also a major factor in the good response to our new program. Young men released from the military and alternative service were ready to attend school.

I began my first school year with a full teaching load plus the very demanding administrative work. Plans for student housing and dining hall facilities required much attention. The library became a critical issue. I spent many weekends in Minneapolis visiting second-hand bookstores to select books to lay the base for a library. Rueben M. Baerg, who had been at Northwestern Bible College and knew the city, was a great help in this selection process.

The lodging of students in private homes could only serve provisionally. Additional facilities needed immediate attention. At first we considered enlarging the existing building. Blueprints were prepared to add a student dormitory and an assembly hall on the second story. But this plan had to be abandoned for lack of building material, plumbing in particular. A plan for a new building was launched.

In spring of 1946 we began construction on the student building, later called Ebenezer and today called the C. A. DeFehr Residence Hall. Building materials were still scarce. The frame of the new building was constructed of two-by-six lumber from a grain elevator that was dismantled in a small town not far from Winnipeg. Plumbing supplies were especially hard to come by, so only one bathroom was built on each end of the first and second floors. These new developments as well as the refurbished heating system would never have been accomplished without C. A. DeFehr. He personally drove from town to town in Minnesota and North Dakota, scouring hardware stores to gather whatever nails, plumbing fixtures and building supplies he could find.

A Man of Vision

Much of the credit for developing the college must go to C. A. DeFehr, a visionary entrepreneur who had a heart for the church. After fifteen years in business in Russia DeFehr lost everything in the Russian Revolution and had to start all over again. When he arrived in Canada in 1925 his only assets were courage, vision and a deep commitment to God and the church. He developed a small import business selling agricultural equipment and milk separators. Over the years his business prospered. By the time we came on the scene in 1945 his three sons and his son-in-law, Bernhard B. Fast, carried the major responsibility for the expanding business, C. A. DeFehr and Sons. He remained the major director of the business but the day-to-day management was largely in the hands of the family.

DeFehr's vision was far ahead of other leaders in the church. He was always dreaming for the future, on behalf of the Mennonites in general and the Mennonite Brethren in particular. The Mennonite Brethren Bible College was the result of the vision of C. A. DeFehr and the Canadian conference leadership. DeFehr saw the need for it well in advance of other conference leaders. He was essentially the initiator and builder of the college.

DeFehr and his wife, Liese, were warm, loving people who cared deeply for the church. Their home on Glenwood Crescent was always open to faculty and students. Through our extensive work together he and I grew into a father-son relationship.

On one of our visits to the DeFehr home Nettie shared her concern for our boys' safety because of the heavy traffic on Henderson Highway. A few weeks later C. A. DeFehr stopped by and invited Nettie to accompany him to look at a house on Noble Avenue, a quiet area of towering Elm trees closer to the college. "Would this home be suitable?" he asked. A few days later he stopped by again to tell us the house was bought and we could move in. He would look after selling the house on Henderson Highway. He sold it for $12,000. We had bought it for $8,000. Nettie would always claim it was the only time in our long marriage that we ever made a profit on anything.

In spring of 1946 we moved to Noble Avenue. Our new home had four bedrooms and a bath upstairs, a spacious living room, dining room, kitchen and a study on the main floor. A beautiful winding stairway led from the entrance to the second floor. The full basement was a delight for our two boys.

C. A. DeFehr remained a close friend to our family, even though he was one of those who could not understand why we would leave the college after only three years. I could not share with him the real reason why we made the decision to move on.

When the new dormitory was dedicated in late fall of 1946, the name Ebenezer—"Hitherto the Lord has helped us,"—applied not only to the building but also to the initial years of the college. In no way could I take credit for the rapid development of the institution in program, facilities, constituency support and credibility attained in the academic community. It was the Lord's doing, and marvelous before our eyes.

Faculty and Curriculum, 1945-1948

The response to the opportunity of a college in Canada was overwhelming. In the fall of 1945 we had seventy-five day-time students and twenty-three evening students and thirty-eight Sunday school teachers who took advantage of special courses in Christian education.

The faculty for the second year, A. H. Unruh, H. H. Janzen, Jacob H. Quiring, Rueben Baerg and I, were ill-prepared for the assignment. This becomes increasingly apparent to me in retrospect as I reviewed the offerings in the catalogue of these years. The two senior members of the faculty, Unruh and Janzen, lacked academic credentials but were especially gifted in Bible exposition and were known throughout the Mennonite Brethren conference and beyond for their great preaching. The other faculty members, though academically better prepared, had to accept assignments far beyond their expertise. Overall, however, we managed to fulfill the objective of the college as stated in the more fully developed 1946-47 catalog:

The Mennonite Brethren Bible College seeks to provide an opportunity for earnest young men and women to prepare adequately for the high calling of Christian service as ministers, teachers, missionaries and workers in other fields of Christian work. The institution, even though a school of the Mennonite

Brethren Conference, recognizes the unity of all true believers and therefore offers its service and opportunities to men and women of all other evangelical denominations in our Canadian land and the northern areas of the U.S.A.

The personalities and the giftedness of A. H. Unruh and H. H. Janzen gave the college the necessary visibility and trust from the very beginning. In character and personality both men outranked many of the choicest academicians. Their annual Bible conferences held in the last days of December attracted hundreds of ministers, teachers, church workers and others who valued good Bible expositions. They were a special gift to the church, and played a key role in the development of the College.

A. H. Unruh, then in his late sixties, did not show his age in the classroom. His strongest contribution was in the exegetical study of the New Testament. He was a scholar who emerged, not from institutional academics, but as a product of prolonged immersion in Scripture, wide reading of German theologians like Adolf Schlatter, and a broad historical outlook. In debate he could easily hold his own against any of his academically trained counterparts. A. H. Unruh was a theologian par excellence and a very popular pulpiteer.

Unruh was a man of broad scholarship, deep piety, and sincerity embodied in a cheerful and engaging personality. His classes were never dull. He made the Bible come alive through stories and experiences from real life situations. In hours of relaxation he would be the entertainer of the gathering. In our faculty meetings he would spice the deliberations with humorous anecdotes that often derailed us from the agenda. At one such meetings, where he told story after story, keeping the faculty in continuous laughter, I finally had to ask that he preserve his humor for a planned social gathering at our home, and for the hour concentrate on the agenda.

H. H. Janzen, though less of a scholar, had strong gifts of exposition and was a forceful preacher. He was with us only one of the three years of my tenure.

Two other key faculty members, Jacob Quiring and Rueben Baerg, both young and growing into their ministries, were an effective stabilizing force for us. Together the faculty was a marvelous provision for the Mennonite Brethren in that era of history.

We all worked together to develop a coherent curriculum that would accomplish the aims of the college. The departments of Old and New

Testament studies were divided among the existing faculty. My part in the instructional program was the department of theology. With limited resources and a library of just a few hundred books, I had to rely on the methods I had used at the Bible school in Hepburn. It took all my ingenuity to scratch together whatever Anabaptist and other materials I could find. These included a book by Collin Cline, my former professor at Western, as well as Osterzee, Kohler, Mullins and Strong. The courses were basically biblical theology with the Scriptures as the main source.

The music department was a strong feature of the college right from the beginning and has remained so to this day. It was a product of the vision of Ben and Esther Horch, whose musical influence has been influential throughout the entire Mennonite Brethren conference. I found myself troubled by the immediate popularity of musical interest. Ben and Esther were so successful that I feared music might detract from the biblical and theological core.

Troubling Undercurrents

While the college was greeted with a large measure of acceptance and success, there were nonetheless troubling undercurrents that cast doubt on whether my tenure should be long-term.

The college board was dominated by Canadian Conference leaders who had shown great vision in bringing the new institution into being even before the constituency was ready. They quickly demonstrated a desire for strict control, however, as well as some isolationist tendencies that I knew would make our journey together difficult. At the first board meeting in the fall of 1945 they already made clear to me that they had a rather fixed understanding of how the college should be run. I found several features of their understanding distasteful.

For one, they indicated a desire to be sharply separate from other Mennonite groups. There was no interest in entering into discussion with the General Conference Mennonites who were also moving to establish a college. I was also concerned about an apparent desire to remain culturally isolated. German, I was told, should be the language of the college, with a minimum of instruction in English. Then there was the matter of stringent rules to govern the social life of the student body. After my years of exposure at schools in the south, I chafed under the "straightjacket" model for a college with mature students.

With all the affirmation and encouragement that came from constituents as they saw the rapid development of the college, I could not reconcile myself to the narrow vision of the board to whom I was responsible. They demanded a full report on the language question at every board meeting: How many chapel services were conducted in English and how many in German? Classes were scrutinized as to the language used in instruction. In the second year the chairman of the board expressed his deep gratitude for the strong progress of the college and ended with the words: "You have been given to us as the brother who will save the Mennonite Brethren Conference from *Verenglishen* (anglicization)." I continued to work hard but began to question whether it was my assignment to wear myself out in a culture struggle that I saw as fruitless.

In February 1947 I participated in a Bible conference at Pacific Bible Institute in Fresno, established three years earlier. Following the conference, I ministered briefly in the Reedley Mennonite Brethren Church. Several people from the leadership approached me as to whether I would consider coming to the West Coast. With the impending retirement of George B. Huebert, they were looking for a replacement.

Only a few months later the Reedley church found itself in a severe crisis. They had called H. G. Wiens, who had just completed his doctor of theology degree in Fort Worth, Texas, as an associate to G. B. Huebert. With the advancing years of Brother Huebert, Wiens surrounded himself with a group of people who wanted a change. The subsequent struggle very quickly divided the church. Through its strong lay leadership, the church demanded the resignations of both Huebert and Wiens. But the loyalties were sharply divided. One group had been committed to G. B. Huebert, another to H. G. Wiens. A third group was deeply affected by Pentecostalism.

One year later, in January 1948, I received a telephone call from Reedley, again inquiring if we would consider the pastorate of the church. A letter followed. For a number of days the letter stayed on my desk in the office. I recalled so well Nettie's statement when we were in California for the 1939 Pacific District Conference in Dinuba, "I am so glad that we will never need to live in California."

Given my uncertainty over leading a college that would increasingly be the focal point of the conference's cultural struggles, I was open to considering a change. The college itself was well established and had gained acceptance at the grass roots of the conference. The faculty was solid and, for the 1940s, well qualified. The relationship with the Bible schools had been resolved, and the future course seemed set. Inwardly I was asking myself whether my task was done. After much prayer I felt free to share the letter with Nettie. On a Friday evening I took it home and handed it to her without comment.

Late that evening while I was working on a sermon Nettie came from behind, placed the letter before me on the desk, and said, "If you want to go to Reedley then go, but do not ask me to go there." I didn't respond. Inwardly I had reached an openness to accept the invitation on the condition that Nettie agreed.

Several days went by. Neither one of us mentioned the Reedley letter. On Wednesday evening, after the boys had been put to bed, Nettie came into my study, bent over from the back, put her arms around me and said, "I have promised to never stand in the way when God would call you to a ministry. If you feel inwardly led to consider the Reedley invitation, I will go with you."

We now had the basis to pray together for the Lord's leading. Nettie was expecting our third child, and a move at this time would be difficult. I also wondered if my leaving the college would injure the cause.

By the March board meeting we had reached a decision, and I handed in my resignation. For several weeks the board was not ready to accept the resignation. Leading brethren from the conference pleaded with us to reconsider, but we felt our decision was the right one.

Our furniture, including the piano, was crated and shipped by train to California. Grace Unruh, Nettie's sister, had taken a sabbatical from her school and was able to assist in the transition. The time of the move for the family was critical. Not only was Nettie expecting, but she was also forty-five years old. Would her advanced age and the move affect the development of the child? We found the departure difficult and depressing.

On June 29 we left Winnipeg by car, heading west. We stopped in Coaldale to visit the family before going on to California. Aunt Grace was a great help to us in a time of the move. She shared the back seat of the car with John, ten, and Paul seven. Nettie, facing the last two months of her pregnancy, appreciated the reclining seat in front.

For me the journey was a time of inner turmoil. Although we had made a clear decision after much prayer and thought, I now found myself haunted by second thoughts. The outpouring of appreciation and affection from friends and colleagues on our departure from Winnipeg, as well as their frequent skepticism as to whether our leaving was really of God, followed me over the endless miles.

Over and over again I replayed the questions. Why had we left just when the college had begun to hit its stride? Why would we want to give that up to accept the pastorate of a large church that was reeling from a painful split? My doubts reached the point of crisis. I realized I was not ready to assume my new position while still tormented by this uncertainty.

We reached Fresno on July 4. I rented three rooms in the California Hotel, one for Nettie and the boys, one for our sister Grace and one for me to be alone and seek the Lord's face.

I struggled for two days and two nights. Nettie, very much concerned, struggled with me. Those days in the hotel in the summer of 1948 became for us a crisis like that of Jacob when he wrestled with God: "And Jacob called the name of the place Peniel: for I have seen God face to face and my life is preserved" (Gen. 32:24-32).

Finally, early in the morning I found victory as I humbled myself before God and declared my uncertainty: "Have I made a wrong decision which may lead to a Waterloo, a defeat in my ministry? If so, I will accept it. I will confess my error publicly and accept the consequences." In my distress I asked for God's mercy in case I had not understood him. If, however, the decision was in keeping with his will, I asked for a threefold confirmation: 1. *A healthy baby.* I asked that the child, due in less than two months, would be normal and healthy, not affected by Nettie's advanced age nor the stress of moving while she was in this condition. 2. *A healthy college.* At the informal farewell at the college one faculty member said to me in an accusing tone: "If our enrollment next fall is way down, you shall know that you are responsible." For a second confirmation that I had understood the Lord correctly was that the enrollment at the college would be equal or beyond the last year of my leadership. 3. *A healed church.* The disunity in the Reedley church was grave. The strained relationship of G. B. Huebert and H. G. Wiens and their respective supporters had defied every effort at reconciliation. Could the impossible become possible? My third request for confirmation was that within the first year of my ministry we would witness the reconciliation of the two men and the restoration of the unity of the church.

Nettie and I committed ourselves again to God, asking that he reveal himself to us while we would continue to wait upon him. On July 7, in the morning, we called the church in Reedley to say we were in Fresno and would arrive by noon. Deep peace had come to our hearts.

CHAPTER 15

Back to the Pastorate

W e settled into a rented house on Reed Avenue. In anticipation of our coming the church had begun plans to build a parsonage. With our furniture (as well as my small library) still on the way from Winnipeg to Fresno, kind people of the church had set up whatever we needed to get settled.

July 9 was my first day in the church office. I planned to spend my first hours praying and preparing for the installation message on Sunday, July 11. But first thing in the morning I received a message from Esther Enns, the church secretary, that a Mrs. Klassen had called and requested a visit. I instructed Miss Enns to phone Mrs. Klassen and explain that we had just arrived and perhaps my visit with her could wait. That afternoon Mrs. Klassen called again. Her message was urgent: "I must see the new pastor today."

Thinking her need must be critical, I set out to find her home. With the help of a map drawn by Miss Enns I finally located her small house, isolated in the middle of a vineyard. I knocked at the door, but no one answered. I knocked again and again. Mrs. Klassen was an old widow who lived alone. She was also quite deaf. Upon repeated knocking she finally appeared at the door.

"Are you the new pastor?" she asked. She set a hearing horn to her ear and I had to speak quite loudly into it for her to hear. "Are you a college president?" was her second question. I said yes, I had come to Reedley from a college in Winnipeg. She stared at me for a while. Then she said, "The *Reedley Exponent* [the local newspaper] has an article about you, telling how great a man you are. It also says you came from Russia. Where in Russia were you born?" I replied that I had been born in the Molotschna Colony, in the village of Alexandertal. "Was your father a teacher?" she asked. Again I replied in the affirmative, always speaking directly into the hearing horn which she held to her right ear. "Was your mother's name Margaretha Janz?" Again I replied, "Yes that is correct."

She was quiet for a long time. I was beginning to wonder what was so urgent to draw me here on my first day. Finally she broke the silence.

"Then you really are not a great man like the *Exponent* says. You are only the son of Miller Janz's Margaretha. I served as a maid in the Janz's house. I know your mother, Miller Benjamin Janz's Margaretha's son. Now I know from where you come. You have nothing to brag about. You are not a big man. You are Miller Janz's Margaretha's boy."

For a moment I was stunned. Did I have to come here, my first house call in Reedley, to have this elderly lady tell me who I really was?

I drove back to the office. I could not continue my sermon preparation. *You are not a big man: you are only Margaretha Janz's boy.* That message stuck. It has followed me through the years of my ministry, not only in Reedley but through life. It was a good reminder that by the grace of God I am who I am. Any identity I had was through God's mercy. The introduction to Reedley through God's messenger, an old widow with poor hearing, was significant then, and continues to be.

Tension from the Start

My installation message was based on 1 Corinthians 2:1-8: "And I brethren, when I came to you, came not with excellency of speech or wisdom, declaring unto you the testimony of God. For I determined not to know anything among you, except Jesus Christ, and him crucified." The text was appropriate, for the disunity in Reedley was so similar to the Corinthian church. The solution there, too, was no different than what we needed in Reedley.

The various "camps" in the church wasted no time making their concerns known to me. At the end of the service I greeted people at the door. Because of her condition, Nettie preferred not to stand with me in line. When all the people had passed, one man came by alone, stopped, peered into my eyes and said, "You will not be my pastor except you exonerate G. B. Huebert." Within the first week two other men from the church approached me to demand the exoneration of H. G. Wiens. Then a delegation of three came to me to ask about my position on the gifts of the Spirit, speaking in tongues, prophecy and healing. The lines had been drawn.

G. B. Huebert, the pastor for fourteen years, was a man of God. By profession he was a banker, a manager with the Bank of America, a successful man in the community. God had laid his hand on him and called him into the ministry. As a student of Dr. R. A. Torrey at the Bible Institute of Los Angeles he had been strongly influenced by fundamentalism. The secret to his effective ministry, however, was that he was a man of prayer and a student of Scripture. He was well known on the wider evangelical scene. Before accepting the pastorate of Reedley, his own home church, he had travelled extensively as a tent evangelist.

Huebert came to Reedley at a crucial point in the church's history. His ministry led first to reconciliation with the church in Dinuba, which had separated from the Reedley church in 1925 in protest of the inroads of charismatic Pentecostalism. Under Huebert's leadership the church grew from a membership of 450 to 1,200 in 1948. Through my earlier ministries in Reedley in 1946 and 1947 G. B. Huebert had become a friend and spiritual mentor.

H. G. Wiens was also well known to me. He had been a member of the faculty at Bethany Bible Institute for two years. I had an open door to both of these men who were now in conflict with each other. This personal relationship proved to be a great benefit during my initial months in Reedley. I sought opportunities for their fellowship whenever I could.

Our Third Son Arrives

On August 24, 1948, only six weeks after our arrival in Reedley, our third son, James, was born. God had given us a normal, healthy child. We united in prayers of thanksgiving. Nettie's age and the stress of our move from Winnipeg had not adversely affected our newborn baby. We had received the first confirmation that we had understood the Lord in coming to Reedley.

That same day, August 24, while Nettie remained in the hospital, I left for the Mennonite Brethren General Conference in Mountain Lake, Minnesota. Aunt Grace was a special blessing during this time. She assumed responsibility for the boys at home, looked after Nettie in the hospital, and cared for both mother and newborn when they were discharged. Grace was an angel of God to our family on so many occasions through the years of our ministry. Not only did she frequently give of her time to our family, but she was also a strong financial support in my worldwide assignments in later years.

The 1948 Conference

The delegation from California had reserved a special railroad car to travel to Mountain Lake. The fellowship on the train was good. There was singing, visiting and two Bible study sessions per day, one in the morning and one in the evening for the trip there and back. My assignment was to provide an exposition of Paul's letter to the Philippians. With us on the train was the veteran missionary from India, John H. Pankratz. It was his last involvement in the Mennonite Brethren Conference before his homegoing just a few years later.

At the previous conference in 1945 I had been elected to the Committee of Reference and Counsel. Now in 1948 I also became a member of the Board of Missions. For the next fifteen years I was privileged to work with both of these committees.

Two decisions of historical significance were reached at the 1948 General Conference. First, a delegation from South America, representing Uruguay, Paraguay and Brazil, had come to North America to apply for membership in the General Conference of Mennonite Brethren. The positive response of the North American body made them a district of the larger conference.

The second major decision was the overture of Mennonite Central Committee to the Mennonite Brethren to accept the responsibility for the postwar relief program in Japan with the intent to make it a stepping stone toward a church-planting mission. The 1948 conference thus marked the beginning of the most effective church-planting program of the Mennonite Brethren in the post-World War II period, the church in Japan.

The proximity of Mountain Lake to the Freeman-Marion area of South Dakota gave me my last opportunity to visit Mother Unruh. She had moved back to South Dakota from Buhler, Kansas, so she could be close to Martha Ratzlaff, her oldest daughter, and her two sons, August and Isaac Unruh.

On Saturday evening, after the last session, Erwin Adrian from Buhler offered to drive me to Marion, a three-hour trip. I spent Sunday morning, September 2, with Mother Unruh, whose health had deteriorated and was being cared for at the Thiessen Home for the Aged. It was an unforgettable morning! We visited together. I reported the birth of our son James and told her about our entrance into the ministry in Reedley. We concluded the visit with a brief study of 1 Peter 1:3-9, meditating on the blessed hope that awaited us in our heavenly inheritance.

Less than two months later Mother Unruh entered that inheritance. Nettie, in her motherly concern for baby James, not yet three months old, chose not to make the long trip to South Dakota to escort her mother to her last resting place.

Shepherding the Flock

I returned from the 1948 General Conference very conscious of the challenging task before us in the Reedley church. In order to have a fruitful ministry, a way had to be found to respond to the two camps demanding exoneration of their respective former pastors, as well as to those who leaned in a charismatic direction.

Days of fasting and prayer followed my return. In total helplessness I came to the realization that only the power of the Word could remove the hindrances. With the consent of the executive of the church council, William Wiebe, H. R. Wiens and Peter Funk, I made it a point to go about my ministry without referring to the problems in the church. I experienced great liberty in preaching the Word and teaching in the midweek services.

Two aspects became central to our ministry in Reedley. First, the Lord led me to systematic expository preaching. The Gospel of John, Ephesians and portions from the Synoptic Gospels provided the subject matter for the fall and winter months. In summer I presented a series of character studies from the Old and New Testaments. God honored the exposition of the Word.

The second aspect of our ministry was visitation. As was the case in Buhler I needed to know the people in order to minister to them. In the first years I made several hundred house visits. I visited the older people during the day and the professional and business people in the evenings. Frequently I would go to homes for supper. I ate very little. The word spread that the pastor did not like fancy and heavy meals. I came not for the sake of the meal but to know the people. Nettie would go with me on Tuesdays and Thursdays, while a baby-sitter looked after baby James and met the boys when they came home from school.

We felt accepted from the very beginning. People were open. They loved us and trusted us. A factor that may have helped in this regard was the neutrality with which we could move among them. We were not allied with any particular faction or groups of friends.

My January 1949 pastoral report to the church stated my position on special favors or gifts from individuals or groups of people, a lesson I had learned in Buhler. For example, all income in the form of honorariums from ministries in other churches or in conferences, above the provisions made by the church for our well-being, was to be turned over to the Board of Trustees for the church budget. Throughout our ministry we found that living modestly and receiving only enough to cover necessities tended to bolster people's confidence in us. This policy was not without struggles. But overall the discipline of serving not for salary but rather as a service to the Lord and to people has brought our family great rewards of a different kind.

During our visits with the former pastors I left it to them to refer to their spiritual hurts and the unresolved tension in the church. All three members of the executive were also their close friends and maintained their relationship with them.

Inner healing began to occur during the fall months. It was clearly a moving of the Spirit from within. Frequently, after the worship services on Sunday morning, small groups of brothers and sisters would meet in the basement for cleansing, reconciliation and restoration of relationships.

God gave me the liberty at the end of November to meet with the former pastors individually and broach the topic of reconciliation. God gave the church that liberation on December 6, 1948. Huebert and Wiens both appeared before the congregation and announced their mutual forgiveness and reconciliation. The past was brought under the forgiving grace and mercy of the cross. Here was the second confirmation I had sought from God. The third confirmation was not long in coming. We had been awaiting information about the college in Winnipeg. Was it going well, as we had prayed? We received a Christmas card with brief words of greeting from John A. Toews, a member of the faculty in Winnipeg. A brief footnote at the bottom of the card said, "Our enrollment for this year is 131." That was one student more than the previous year.

Christmas 1948 was special for us. Both Nettie and James were healthy; the church was experiencing renewal; the former pastors had found grace in forgiveness and reconciliation; and the enrollment in Winnipeg had not declined because of our leaving. It was clear to us that we had understood the Lord in coming to Reedley. We were in the place he wanted us.

It was not until the next spring that we discovered one of the secrets underlying the workings of the Spirit of God in the Reedley church. One Saturday evening I needed to make an unannounced visit to one of our deacons. I drove to his home, located in the midst of a large vineyard, and was surprised to see a number of cars parked on the yard. My first reaction was: "What, a party in a deacon's home on Saturday evening?" I paused in my car, wondering if I should leave without pursuing the purpose of my coming. I decided to follow through and proceeded to knock on the door.

Mary Leppke, the deacon's wife, answered the door. "Brother Toews," she said with a tone of surprise. After a brief hesitation she invited me to step inside. In the midst of the spiritual struggle of the church over the past two years, a group of four couples had banded together to urge God's intervention on behalf of the church. They had promised to make the intercession for the church a daily responsibility, and to set aside each Saturday to fast and then meet in the evening for united prayer. The focus of their intercession was threefold: (1) the unification of the church; (2) the reconciliation of the former pastors; (3) the provision of a pastor who would preach the Word strongly and who had compassion and love for the people of the church. "We did not want you to know about these prayer meetings," said one of the women. "It was a commitment between us and God."

The secret of God's leading of the past year was clear. The committed prayer of the group was an important part of the answer to the events of the past months. Our struggle to leave the college in Winnipeg, our coming to Reedley and the moving of God's Spirit in the events toward liberation of the church could not be separated from the intercessory group I met that evening.

A Highlight of Ministry

Soon after our arrival the church had decided to build a parsonage only a few blocks from the church. It was dedicated on February 20, 1949. With three spacious bedrooms, kitchen, dining room, a spacious living room and a study, the new parsonage was a very gracious provision for our growing family.

We entered into a period of rich and stable ministry. The years 1948 to 1953 could be described as the highlight of my sixty years of public ministry. The most appropriate thing to be said about this period is, "This is the Lord's doing" (Ps. 118.23.

The core of the church had retained its spiritual vitality through the difficult years of tensions and disunity. On November 3, 1948 the church baptized thirty-one people who testified of having found salvation through faith in Christ. Other baptisms followed in the years 1949 through 1954. A special phenomenon that may account for the blessings of God upon the Reedley church in those years was the church's continuous concern for sanctification. At numerous meetings there were public confessions as people grieved over inconsistencies in their lives and asked the church for forgiveness for having harmed the testimony of the church.

From 1949 to 1953 the church ordained seven missionaries and sent them to foreign assignments. The ranks of the church workers were strengthened in the selection of more deacons. Ongoing attention was paid to the calling out of new workers from the congregation. The entire music, Sunday school and youth programs were staffed by volunteers.

On May 21, 1950, Henry R. Wiens, the principal of Immanuel Academy, was called as a full-time associate to the pastor. His leadership and ministry had been crucial in the previous times of trouble. The value of his contribution to the restoration of the church cannot be overestimated. His major strength was in relationships. Because he had the spirit of a true and loving shepherd, people extended him an unusual degree of confidence. He was a man of prayer, an intercessor for the people. He and I were quite different in character and temperament, but we worked very well together. In fact, as I reflect on our ministry together I consider H. R. Wiens to have been the real pastor of the church; I merely carried out the preaching ministry.

Other members of the church council executive were also vital supporters in the Reedley ministry. William Wiebe, a raisin farmer, was a man of wisdom and leadership ability who knew his people and had earned their confidence. He was a counselor to many people, young and old. He was one of the group that established Hartland Camp in the Sierra Nevada mountains. The cause of the church always took precedence over his own plans and aspirations. His wife, a school teacher, shared his commitment. With no children of their own, the church became their family.

I need to also mention Luther Linda and Peter Funk as members of the core leadership of the church. Luther, a pilot and a fruit rancher, could always be counted on. The cause of the church always took precedence over his own interests. He chaired the building committee from 1949 to 1952 when the new building was erected. His own stewardship motivated others to help support this project.

Peter Funk, an insurance broker, was a sparkling supporter of the church. As a member of the Navigators he made it a point to memorize Scripture and to disciple other young men. His freedom in witnessing to people in the community was irresistible. He and his wife, Martha, and their two children maintained a home that had a magnetic attraction to both friends and strangers.

Dozens of others provided the context in which the church prospered. There was Sam Knaak, who gave two years of time and talent to build the sanctuary; the deacons, Abe Leppkes and John Brauns, both fruit farmers; and Ernie Enns, a banker who gave his time for the music department as leader of the large church choir and the male chorus. August Schroeter was the parliamentarian of the church and conference. Ben and Anna Marie Nachtigal, business people struggling for economic survival, had room in their hearts for everybody. John Enns, a pilot of a small plane who operated an automobile repair shop, chaired the board of trustees. Henry R. Martens, a car dealer, was always concerned for the church. His wife Lydia, served as the soul of the Ladies' Missionary Circle and the leader in the conference women's organization. The Otto Reimers, a deacon couple, could always be counted on.

There were many more who carried the church in love and devotion. In the midst of joy and appreciation for such a fellowship one is inclined to forget the sad experiences when some members strayed from the narrow pathway of following Jesus. In those cases there were tears and sorrow as people were disciplined and even excommunicated. The pain of such occasions was shared by many people and often resulted in restoration of the lost sheep to the fold.

Congregational records show that the church had already begun to feel crowded in 1946. Thanks to the growth of renewal, this became a pressing concern in 1949. On several occasions there had been talk of remodelling the existing sanctuary to provide more room. Another option, considered at the congregational meeting of January 31, 1949, was to establish a second church of four hundred to five hundred members. I personally supported this solution, but the general response was weak. The church wanted to stay together.

On February 20, 1949 it was decided to build a new sanctuary with seating for two thousand. Of special note was the insistence that this project not erode existing budget commitments to the mission program of the local church and conference. As it turned out, construction would be interrupted twice over the next two years when our mission obligations fell short. As the largest Mennonite Brethren congregation, we needed to give priority to our obligations to the conference mission program.

A unique feature of the financing plan was its inclusion of all households in the church. The original cost estimate of $323,595 was apportioned among all members, each to give according to their means.

Sam Knaak devoted two years to serve as construction foreman. Whatever work could be done by laypeople was handled by volunteers from the church. This involvement in a common cause strengthened our sense of unity and commitment. The small minority who did not participate for various personal reasons did not dampen the enthusiasm of the others.

The new church was dedicated on May 4, 1952. The cost, somewhat beyond the original estimate, was $423,000, of which $72,000 was borrowed. The volunteer labor, not included in the cost, was estimated at $29,665. On October 6, 1952 another $17,315 was committed, leaving an indebtedness of $56,432.

Two passages of Scripture served as the basis for the dedication message: 2 Chronicles 2:4, "Behold, I build a house to the name of the Lord my God, to dedicate it to him," and Psalm 26:7-8, "That I may publish with the voice of thanksgiving, and tell of all thy wondrous works. Lord, I have loved the habitation of thy house, and the place where thine honor dwelleth."

This was a great day in the history of the Reedley Mennonite Brethren Church. A spirit of thanksgiving and praise rang through the hearts of the people. "The Lord hath done great things for us, whereof we are glad" (Ps. 126:3). For Nettie and me this day was an Ebenezer: "Hitherto the Lord has helped us." That evening, after our boys had retired, we reviewed the leading of God in our life and ministry since coming to Reedley nearly four years earlier. What we had experienced was "more than we could ask or think." The day concluded with a prayer of new dedication to God who had been so gracious, longsuffering and kind to us.

Wrestling Against Principalities and Powers

Our ministry in Reedley taught us how the sufficiency of God can triumph over human frailties when people take responsibility for their actions and humble themselves before him.

The reconciliation of the two pastors followed deep self-searching on the part of the church. A statement of confession and repentance on the part of the church was presented. The statement spoke to the character of the church as a body, which shares in or may even be the cause of sin in their midst. The body humbled itself before the Lord, asking for forgiveness where its failures had created a climate that made the leadership struggle possible. The statement of confession filed in the council minutes of November 29, 1948 became the basis for the subsequent reconciliation in December 1948.

A major lesson for me was the realization that the church shares the responsibility for the sin and relationships within the body. That December meeting marked not only the confession of two men, but also a time of restoration for the entire church.   Among the darker moments at Reedley were having to deal with members' moral failings. We experienced both defeats and restoration in this area. On some painful occasions the church body had to excommunicate members because of sin or wrong relationships.

The Korean War from 1950 to 1953 also created problems in the local church. A number of our young men accepted the draft into the regular army, both in noncombatant and combatant classifications, rather than choosing alternative service. The teaching of our Mennonite Brethren position of biblical nonresistance had been neglected. For me, as pastor, this became very painful.

Because of our size the Reedley church was a major force in the larger community. This became clear in our deep involvement in school issue. Immanuel Academy—now Immanuel High School—operated by the Reedley, Dinuba and Zion churches, was a point of tension. We as a church were a large voting block. To wield power in the community as a body that operated its own school carried many implications, especially when the vote of the church put one of our members into the position as school superintendent. I wept when we as a church failed to be salt and a light within the community.

An Expanding Ministry

Requests for my involvement in external ministries, both in the Mennonite Brethren Conference and beyond, grew during this time. The fourth Mennonite World Conference took place in Newton, Kansas, August 3-10, 1948. I declined participation because of our recent transition from Winnipeg to Reedley. My absence did not prevent my appointment to the World Conference Presidium. The assignment necessitated several meetings in the interim, 1948 to 1952. The fifth Mennonite World Conference convened in Basel, Switzerland, August 10-15, 1952. The theme for that conference was "The Church of Jesus Christ and Its Mandate." I was asked to bring a message titled "The Church—A Living Faith."

My membership on the Board of Missions from 1948 onward required my attendance at two meetings per year. As secretary of the board I was also responsible for correspondence. Since the 1945 General Conference in Dinuba I also served on the Board of Reference and Council, requiring an additional two meetings per year.

I also kept up my involvement in various Bible conferences, which occupied several more weeks. The Reedley church showed great understanding for the importance of these services, even though they took me away from the duties of the church, especially in the visitation program.

A Taste of Africa

In 1952, as a member of the Mennonite Brethren Board of Missions I was asked to visit the Belgian Congo (now Zaire), the fastest-growing area of our ministry abroad. The Mennonite World Conference, meanwhile, would be in Switzerland. This leg of the trip grew in scope as an extension was planned for some of us to also visit the Middle East and examine the broader implications arising after the Second World War. The Reedley church accommodated these demands, permitting my absence for several months that summer. This was made possible by the pastoral strength of H. R. Wiens, who ably took over my duties.

We made special family arrangements to lighten the load on Nettie during my prolonged absence. John, then fifteen, was sent to our farm in Saskatchewan. The previous year we had built a new house on the farm, then occupied by the Toby Schmidt family. We felt that working on a farm with cattle and a large pasture would provide plenty of interesting work for a teenager. We built the house in the hope that one of our sons might eventually become a farmer.

Paul, eleven, was "adopted" for the summer by a kind family in our church, the W. W. Wiests. They would bring him home each Saturday evening and call for him again on Sunday evening.

Nettie, with four-year-old James, remained in the Reedley parsonage and maintained weekly communication with the other boys. The summer of 1952 was our introduction to a new way of life that would become a pattern for us: Nettie and the boys spending weeks and months alone while

I gave time and energy to wider ministries. Not everyone would always agree with my choice of kingdom priorities.

Only two weeks after the May dedication of the new church Sanctuary I left for six weeks to our Congo mission field, followed by a visit to other missions on the vast African continent.

The Africa work, begun by Aaron A. Janzen as an independent faith program in 1914, had been accepted as a conference responsibility at the Buhler conference in 1943. A missions official had visited the work in 1949 to check on its status but since then the program had mushroomed to thirty-two missionaries. Some significant issues demanded attention.

The work of the Africa Mission Society was located in the Kassai Province, in the northern part of the Congo. The larger field was in central and southern Congo. Distance and different languages made it impossible to rotate missionaries between the two fields, affecting the total ministry of evangelism, education and social services, including the health program. A second difficulty on the field was the development of a program of education that would be recognized by the Belgian government and qualify for government subsidy. The missionaries themselves were seriously divided about how to proceed on this question. A third issue concerned the establishment of a missionary children's school in cooperation with the Congo Inland Mission.

There were no principals and policies to govern the expanding program. Relational tensions arose that hindered the work of the Holy Spirit. The report to the Board of Missions for the October 1952 meeting contains the details of our negotiations and the directives that were set for the future.

That trip, however, had further implications that would affect our entire future ministry. Missionary A. A. Janzen, who had pioneered the work in the Congo since 1914, was anxious for me to gain a broad exposure to local conditions. He wanted me to travel with him through some of the areas that were still without missionaries, schools or medical programs, and where witchcraft and superstition still prevailed. With deep emotion he related the plight of the elderly who were carried into the jungles far from their native village and left to die, their bodies prey for wild beasts.

We travelled from village to village by jeep, loaded with the necessary provisions of water and food and accompanied by two natives. Missionary Janzen, then at retirement age, reflected with deep emotion on the spiritual condition of these people.

For the night we camped in a clearing in the jungle, with a small tent serving as our bedroom. The natives slept next to the jeep to protect us and guard our food and water. I awoke in the middle of one night, and realized I was alone. Janzen was not in the tent. I took a flashlight and surveyed the strange surroundings. One of the natives noticed my concern but could not explain where Brother Janzen had gone.

In the dead silence of the night I heard some groaning off in the distance. Probing with the flashlight I crept through the thick of the jungle in the direction of the sound. There I found A. A. Janzen kneeling in prayer. His burdens so consumed him that he did not notice my approach. I could hear his prayer. In deep agony he pleaded for the multitudes who had not yet heard the gospel. He mentioned me by name, asking God to place upon me the burden for their spiritual condition. He asked that I not find rest until I filled the gap that needed leadership. I withdrew quietly. About an hour later he returned to the tent, not aware that I had heard some of his pleading. Unable to sleep I lay quietly until dawn.

The natives had prepared us a breakfast of cooked eggs, bread and a hot drink. I did not let on to my host that I had overheard his agonized intercession, but I was deeply touched by his request that God move me to consider the leadership of this work. However, I sought to put the whole incident out of my mind. I had been given the great privilege of a ministry in Reedley, a challenge that captivated me. In no way was I open to give ear to the missionary's prayer.

I spent the concluding weeks of July visiting other missions to survey their methods of evangelism and study the indigenization of their institutions, schools and dispensaries. In the Congo I spent some time with the Congo Inland Mission, the Baptist Mission and the Catholic missions. My visit was extended to French Equatorial Africa. Here a Swedish mission had developed an industrial complex operated by the national church with only minimal supervision from abroad.

I made a stopover in Nigeria and travelled extensively to see the work of the Sudan Interior Mission which was a leader in building true indigenous churches. The methods of the Africa Inland Mission also gave me insights I had not grasped before.

My remaining travels to Europe and the Middle East were highly in-
formative and enriching. In Europe I spent a week with Cornelius Wall,
who introduced me to the many refugee camps that had sprung up in the
aftermath of World War II.

Up to that point my knowledge of the greater worldwide Mennonite
family had been largely limited to the Dutch Mennonites during our stay in
the Netherlands from 1926 to 1928. Now, at the world conference, I was
able to enlarge my acquaintance with other Mennonite branches. I was
also able to witness the efforts that were made to heal the rifts that had
been created during the war as Mennonites from various countries had
been forced to confront each other on opposite sides of the conflict.

Touring the Middle East with a delegation representing various Mennonite groups was likewise enriching. Getting a firsthand glimpse of Italy,
Cyprus, Israel, Egypt, Jordan and Greece enlarged my grasp of biblical
history. Only a few years had elapsed since Israel had become an independent state. The political tension throughout the total Middle East was
evident everywhere.

By September 1 we were finally together again as a family. We had
many experiences to share—John from Hepburn, Saskatchewan, and Paul
from the Wiest farm. Nettie and James, the keepers of the house, had
experienced a major earthquake, which Nettie had found very unnerving.
Little did we realize that this kind of family separation would become increasingly common.

A Crisis Decision

The insights from the summer of 1952 required a time of processing.
The post-war period had created unlimited opportunities for the expansion of missions abroad. Two centuries of colonialism had come to an end
and all the colonies of western Europe were crying for independence.
Around the world old political structures were being dismantled. India
gained its independence in 1948, the same year that the nation of Israel
was born.

As I pondered the great need I had seen and the urgent prayer I had
heard in the jungle, I got a clearer picture of what would be needed for the
Mennonite Brethren Church to remain a faithful steward of the gospel. A
new era in the history of missions was dawning. The leaders of the Sudan
Interior Mission in Nigeria and Ethiopia, with whom I had spent much

time, had pressed upon me the need to change our mission approach, both in relationships and strategies.

My report to the board in October 1952 urged a review of our mission programs in India, Africa and South America. The board acknowledged the need for change and decided that if we were to set a new direction we would require additional leadership. Abraham E. Janzen, the executive secretary, was preoccupied with day-to-day administration of the world-wide program, which at the time included Europe, India, Japan, Africa, Colombia, Mexico, Brazil and Paraguay. Another administrator was needed to look after promotion and overall direction.

I was not open to this assignment. I felt the right person for the task was G. W. Peters, then the president of Pacific Bible Institute in Fresno. He taught missions and was well-versed in the changing currents in world affairs and their effect upon missions. The question was delayed to the spring meeting. When the board met again on April 9-11, 1953 the matter of a promotional secretary was high on the agenda. Several candidates were considered, among them Orlando Harms, G. W. Peters and J. B. Toews. After lengthy deliberations there was a unanimous vote to ask me to assume the position.

Inwardly smitten, I returned to Reedley. I was not open to leaving the church where we had experienced the working of God in such a marvelous way. I had told the board that I would take their request under advisement, but inwardly I was committed to continuing my present ministry. In my view the request was not even realistic. The new position would demand continual absences from my family at a time when they needed me most. The Reedley church, with its fervent commitment to missions and evangelism, was my first love. In my devotional hours over the next months the call to missions emerged again and again. Nettie, of course, shared the struggle with me. For me to leave Reedley at the time would be a sacrifice not unlike that of God asking Abraham for his son, Isaac.

The words of Genesis 22:2 continued to ring in my ears: "Take now thy son, thine *only son Isaac*, whom thou lovest . . . and offer him for a burnt offering upon one of the mountains which I will tell you of." In July I shared the struggle with the Reedley church leadership. At first I found very little sympathy for my inner conflict. The evidences of God's blessings upon the church ministry were too convincing. How could we consider interrupting them?

An additional factor that entered our deliberations was Nettie's health. The fiercely hot summers sapped her energy. She was always tired. It appeared that the water cooler was also a culprit. The atmosphere in the parsonage was too damp. Modern air-conditioning systems were not yet common.

Finally we made our decision, and on Sunday, August 18, I read my letter of resignation to the church. Many people in the audience wept. I managed to contain my emotions in public but back in the office I broke down and wept like a child. Some brethren from the leadership followed me into the office and put their arms around me. Standing in a circle, we wept together. For me this was akin to the offering of Isaac.

The date of my departure from the church was set for December 1953, in consideration of the boys' school schedule. John, sixteen, was in high school; Paul, thirteen, was in grade eight; James was in kindergarten.

The farewell Sunday was very difficult for all of us. With a trailer behind our eight-cylinder Pontiac we left Reedley early on a Monday morning. For the first few hours we were all very quiet. Here and there we wiped tears from our eyes. Our attachment to the Reedley congregation had been deeper than we realized.

The three-day journey to Hillsboro, Kansas, was uneventful. A stopover in Buhler, where we had left eight years earlier, brought back some of the pain of leaving that pastoral ministry. Looking back now on six decades of public ministry, I have to say the combined eight years of the pastorate in these two communities has remained the highlight. The sense of being physically part of a people and serving them in the varied stages of life, seeing God working in their lives, providing leadership, ministering to their needs in the congregation and in their homes, has never been equalled in my nearly forty years of service to other segments of the community of faith.

If relinquishing the Reedley ministry was a personal sacrifice to me, it would pale when compared to the sacrifice my family would end up making for the cause of missions. The next ten years would be a time of continuous irregularity in our family life as I would be gone from five to eight months per year.

Nettie, in her unflinching devotion, became more and more the center of the family while I saw my arena of duty as being the wider North American and international community of faith. Steadfast in her devotion to Christ, she never wavered in her support of the public ministry to which we were called. Raising our three sons and providing hospitality for the many missionaries and the constant flow of conference-related personnel who passed through our home, tested her to the uttermost. In her quiet and unassuming way she reflected the qualities of both Martha and Mary.

The parental home of Nettie on the farm near Freeman (compare with the Toews' farmhouse in Coaldale).

The Unruh sisters: From left to right, Martha — Mrs. Pete Ratzlaff, Nettie, my wife, Grace, a teacher by profession who related very close to us in our ministry. She financed most of my travel during the years I served as mission secretary. Emma, a store clerk, circa 1972. Other members in Nettie's family were two brothers, August and Isaak.

Freeman College where I taught 1940-1942.

Buhler parsonage which the church bought to provide a home for us. In front our car, a gift from Mother Unruh.

Mennonite Brethren Bible College administration and classroom building.

Student housing, Ebenezer Hall dedicated fall 1946.

College Board. From left to right, Heinrich Neufeld, Herbert, David Wiens, Vancouver, B. B. Janz, Coaldale, C. F. Classen, Winnipeg, Heinrich Toews, Arnaud, Chairman, C. C. Peters, Yarrow, A. H. Unruh, Winnipeg, J. B. Toews, college president, C. A. DeFehr, Winnipeg, Abram Voth, Winnipeg, B. B. Fast, Winnipeg.

Our family in Reedley, 1953.

One of many departures during the years in mission administration. A. E. Janzen to my left.

The Indian oxen cart with P. V. Balzer and from left to right, myself, C. A. DeFehr, mission treasurer for Canada and J. P. Kliewer, board member.

Leaders of the church in Zaire. From left to right standing: myself, Matshitsa Matsi, Djimbo Kubala, Kilabi Balulu, Arnold Prieb. Front row: Ngangu Diyoyo, Ernest Dyck, Makose Mbavu.

A congregation of the Japan Mennonite Brethren church.

CHAPTER 16

A Decade in Missions

Before my arrival, A. E. Janzen had been the sole administrator of an international ministry of nearly 150 missionaries in Africa, India, Brazil, Colombia, Paraguay, Mexico and Japan. He was assisted by only two office workers. The budget for the 1951-54 triennium was $285,435, an astonishing low amount even in those days. My new position had a broad mandate. As "promotional secretary," I was to re-examine the theology, philosophy and practice of Mennonite Brethren missions, implement appropriate changes, and generate understanding in the constituency for the new approaches.

Colonial Legacy

The status of Mennonite Brethren missions in 1953 can be understood only in the context of a colonial system where each missionary or group of missionaries functioned as an independent entity. The task of these entities was to "save souls." The first principle of missions clearly stated, "He that winneth souls is wise" (Prov. 11:30). The millions who had never heard the gospel were lost. They must hear. The dedication of the Mennonite Brethren Conference, the missionaries and the administration was deeply sincere. The orientation of our missions thrust up to that point may seem simplistic, but the evident blessings of God were convincing.

At this time the Mennonite Brethren mission program was still based on the concept of a mission station as the center of operational outreach. The Mission Council, consisting of all bona fide missionaries on the field, took full responsibility for the program of evangelism and institutional services (including schools and hospitals). Missionaries were given a permanent place as "fathers and mothers in Christ" in the indigenous church. They would remain part of the indigenous congregation for life. These practices, outmoded as they seem, were nonetheless an accurate reflection of the colonial mindset that had prevailed up to that point. The mission board and some in the constituency saw that missions had to change following the worldwide collapse of colonialism in the postwar era.

My assignment as promotional secretary related to the home constituency as well as to the overseas programs. Both parts of the task were very demanding. All travel among the churches in the U.S. and Canada was either by car or by train. Each year I would drive for weeks on end, criss-crossing North America, from east to west and north to south, visiting the churches. Missionaries often would travel with me to report at mission conferences. Train travel meant spending many nights sitting up, as Pullman cars were too expensive for a mission agency.

The days and weeks of close contact with missionaries provided opportunities for counsel and confidential exchanges. Beneath the sincerity of our missionaries I found deep spiritual needs, tensions in relationships with fellow missionaries, and problems with the structure of mission ministries. In the missionary pecking order, older workers dominated the program and the younger missionaries and single women were relegated to secondary roles. Seniority had to be earned over a period of years.

In the years 1955 through 1957 I had the opportunity to visit India, Belgian Congo, Colombia, Brazil, Paraguay and Uruguay. On first arriving in India in 1955 I was greeted by two senior missionaries with the gruff question, "What do you want here?" With the approval of the board I had prepared an extensive set of questions related to the work on each station and the work schedule for each missionary. The tone of these missionaries' greeting implied some resentment to the detailed inquiry. On my second day in India I received a request from the nationals for a private meeting, with no missionary present. When I mentioned this request to some of the missionaries they openly protested. In spite of the protest I did arrange a meeting with only national leaders, who then shared some of their deep tensions. They pointed to the changes that had occurred in India following the country's independence in 1948. They felt the missionaries should have transferred more responsibility to them in recognition of their new nationhood.

A Matter of Money

The notion of an active missions administrator who actually travelled to the fields on a regular basis was a new one to many in the constituency. It took time for them to recognize this as a wise use of funds.

In the 1950s the study and evaluation of programs was seen as the task of the missionaries. The task of the board and the churches was not to interfere but to enable the missionary to go to the "heathen," bring them the "good news" and report back to the churches.

At the 1956 Pacific District Conference a brother from Shafter, California, who had followed my extensive travels, came to me with the question: "J. B., where can we now send our money for missions so that you cannot use it for traveling around the world?"

"Brother Siemens," I replied, "none of the money that is sent in for missions is spent for my travel."

"Who then pays for it?" he persisted.

"It comes," I said, "from private sources designated for travel in the study of our mission programs abroad."

Most of my overseas travel on behalf of Mennonite Brethren missions was paid for privately. The largest share of it was provided by Grace Unruh, Nettie's sister, and our personal resources. Our sister Grace, a teacher all her life, had many questions about the glowing missionary reports she had heard over the years. Her desire for an unvarnished version of the truth was such that she was willing to finance a good deal of my foreign travel in an effort to gain an accurate report. The only trip that was completly charged to the agency was an emergency trip to Africa in 1960 when the revolution forced all our Congo missionaries, staff and families—more than ninety persons—to be evacuated.

A New Direction

My visits abroad and my consultations with many other mission agencies in various countries gave insight into the radical changes we would need in mission relationship, theology, methods and structure.

Some members of the mission board, in particular G. W. Peters and H. H. Janzen, agreed with my concerns. From 1955 to 1957 I shared openly with the constituent churches the need for major readjustments in our worldwide ministry. Some found these views hard to accept. In the mid-1950s the Mennonite Brethren Church had nearly 200 missionaries in foreign lands. Their motives were genuine. The support from the churches had been amazing. It had been the golden age of Mennonite Brethren missions. Why change now?

With the help of people like G. W. Peters, we prayed earnestly for the future of Mennonite Brethren missions. The struggle found expression in a document I wrote that was first accepted by the board and then presented to the 1957 General Conference. Extensive travel to the churches and consultation with leaders in the constituency preceded the conference, held in Yarrow, B.C., on October 20-23. By now the delegates were ready for the changes outlined in the document and voted their approval.

The document projected the role of the missionary to conform to the New Testament expansion of the gospel. Like Paul, the missionary proclaims the good news and serves as the planter of the church. The mission is only the enabling agency to help plant the church and then provide assistance in teaching and nurture with the local church becoming responsible for its own expansion within its respective culture.

Some of our older missionaries found the new direction very difficult to accept. They were products of a time that had passed. One incident illustrates the tension some of them felt. At a missions conference in Greendale, B.C. following the 1957 conference, two missionaries from India presented reports. The first one concluded her report in tears and said, "What will happen with the work in India now, with the decision of the conference, we do not know." The other missionary also concluded his report with deep emotions, adding, "How the work in India will continue with the new direction accepted by the conference only God knows, and if it fails, J. B. Toews will need to accept the responsibility."

I was stunned. I was to speak next. To gain time for a reply I asked the choir to sing two songs. By the time the singing stopped I had decided not to reply directly to their comments. I changed my text to Acts 28:28, "Be it known therefore unto you, that the gospel has been sent to the gentiles and they will hear it." My message expressed confidence that God had made provision. The work would go on.

The older missionaries can perhaps be excused for finding the new direction so difficult. As recently as 1947 their relationship with the national churches had been officially defined as one of parent and child. The new approach anticipated their removal from the churches as early as was feasible to give nationals liberty for self-identity in the context of their native culture. For some missionaries this implied the end of what they had understood to be a lifelong relationship to the national churches. Their struggle was somewhat like parents having to separate from their children. The next triennium, 1957-1960, was very demanding. In consideration of A. E. Janzen's advancing age I was asked to take additional administrative duties as executive secretary. The new policies and their implications for each of our fields needed to be worked out. National governing councils were created for each field to take over decision-making. The missionaries were asked to serve only in advisory capacities. The missionary council, formerly the legislative body, was now to function as a fellowship. The implementation of the new policies was difficult. The older missionaries from India were withdrawn. A younger generation of workers was assigned to help the church develop its independence. The overall relationship of the North American church to the national churches abroad found expression in the statement, "Partnership in Obedience."

The years 1960 to 1963, my concluding years in the mission program, were spent on implementation. Written policies are one thing, but the realization of the ideal was something else. The General Conference of 1960, the Mennonite Brethren centennial, was a milestone. Our mission report was titled "A Century of Grace and Witness." For a hundred years the missionary emphasis had been on "saving lost souls." The initiative had come entirely from the West—Europe and North America. Theoretically we had turned the corner with the 1957 resolution that made our chief objective the establishing of national churches that could more effectively evangelize their own people.

The 1960 centennial featured representatives from the national churches India, Japan, Africa, Mexico, Colombia, Brazil and Paraguay. The "Partnership in Obedience" principle was confirmed. I saw it as a great day in the history of Mennonite Brethren missions. In theory, at least, the focus had shifted from an outmoded paternalism to a new era of indigenization. The commitment to partnership with the churches abroad was again strongly affirmed at the 1963 conference in Winnipeg.

A Disappointing Process

Little did I realize that the actual implementation of this new partnership would not be fully realized for another thirty years. Despite good intentions, it has been difficult for North Americans to change the practices of the past. Into the recent past some Mennonite Brethren missions retained their colonialist flavor while others moved more rapidly toward indigenization.[10]

When asked to comment on the commitment to Partnership in Obedience, one Colombian Mennonite Brethren leader responded, "Obedience to who?" and "Partnership with whom?" He said it took at least a decade before attempts to develop a fraternal rather than paternal relationship began to appear on the field. Even then, the changes were largely cosmetic in nature. He adds:

The Colombian leaders continued to have the mindset that they had to be obedient to the decisions made by the missionaries and, in the end, Hillsboro always had the last word. Of course, it was said that the Colombian Conference was autonomous to make decisions but since we were partners with the Mission, this partnership was understood to be in only one direction and not reciprocal. Hillsboro was the "Vatican" for us. The mission board who insisted that they were partners with the national conference always found ways to subtly impose the decisions that they wanted in relation with personnel, projects and finances. It was obvious that we Colombians understood partnership in one way and in Hillsboro it was applied another way. How can you be a partner at the same level, fraternally speaking, when everything is decided vertically, i.e., from the top power downward?[11]

This leader also complained that missionaries found it difficult to relate on an equal footing with national leaders, partly because they tended to be people with a domineering middle-class mindset and lifestyle. "The missionary goes as a chief and not as a facilitator," he said. The national churches feel they have little to contribute to the dialogue because "Big Brother has all the answers."

Reflections

Were my ten years of administration in Mennonite Brethren missions a failure? Were we three decades ahead of our time? Or did we expect change to come too quickly?

Reflecting on this part of my faith pilgrimage I make several observations:

1. To serve in leadership during a time of major fundamental change is rewarding. The process of change, however, can be very painful for those directly affected, in this case the older missionaries.

2. The commitment of the Mennonite Brethren Church to the cause of missions in the 1950s and 1960s reflected a high degree of understanding and unflinching support.

3. The personal relationship to the missionaries over a period of a decade provided unlimited opportunities for close fellowship. Missionar-

ies are not saints. Their calling requires continuous affirmation and spiritual nurture. In general they are a lonely people, often separated from their children and extended family. Singles feel this isolation most keenly. Maintaining a continuous sense that their assignment is a service unto the Lord is difficult. The weakening of this priority expresses itself in personal spiritual struggles which generate many tensions in inter-personal relationships. Providing a spiritual ministry to the missionaries, though rewarding, constituted the most difficult aspect of my ten years in mission leadership.

4. Maintaining my personal spiritual resources was no easy task. My energy and strength were sapped by the demands of relating to some 200 missionaries and making daily decisions affecting our program of spreading the gospel.

5. For half a century the missionaries had been the center of the missions program, with little accountability. Their reports to the constituency tended to be highly inflated. To change the structure was very difficult. In the churches the missionaries carried an image of holiness and exemplified the highest degree of spirituality. The contrast between this elevated image in the churches and the reality as reflected in personal relationships on the field was very difficult for me to accept. But they were a product of our making. For decades they were isolated from the home environment, responsible only to themselves and to God. When they came home on furlough they were celebrated as exhibits of godliness. No wonder there was a gap between image and reality. Adjusting to this dissonance served as a maturing influence in my own spiritual pilgrimage.

6. Finally, my years in missions took a toll on my family. Nettie and our three sons, the older two both teenagers, were asked to accept the continuous absence of husband and father. Their acceptance of having to take second place may have been the greater contribution to the cause of missions during this period of my life.

CHAPTER 17

The Seminary Presidency

I n the early 1960s I was invited to consider a teaching position at the Mennonite Brethren Biblical Seminary in Fresno. The invitation was tempting for a variety of reasons. For one thing, the years of intensive travel as a missions administrator had taken their toll, and the prospect of a more relaxed assignment for us as a family was appealing.

I was also drawn to the idea of making a significant contribution to Mennonite Brethren higher education, particularly in the area of fashioning a more specific Mennonite Brethren identity.

I had spent nearly ten years in Mennonite Brethren education at Bethany Bible Institute and the Mennonite Brethren Bible College. I had spent another ten years in the pastorate, and ten more in missions administration. I was concerned that the character of our educational efforts did not reflect the passion for a lifestyle of faith and discipleship that had been such a distinctive stamp of our Mennonite Brethren and Anabaptist forbears.

The Vision for a Seminary

The Mennonite Brethren journey in seminary education had not been smooth. In 1948, the Mennonite Brethren General Conference agreed to consider the need for a seminary and a commission was appointed to study its feasibility. The 1951 General Conference Yearbook records a plan to establish a General Conference seminary close to one of the existing schools. But in 1954 when the General Conference began to lay the foundation for such a seminary, the Canadian Conference delegation withdrew from the negotiations.

At the following year's Canadian Conference the Mennonite Brethren churches of Canada took a position that removed them from any obligation to such a program of seminary education. At this conference I delivered a message titled, "The Bible and Higher Education in the Context of the Spiritual Conflict of our Day." The response to my message was very positive, but it failed to change the Canadian Conference position of non-participation in theological education at the General Conference level.

Some of the Canadian leadership from the 1920s (B. B. Janz of Coaldale; Johannas Harder of Yarrow, British Columbia; Aron A. Toews of Namaka, Alberta; Jacob Thiessen of Dalmeny, Saskatchewan, later Vancouver; Heinrich Toews of Arnaud, Manitoba; and others) carried a deep prejudice against the Mennonite Brethren educational program in the south. I well recall B. B. Janz's reaction after he visited Tabor College in 1932. The guide who took him through the campus showed him the old gymnasium where a group of young people dressed in shorts and sleeveless shirts were playing basketball. In his report to the Coaldale church he described the spirit of worldliness he had observed in the Tabor gym, referring to it as a "culture of nudity, void of any degree of modesty."

Other Canadian leaders wanted to avoid any involvement with American Mennonite Brethren in matters of education. The establishment of the MB Bible College in Winnipeg had been intended by some as a move toward isolation.

The U. S. churches were also not united on educational issues. Historically, the center of the Mennonite Brethren Conference had been Hillsboro, a small rural town. It had Tabor College, the MB mission board offices and the MB Publishing House. The establishment of Pacific Bible Institute in Fresno, Calif., in 1944, was the beginning of a shift in this dominance. But the question remained: how could a conference of only 10,500 members support a four-year college in Hillsboro, a Bible institute in Fresno, and now also a seminary program as a new department of the Bible institute? It seemed like an impossible task.

The key to making the impossible happen, was the U.S. Conference Board of Education, specifically its chairman from 1954 to 1971, Ed J. Peters. He had accepted the call of the U.S. Conference to the Board of Education as a call from God. Peters, a prominent business man, was a founding member of Mennonite Economic Development Associates (MEDA) and a director of Hume Lake Christian Conference. He held many other positions of responsibility in church and community ventures. Various slogans that he liked reflected his energetic spirit: "The job assignment is not too big, maybe the man is too small for the job." "If you can't do the job, God will surely find someone else in your place to do it." He understood prayer as related to human responsibility: "Do not fight your prayer in waiting for God to act, rather go to work and implement your prayers." In the struggle for finances for education he would say, "God made too many Christians and not enough dollars." Many other slogans were common with Ed Peters, who believed that "nothing is impossible if God has assigned it to you."

Peters, together with Peter A. Enns and Dr. Menno S. Gaede, were the key movers in the development of the seminary. Despite the tension among midwesterners who visualized a seminary in Hillsboro, Enns and Gaede took a leap of faith and purchased property for the seminary next to the new location of Pacific College in Fresno.

In the spring of 1955 the Board of Education approached me to accept the presidency of the new seminary. I declined for several reasons: First, the seminary program was considered only provisional, subject to ongoing negotiations towards a joint sponsorship by the U.S. and Canadian conferences. Second, the Fresno location for the seminary was also considered provisional; the permanent location was to be selected by the two conferences when agreement was reached with Canada. Third, the faculty already appointed from the Bible departments of Tabor College and Pacific Bible Institute did not project an Anabaptist character for the seminary. It was to be known as an evangelical seminary, and all publicity identified it as such. With the rising religious pluralism and individualism of the 1950s I could not see myself leading a program that did not project a distinct Anabaptist identity. Fourth, I had just taken on responsibility for the Mennonite Brethren mission program and its major thrust of moving beyond the colonial captivity of the past. I could not leave this task unfinished to tackle another need that was no less worthy but had a very uncertain future.

A decade later, however, I felt differently. Somewhat exhausted from the ten years in missions, having guided the transition from colonialism to the policy of "Partnership in Obedience," I was open for a change. Now R. M. Baerg invited me to come to the seminary to fill a void in the faculty. The prospect of teaching missions and theology appealed to me. I accepted the invitation and the Board of Education approved my appointment at its August 20-21, 1962 meeting. At the fall 1962 Board of Missions meeting I resigned as executive secretary, effective September 1, 1963.

Our Need for Change

After so many years of various types of administration I was now, at age fifty-six, ready for a quieter assignment of teaching. Nettie and I felt a need to be closer together as a family. Our youngest son, James, was then a teenager. Our relationship as husband and wife also needed more relaxed time together than the previous thirty years of ministry had allowed.

I accepted the invitation to the seminary on the condition that I would not be required to be involved administratively. I needed a rest. I also envisioned completing my doctorate, which I had given up twenty years earlier because of the prevailing lack of understanding in the conference for advanced theological education. With summers free from teaching, resuming my studies became part of the attraction to the seminary.

The fact that our son John and his family were already in Fresno was also a factor in our decision. He was studying at the seminary and teaching at Pacific College. John negotiated the purchase of a house for us on East Townsend, a half block from the seminary.

At the time we viewed the change from Hillsboro to Fresno as a transition. Inwardly I longed to return to the pastorate. There were openings for us in churches in both Canada and the U.S. The future of the seminary in the summer of 1963 was still not clear. The seminary property, adjoining Pacific College, needed development. The building, a stately old mansion, needed major renovations to meet the city's building code. The seminary faced significant questions. Should it become the theological department of the college, a continuation of the College of Theology at Tabor? Could the prospect of a joint seminary with Canada be realized?

Amid many questions we moved to Fresno and I began teaching. Nettie, James and I basked in the prospect of spending more time together. The chapter of mission administration was behind us. We were looking for direction for the future.

Pressure, Again

September, October and the first part of November were quiet months for us. But the calm would not last long. By mid-November 1963, I came under pressure from members of the board to consider the presidency. R. M. Baerg had notified the board that he looked for an early relief as acting president.

I soon realized the future of the seminary was at a crossroad. Ed Peters, Menno Gaede and Peter Enns, put great pressure on me, suggesting that the future of the seminary depended on my affirmative response. The time from mid-November 1963 until February 1964 thus became another time of crisis for us. We had anticipated relief from administrative responsibilities and now we were again in a squeeze. Looking back I find it difficult to interpret my naivete in coming to Fresno.

I had no interest in accepting the leadership of a provisional program, as the seminary essentially had been up to that point. Only upon the board's decision to proceed with the seminary development, envisioning a permanent independent institution subject to the ratification of the U. S. Conference in 1965, would I even think about such a position. After lengthy consultations with members of the Board of Education and with the leadership of the Canadian Mennonite Brethren Conference about the prospect of finding a basis for a future joint seminary, Nettie and I finally agreed to accept the assignment, though not without major reservations. On March 6, 1964, after being with the seminary only six months, my appointment as president was announced.

My commitment in accepting the position was threefold: First, to redefine the seminary's identity as an institution committed to an Anabaptist approach to the interpretation of Scripture and to the life and character of the church. Second, to upgrade the faculty and other resources to meet the demands for a graduate-level academic program. Third, to develop the campus to provide adequate facilities for a graduate institution with the prospect that it could become the permanent location for a joint seminary with Canada.

Struggle for Anabaptist Identity

The initial step toward developing an identity more consistent with our historic understanding of the faith was a statement of purpose and philosophy released in 1964. This statement called for graduate-level theological education that was committed to a bibliocentric curriculum, an experiential faith, an Anabaptist concept of a disciplined church, and a New Testament understanding of mission and evangelism. These commitments would require major changes in the curriculum.

The guiding principles identified the seminary as being historically committed to the Anabaptist view of the church and introduced the requirement of a full four-unit course in Anabaptist history and theology. The name became the Mennonite Brethren Biblical Seminary to identify the core character of the institution.

The content of the curriculum was further tested and focused on areas such as:

• *The meaning of Christian experience*: A creedal faith, or genuine relationship.

• *The style of life*: Easy Christianity, or Christian discipleship and self-denial.

• *The interpretation of Scripture*: A particular system, or a hermeneutical community.

• *The nature of the church*: A covenant community of biblical disciples, or a highly-organized institution.

• *The nature of the ministry*: A professional pastor who does the work of the church, or a gift that God gives to the church for the purpose of equipping the saints for the work of the ministry.

• *The mission of the church*: Evangelism versus social concerns, or proclamation in both word and deed.

• *The centrality of ethics*: A question of only war and peace, or the lordship of Christ in all of life, including suffering love for enemy.

The dialogue of the initial years involved a larger circle of participants, including faculty from the college in Winnipeg. The conversation with leaders from Canada with regard to a joint seminary continued.

Developing A Faculty

In order to work toward an accredited seminary we needed to strengthen the faculty. For the initial years, 1964 to 1970, we sought to fill this need with qualified part-time faculty: Peter J. Klassen in history, Elias Wiebe in Christian education, Dalton Reimer in public speaking and communication, and pastor Werner Kroeker in homiletics and preaching. Abram J. Klassen was added to the faculty as professor in theology in the second year. George Konrad joined us in 1966 as professor in Christian education. Orrin Berg from Pacific College introduced the first course in counseling in 1967. Other part-time faculty over the years were Melvin J. Loewen, Henry J. Krahn, Larry Warkentin, R. M. Baerg and Waldo Hiebert, who in 1968 had left the faculty to pastor the Reedley Mennonite Brethren Church. A. J. Klassen became the academic dean in 1967, and completed doctoral work at Claremont Graduate School. While we waited for Elmer A. Martens to earn a doctorate in Old Testament, Dwight Acomb served as professor of Old Testament. Paul Hiebert served as professor of anthropology and missions for the year 1970-1971. To make graduate studies for members of the faculty possible we needed to provide financial subsidies, which were provided from individual donors and special friends of the seminary.

We continued to work on strengthening our course offerings. We consulted with other Mennonite seminaries in Elkhart, Indiana, and Harrisonburg, Virginia, to help us rebuild a curriculum consistent with our denominational identity. Recognition must be given to the new dean, A. J. Klassen, for his role in restructuring the curriculum. As a student of Harold S. Bender, the Mennonite church leader and historian, he was well versed in the field of Anabaptist studies, which were incorporated into the core program.

In 1969 the seminary attained associate membership in the American Association of Theological Schools. Full accreditation was delayed subject to the expansion of the library holdings. In January 1972 we received full academic accreditation with the Western Association of Schools, Colleges and Universities. Full accreditation with the American Association of Theological Schools followed in 1973.

Campus Development

In 1955 the seminary had begun in the Pacific Bible Institute facilities in downtown Fresno. In 1961 it was moved to its present location at 4824 E. Butler. This property consisted of six and one-half acres of land and a mansion built in 1917. The home was surrounded by a large variety of trees. A narrow gravel road ran from the northwest corner of the property and wound through the forest of trees to the southeast corner. There was also a swimming pool and a maintenance shop.

As long as the seminary location had been only provisional, few efforts to develop the campus had been made. Now that the Board of Education had committed itself to this permanent location, campus development became a pressing issue. Since we had no provision for this in the conference budget, the task appeared impossible. The Southern District, specifically Kansas, opposed the development of a seminary on the West Coast and contributed nothing to campus development. They continued to argue—naively, I thought—that the seminary should be established in Hillsboro, close to Tabor College. Both Tabor and Pacific College, meanwhile were appealing to the constituency for resources for their own expansion.

I remember the spring, summer and fall of 1964 as a time of inner crisis. Had I committed myself to an impossible task? What about our family needs, which had been a major factor in leaving the mission administration?

I recalled a slogan that had become a guiding principle for me while I was in missions administration: "God's work done in God's way will not lack God's provision." For me the burning question then became whether developing the seminary was really God's will. Could this assignment be a step that would lead to a more positive response from Canada for a joint venture in seminary education? A student body of thirty-five (the enrollment of the 1964-1965 academic year) was not enough to sustain a program that would earn the respect of accrediting agencies. I came to rest in the story of Abraham who was asked to obey without knowing the future.

As it turned out, relationships from the distant past came to my aid. In October 1964, while at a conference in Delft, Minnesota, I shared my concern with a group of people whom I knew from my early years of ministry in the Central District. I made contact with A. N. Dick, a builder I had learned to know in Montana in the 1930s. A lengthy discussion with Brother and Sister Dick planted the seed which would provide the answer to our campus development needs. From the fall of 1965 through the fall of 1969 the Dicks gave us six months of their time every year.

October 1965 through March 1965 was spent renovating the main building to meet the city code. The whole heating system and the plumbing needed replacement. Two bathrooms were converted into faculty offices and a third bathroom was relocated. One large bedroom was subdivided into two offices. The kitchen on the main floor was torn out to provide a workroom. Major foundation work was necessary. During the rainy season the basement floor would take in up to an inch of water. A deep ditch was dug around the foundation to the north and east of the building to install the appropriate drainage. City regulations also required installation of a complete sprinkler system, at a cost of $16,000. Dan Loewen, a plumber from the Bethany Church, did most of the plumbing for this major renovation, donating his time.

The plan for the seminary campus was laid out carefully in consultation with members of the Board of Education, faculty, architects and specialists in landscaping, and finally approved by the City of Fresno. Many trees had to be removed to make room for an entrance from the north side on Butler. Landscaping was necessary to provide space for other build-ings. The initial expense of the renovation and campus development in 1965 and 1966 was $23,673.

Basic student housing was also urgently needed, but again there was no budgetary provision. Once again the answer was in the donated labor of A. N. Dick as well as Hugo Wiens of St. Catharines, Ontario, and others who volunteered for shorter and longer periods.

We began the development program with the understanding that we could not go into debt. The financial provisions would determine our rate of progress. The example and influence of A. N. Dick attracted other vol-unteers from the Central District. There were times when all work had to be stopped because funds were exhausted. Here the volunteers them-selves stepped in, calling their friends in Minnesota, North Dakota and Montana to tell them work had stopped for lack of finances. Their voices were heard, and more contributions came in.

Mission Memorial Court, the complex of ten two-bedroom apartments for student families, was made possible by donors who wanted to com-memorate missionaries and family members. Major contributors were Mr. and Mrs. D. W. Gloeckler, San Jose; missionary John H. Lohrenz, India; John W. Friesen, Big Bow, Nebraska; the Cornelius C. Reimer family of Shafter, California; Mr. and Mrs. Menno Siemens, Shafter; and friends of Krimmer Mennonite Brethren missionaries from Dinuba, California. The modest monument inscribed with the names of all Mennonite Brethren and Krimmer Mennonite Brethren missionaries who were called to their reward before 1967, stands in the center of the court. For me personally, Mission Memorial Court is a monument of God's faithfulness to his people who know how to pray and to trust him for the humanly impossible.

Another important symbol is the Prayer Chapel, erected in memory of Herman Warkentin by his parents, Mr. and Mrs. H. K. Warkentin. This chapel reflects the centrality of prayer in the life of an institution dedicated to the preparation of church workers and missionaries.

The idea of a prayer chapel came to me during a visit to Westmont College in Santa Barbara, which had a prayer chapel in the center of the campus. I spent some time in that chapel, and became convinced that we, too, needed a similar center to symbolize the focal resources that would determine the future of the institution. Months later I was led to think of Herman Warkentin, a missionary who lost his life in India in 1953. I gathered my courage and shared the vision with Herman's parents. I took their favorable response as another sign of God's purpose for the seminary.

Despite all this activity, the campus remained inadequate. The central building housed the administrative offices, faculty offices and three classrooms. My vision for the seminary was a faculty of eight and a student body of seventy to seventy-five. The enrollment in 1968-1969 was sixty. Additional office and classroom space was an absolute necessity. We needed a chapel large enough for faculty, staff and sixty students with their families.

The Pacific District Conference and the U. S. Conference also needed office space, and after long negotiations it was decided to locate these facilities on the seminary campus. This combined interest enabled us to make plans for a joint seminary-conference building. A. N. Dick, together with volunteers from Minnesota, North Dakota and Montana, again pitched in to erect a facility to house a chapel with a seating capacity of 120, a large classroom, and offices for faculty and conference personnel. The total cost, with furnishings, would be $106,042. Gathering a third of this amount was again a step of faith. The building was completed in the spring of 1970.

Looking back on these six years of campus development, I am amazed at the way God provided. This does not mean there were no crises along the way. One memorable experience occurred in December of 1969. My spirits had dipped to a low ebb. We did not have money to pay the meager salaries of the faculty, nor was there money to continue work on the conference building.

Close to despair, I drove to the farm of William Wiebe, a deacon of the Reedley MB Church. He had been a very close friend during my time there. William and his wife, Renetta, were at the supper table. I walked in without greeting them, went to the fireplace, sat down on the ledge and burst into tears. The Wiebes were taken aback. William drew near and sat beside me. I could not control my emotions for some time. Had God forsaken me? Was there some hindrance that prevented am answer to our prayers in this time of need?

After some time of silence I could open up and share with my friends the desperate situation in which I found myself. An hour passed. I regained my composure. William led out in prayer; Renetta followed. I, too, managed to pray, pleading with God to find a way out.

A long period of silence followed. Suddenly William got up, went to his desk, and wrote out a check for $1,000. "Here," he said, "take this as the down payment, and exercise faith that God will provide your needs."

In the weeks that followed, the last week of December and the beginning of January, our needs were met through people whose hearts God touched. The dedication of the conference building in the fall of 1970 was a day of deep gratitude. My faith in the slogan, "God's work done in God's way will not lack God's provision," was confirmed.

Reflections

By 1970 I felt I had accomplished the major task of my assignment: to lead the seminary towards a Mennonite Brethren-Anabaptist orientation; to upgrade the faculty and program; and to gain accreditation as a graduate-level institution. I enjoyed the half-time teaching load I carried in order to remain closely involved with the academic program and the student body. Here I found a level of satisfaction that had eluded me as an administrator.

The resistance of the Southern District Conference to the West Coast seminary had gradually diminished. The U. S. Conference as a body had accepted the seminary as its responsibility. At the convention in Dallas, Oregon, in 1965, the conference participated in pledges that liquidated the indebtedness on the original purchase of the seminary property.

Discussions with Canadian Conference leaders had continued. My good connections with them provided a basis for ongoing conversation. My Canadian background, my years at Bethany Bible Institute and the Mennonite Brethren Bible College, and my ten years of mission administration were all factors in the continued relationship.

The Winnipeg college had tried in 1965 to add a seminary program leading to the bachelor of divinity degree but was not successful. The basic issue was one of exposure. Students who had already spent three years at the college could not be expected to remain in the same environment for an additional three years. The faculty of the college was well-qualified, but could not meet the demand for new academic exposure and environmental stimulant.

Thus the question of a unified program for the Mennonite Brethren General Conference remained alive. A proposal surfaced in 1969 to consider establishing a unified seminary in the Vancouver area of British Columbia. The Americans rejected this recommendation and proposed instead "that the U.S. Conference extend an invitation to the Canadian Conference to join the U. S. Conference in our seminary program." This proposal was rejected by the 1969 session of the General Conference.

At the 1971 Canadian Conference John H. Redekop, then chairman of the college board, presented an analysis of the status of the Mennonite Brethren Bible College in which he pointed to the "blurred" image of the college in its academic program as well as in the view of constituents. As a result of this realistic reappraisal, the Canadian Conference appointed a commission to "study the future of theological training in terms of: (a) a cooperative arrangement with the Fresno seminary; (b) a transdenominational or cluster seminary; (c) other possibilities." At the same time the Canadian Conference appointed two observer participants to the Fresno seminary board.

In January 1972 this study commission suggested to the Canadian Council of Boards that it initiate the process of joining with the U. S. Conference to develop the Fresno seminary as a General Conference school for theological training. The direction toward a North American Mennonite Brethren seminary was now set. Further decisions in 1974 and 1975 would complete the process.

I reached the age of sixty-six in September of 1972. The pressures of eight years of administration had affected my health. Periodically I would experience chills and insomnia. Nettie, who was very sensitive in observing the symptoms, pressed me to terminate administrative duties.

At the fall meeting of the Board of Education I shared my concerns and my wish to step down from the presidency. Some board members felt this would be premature because my key relationship to both the Canadian and U.S. Conferences was still needed. "You must wait to complete the merger," they said.

The January 1972 recommendation of the Canadian study commission found wide support. I was told privately by Canadian Conference leaders that the process towards a joint seminary was virtually assured.

I confirmed my decision to terminate my presidency on July 1, 1972. By the grace of God, the objectives of the assignment had been met. The seminary had stabilized academically, an Anabaptist direction had been set, and accreditation had been attained. The campus had been developed to a degree adequate for the program visualized. The prospect of becoming a General Conference seminary was close at hand, subject to the process of defining the principles and policies of cooperation. I felt at peace about stepping down.

Economically we were in a position to live comfortably. The frugal lifestyle that had governed the years of official ministry prepared us to manage on a reduced economic income (minimal Social Security because of the low salaries throughout our ministry, a monthly pension of $100 from the seminary and $80 from the mission board, and a small income from some limited investments). We had paid for the house on East Townsend in 1963 with proceeds from the sale of the farm in Saskatchewan. Nettie's health, never robust, gave us some concern. Nonetheless, we were generally comfortable with the circumstances in which we found ourselves in 1972.

My decision to decline one more term as president necessitated appointing an interim leader until Canada was officially on board and could fully participate in the selection of the president for the future. Henry H. Dick, at the time the minister-at-large for the U.S. Conference, was asked to assume the interim position.

I considered it prudent to be gone for the first semester of the 1972-73 school year in order to free the interim administration to begin on its own. I accepted a ministry in the churches of Austria and Germany and at the Mennonite Bible school in Bienenberg, Switzerland. I would return to a full instructional assignment at the seminary for the second semester.

When I got back from Europe in November, I was approached by the Mennonite Brethren Historical Commission to consider the position of its executive secretary. The assignment was to promote the historical consciousness of the Mennonite Brethren and the publication of historical material. The invitation appealed to my lifelong interest in the history of the Mennonite Brethren in the context of the larger Anabaptist movement and I accepted. In addition to a full teaching load, I began to project the enlargement of an archival and research center at the seminary and adjacent college. I. G. Neufeld and Peter Klassen had already begun a Mennonite historical library and archival collection. I now began to invest energy in building on their foundations.

A Test of Motives

Not long after beginning this new phase I faced a difficult and painful experience that I had not previously encountered: my motives for ministry were questioned.

As recounted earlier, I had in my younger years struggled to obey the Lord's call. The matter had been settled that evening in the Hillsboro park in 1932 when Nettie said, "It is all right to be poor." Never, in the years since, had we doubted our "yes" to God's call. But now, in the fall of 1973, the integrity of our commitment was tested.

I had begun a full schedule of classes at the seminary. After twenty-five years of administrative responsibilities Nettie and I were happy to be free of such concerns. Our joy and sense of fulfillment was short-lived. On October 3, 1973, Henry H. Dick, the new president, questioned me about the appropriateness of my continued relationship with the school. He also had questions about my continued ministry in the broader Mennonite Brethren Conference and beyond. I recorded his concerns as they were presented to me:

1) He wondered whether my teaching schedule, which was a response to the request of the academic dean and approved by the faculty, was really my own attempt to exert continued influence.

2) He did not think it appropriate as an ex-president, even though I was now a full-time faculty member, to attend faculty meetings.

3) Now that I had resigned from the seminary presidency he felt that I should also withdraw from other conference positions because of their direct and indirect relationship to the ongoing development of the seminary.

4) He likewise questioned the impact on the seminary of my continued ministry in the conference.

5) He was concerned about the appropriateness of my considerable personal correspondence with many individuals in the conference and specifically with Frank C. Peters, a leading figure in Canada, whom I had encouraged to consider joining the seminary faculty.

The incident took me by complete surprise. Had Nettie and I drastically misunderstood the Lord and the circle of believers who we consulted before deciding to remain with the seminary when we had numerous other open doors for ministry? A full week of heart-searching followed.

Nettie and I reexamined our entire past ministry together, laying ourselves open before God. The psalmist's cry became our honest and longing desire: "Search me, O God, and know my heart; try me and know my anxieties; And see if there is any wicked way in me, and lead me in the way everlasting." (Ps. 139:23-24) For days and weeks we sought the Lord, acknowledging that we could not claim our motives through decades of ministry had always been pure. Deep in my inner being I had found satisfaction and affirmation. But I recognized again that I was no holy man without fault.

Our conclusion, after this earnest soul-searching and consultation with various faculty members, board members and conference leaders, was that I should neither leave the seminary nor withdraw from broader ministry. Nettie and I eventually came to peace about the decision. In our view, the events of the next twenty years confirmed that we had understood the Lord correctly.

In retrospect, this difficult experience had a positive outcome. It led to a serious self-examination that turned out to be beneficial. Today I thank God that he permitted the test to come my way.

The Seminary when it was purchased in 1955.

Left to right Mrs. and Mr. A. N. Dick, Mountain Lake, Minnesota who gave five years as volunteers to develop the Seminary campus, myself and Nettie.

Administration building after its restoration.

Ten two bedroom apartments known as the Mission Memorial Court.

Some Seminary board members in 1972, the day the institution was accredited. From left to right: Marvin Steinert, John Friesen, Dr. M. S. Gaede, myself, Peter Enns, E. J. Peters (chairman).

Faculty and adjunct faculty in celebration of accreditation of the Seminary. Left to right: Elmer Martens, Henry Krahn, Ken Berg, D. Edmond Hiebert, Adonijah Pauls, Hans Kasdorf, J. B. Toews, Orrin Berg, A. J. Klassen, Dalton Reimer, Loyal Martin, Delbert Wiens, George Konrad, John Friesen, seminary board member.

The prayer chapel built by Mr. and Mrs. H. K. Warkentin in memory of their son, Herman, missionary to India.

CHAPTER 18

A Continued Ministry

The Historical Commission

I grew up in an environment of historical awareness. My father's library, though limited, included a core of world history, Anabaptist history, the history of Pietism, and Peter M. Friesen's noted history of Mennonites in Russia. One of Father's favored expressions was that "the present is a continuation of yesterday and influences the direction for tomorrow."

My uncles B. B. Janz and Jakob B. Janz also had an impact on my historical consciousness. When they and my father spoke of specific persons in leadership or in social and family relationships, they would always ask, "Who were the parents? What was the family background?" They invariably asked about the past to understand the present.

The last message B. B. Janz, my uncle, delivered to the Canadian Conference in Ontario in 1953 was entitled "Mennonite Brethren: From Where to Where." And a typical expression of my cousin the late John A. Toews, another historian in the clan, was that "a church without the past will soon be a church without a future."

Besides the broad influences that shaped my historical patterns of thought, the statement of Alvin C. Porteous in *The Search for Christian Credibility*, has nurtured my spirit: "In order to do justice to the elements of both continuity and change in formulating Christian beliefs, our theological reflections must keep in fruitful tension all three modes of time: past, present, and future."

From 1972 to 1982 I concentrated my efforts on establishing the Mennonite Brethren archives and a historical research center, in addition to continued part-time teaching at the seminary and broader ministries at home and abroad. To get some professional direction for the assignment I spent a few weeks at the George Washington University in Washington, D.C., and earned a certificate in archival classification.

Initially, the archives were located in the northwest corner of the Hiebert Library (1972-1980), but that did not provide room for proper organization and classification. The remodeling of the library in 1980 provided adequate space for the development of the center.

Rachel Hiebert, a professional librarian, was a godsend for the project. She assumed responsibility for the organization and classification of the archives from 1976 to 1984, and then served as cataloger from 1984-1987.

In 1974 the plans for a Historical Commission were processed by the Canadian Conference in July in Vancouver, and the U.S. Conference in September in Henderson, Nebraska. The August 1975 meeting of the General Conference in Winnipeg, granted approval to the structure of the Centers for Mennonite Brethren Studies to be attached to the conference-operated schools in Winnipeg, Hillsboro and Fresno. That action marked the official beginning of the Fresno center as the General Conference archival repository.

In the meantime, work was under way on producing long-needed materials to undergird our historic understandings. In 1973, with the encouragement of the Historical Commission, I accepted the task to translate P.M. Friesen's *Alt-Evangelische Mennonitische Bruderschaft in Russland (1789-1910)*. The first plan was to distribute sections of the book to several people qualified for translation, such as college and high school teachers with competence in English and German. It became clear in two years that this process was producing an uneven translation. An editorial committee was selected, consisting of myself as chair, along with leading historians Abraham Friesen, Peter J. Klassen, John B. Toews, and Harry Loewen. Large sections of the first translation were redone, and other sections edited. This process required another two years of intensive work.

The small honorariums and travel for the joint meetings of the committee required a budget of $32,000. The Kroeker Foundation of Winkler, Manitoba provided the initial $15,000 and C. A. DeFehr and Sons of Winnipeg provided another $5,000. The remaining $12,000 came from individual business people and churches. The English translation was released in the summer of 1978 under the title *The Mennonite Brotherhood in Russia (1789-1910)*.

The year 1978 also marked the release of my book *The Mennonite Brethren Church in Zaire*. As time permitted, I had worked on the manuscript for four years. To have the church in Zaire share in the process I had made a special visit there in 1973 with the first draft of the manuscript. Their contributions were helpful in preparing the final manuscript which I presented to them for approval in 1976.

Attics and Closets

The 1975 General Conference approval for the Center specified that its permanent location was to be at the seminary. The first step in establishing the archives was to gather a full set of conference yearbooks from private collections. My broad ministry in the churches was the channel for gathering these materials. In many cases we searched attics and closets for long-neglected books and records.

A second phase was the search for minutes, agenda and correspondence of the various conference boards. This required tracing the names and addresses of the board and committee secretaries of the past, writing to them, and searching for what could be retrieved. This required much time and energy. The most complete records were found in the Board of Foreign Missions files located in the Tabor College Library. H. W. Lohrenz and A. E. Janzen must be credited for their foresight and initiative in preserving these materials.

The hardest task lay before us: gathering the historical records and minutes from individual churches. In 1977 I determined to visit every church to see what records and minutes could be found and then to microfilm the material for our permanent collection.

I first made several trips to San Francisco to consult with firms that specialized in microfilming. I learned that what we needed was a camera set for a specific light environment. We then decided to purchase a travel trailer and equip it with a microfilm camera and appropriate lighting. With the assistance of Jake Riediger, then the General Conference treasurer, we estimated the cost of the project and came to the conference with a plan and a budget.

The proposal was approved. I purchased a new travel trailer, had the equipment installed by a specialist and tested the process on the seminary campus. The good results in microfilming the records from local Fresno churches bolstered our confidence that the undertaking could work. We purchased a new truck and began to plan the journey to the churches across Canada and the U.S.

In the providence of God, Jake Riediger suggested that his nephew Bill Reimer, at the time a student at Columbia Bible College in Clearbrook, B.C. and a very knowledgeable and gifted young man, be recruited to do the microfilming and to drive the truck. Bill, open to adventure, responded favorably to the opportunity.

After the close of school in spring 1978, Bill and I drove to Montana to begin our task. From the town of Lustre, Montana, we went to British Columbia, and then east through the Canadian provinces, then down to North and South Dakota, Minnesota and Nebraska. We left Kansas and Oklahoma to be done from the Tabor College Center. When we were finished the trailer and truck were sold. The entire process took nine months.

Open Heart Surgery

I took the place of Hans Kasdorf on the seminary faculty for the second semester of the 1978-1979 school year while he had heart by-pass surgery. Little did I know that by spring of 1979 I would be a candidate for the same operation.

My case was critical because the obstruction was in the main artery close to the entrance of the heart. The nine months of travel among the churches had been hard on me, and were followed by a full teaching load upon my return.

The physician, "Dr. Sam," spoke candidly of the risk of the surgery. Recovery was not a foregone conclusion. Nettie, always a realist, wanted to make preparation in case of my death. She insisted that together we select a burial place. After a visit to several cemeteries we heard of Belmont Memorial Park. The park-like setting, with large trees and a bell tower in the center, struck a chord in her heart. "John," she said, "would it not be nice to put you in the shadow of the bell tower?" "Yes," I said. Little did we realize that she would be first to rest in this beautiful spot.

The surgery was successful. I spent a whole week in intensive care. God's grace and providence spared my life. I was told that recovery would take six months, but it went faster than anticipated. My recovery from heart surgery was remarkable. I have accepted the additional years as a special gift of God, an extension of my days for a specific purpose.

Eighteen months before the surgery I had learned that one of my old friends, Heinrich Woelk, a fellow student in high school in Russia, had survived the communist purges. While convalescing, the message came that he and his family had come to Germany. Because I was forbidden to teach and preach for six months after the surgery, I decided to go to Germany and meet the classmate I though had been dead. Nettie was hesitant, but finally agreed to let me go.

In October 1979 I travelled to Germany. We had a wonderful reunion at the Frankfort airport. What an experience after fifty-three years, to meet a cherished friend whom I had considered dead along with all the rest of my friends and classmates. (To my knowledge, only one former classmate succeeded in leaving Russia in 1924. He was Johann Janzen, for many years a teacher in the Manitoba school system.)

The two weeks of my stay in Germany laid the groundwork for the book *Die Mennoniten Brudergemeinde in Russland, 1925-1980* by Heinrich Woelk and Gerhard Woelk, a very valuable chapter of history of the Mennonite Brethren Church.

The Cloud of Witnesses

The extensive travel in our North American churches and the new trends I saw emerging at home and abroad, impressed me deeply that the church in general, and the Mennonite Brethren fellowship in particular, was facing a major shift at its center. The conference seemed preoccupied with programs and structure rather than with matters of inner character and spiritual moorings. I became deeply concerned that our historical and theological consciousness be nourished on an ongoing basis.

To assure resources for the future historical research and writing I came upon the idea of establishing an endowment for the Center of Mennonite Brethren Studies to be known as "The Cloud of Witnesses." With the approval of the conference in 1987, an endowment fund—projected to eventually reach $500,000 to $750,000—was launched. The first contribution came from the estate of J. C. Ediger of Henderson, Nebraska. The second contribution came from the estate of Otto B. Reimer of Reedley. These plus some smaller contributions from individual donors helped us pass the $100,000 mark. At this writing some $200,000 has been committed from various estates. I maintain the hope that in the providence of God more resources will be forthcoming to meet this need.

I retired from the center in 1982 at the age of seventy-six. I was deeply grateful that Paul, our second son and a professor of history at Fresno Pacific College, was appointed as director to succeed me.

CHAPTER 19

A Conference Servant

L et me pause here to reflect on other conference ministries with which I was involved over the years. They illustrate some of the issues that have occupied the Mennonite Brethren over the years, and point to larger concerns.

Perhaps this is also the appropriate place to explain my use of the term "brotherhood." Today this term has fallen out of fashion, but for much of Mennonite Brethren history it represented a bond of spiritual fellowship and mutuality that transcended gender. Ironically, it originally expressed the inclusive nature of the renewal movement that broke away from the larger Mennonite church in 1860. The mutual connectedness and interdependency that this term sought to convey appears to be declining as Mennonite Brethren approach the twenty-first century.

Youth and Education

I entered the ranks of the larger conference in 1936, at the age of thirty. I was chosen to serve on the General Conference Youth Committee from 1936 to 1939. From the start, my involvements brought me in touch with controversy. In 1937 the conference launched *The Christian Leader*, an English language publication aimed at young people. As a member of the Youth Committee executive I was directly involved in the editorial responsibility.

The introduction of the *Leader* can be seen as a milestone in the conference's struggle to shift from German to English. The youth who descended from the 1870s migration of Mennonite Brethren to North America had lost their literacy in German, even though many churches still used German as the language of worship. Those churches composed of more recent immigrants from the 1920s and 1930s opposed the publication of the *Leader* because they saw it as a threat. The refusal of the Coaldale Mennonite Brethren Church to ordain me, referred to earlier, may have been related to my membership in the committee that published *The Christian Leader*.

In 1943 I was elected to serve on the Tabor College board. Here again I soon found myself in the midst of turmoil, namely the seismic shift from one generation of leadership to another. Up to 1942 the reins of the college had always been in the hands of trusted churchmen like H. W. Lohrenz, P. C. Hiebert and A. E. Janzen. The arrival of Peter E. Schellenberg, however, represented a departure from this tradition.

He was a grandson of Elder Abraham Schellenberg, one of the founders of the Mennonite Brethren Church in North America. He was a scholar, a psychologist, with an analytical faith that was deeply rooted in salvation history. But some constituents were suspicious: Could a psychologist be a true Christian? At the 1943 General Conference in Buhler he publicly shared his testimony, and the board affirmed his leadership.

I personally had profound respect for P. E. Schellenberg. I felt he was a man of great commitment who saw a clear direction in the overall purpose of the college. But a small group of older students in the Tabor bible department continued to question his integrity and to agitate against him. Their suspicions spread into the constituency and undermined his leadership. At work here was a larger public conflict between fundamentalism and liberalism that affected Mennonite Brethren more than we recognized on the surface. He was not understood by the constituency, nor by the board that came into office in 1951. Schellenberg terminated his presidency in 1951, but the tensions that led to his departure were not so easily resolved.

Reference and Counsel

In 1945, at the conference in Dinuba, Calif., I was elected to the Committee of Reference and Counsel and subsequently served a total of fifteen years. Those years marked the beginning of a profoundly destabilizing era in Mennonite Brethren history. In one generation, 1950-1970, the church went through a cataclysmic cultural and spiritual transition. A rural, agricultural, homogeneous people shook off their migrant past and became urbanized, professional and fully integrated into the culture of their day. (This transition is explored in chapters 16-21 of my earlier book, *A Pilgrimage of Faith*.) The church found itself groping for moorings amid this sea of change, and the Committee of Reference and Counsel was at the forefront of the struggle. Its 1948 conference report highlighted some major concerns. First, the strong infiltration of parachurch organizations that came into our churches like a wave after the switch from German to English. Second, for the first time, the issue of divorce and remarriage became an urgent issue. Third, deep concern was expressed over the spiritual welfare of the churches. Fourth, nonresistance was a burning issue in light of the Second World War experience, and continued to remain a concern through the 1980s.

A major task that came to me through the 1951 conference was to carry out negotiations with the Krimmer Mennonite Brethren Church, which had made overtures to merge with us. One of the hurdles was the KMB program of overseas missions. All their missionaries served with parachurch mission agencies. The repeated meetings with KMB leaders from 1951 until the actual merger in 1960 took much time, as we sorted out how to integrate their mission interests with ours. The fact that there was a notable lack of unity within the KMB constituency did not help.

Early Fragmentation

The 1951 conference saw the beginning of a slide away from our historic sense of brotherhood and a rising sense of individualism and autonomy. The record of that conference contains a lengthy document that I authored: "A Frank Analysis of Our Spiritual Status (our duty as we see it)." This document pointed to the "revolutionizing changes" affecting the church and made "An Appeal for a Reaffirmation of the Historic Principle of the Interrelationship of Mennonite Brethren Churches" with Proposed Ways and Means to be Considered to Strengthen the Existing Weaknesses."

The conference response was to refer the document to the local churches for review and reaction. By doing so we lost the full intent of the document. The churches had changed, and there was a reaction to the central authority of a special conference committee as suggested in the document. The 1954 conference handed more General Conference authority to the provincial conferences in Canada and the regional conferences in the U.S. where implementation of the directive control of the conference was gradually lost. We on the Committee of Reference and Counsel during this time felt that the basic principle of central authority was now gone. This accounts for the fragmentation we find in the Mennonite Brethren Church today, with regional conferences and local churches (and their pastors) being increasingly independent of any larger sense of accountability. (See also chapter 21 of *A Pilgrimage of Faith.*)

The 1957 conference drew attention to the spirit of individualism and called for greater unity and love for the church. The contentious issues being dealt with at the time had to do with baptism and nonresistance. The concern over disunity led to a resolution calling for the preparation of books that would shore up Mennonite Brethren identity in the areas of history, biblical doctrines, polity and practice, and missions.

I was asked to prepare the book on "Mennonite Brethren Theology (Biblical Doctrine)." I worked on it, as my schedule allowed, for the next several years and prepared a tentative outline. I read all the writing of Mennonite Brethren in the *Friedenstimme* in Russia, the *Zionbote* in North America and other papers by Mennonite Brethren to gain insights into the various trends in our history. My conclusion, after all this research, was that Mennonite Brethren had an implicit biblical theology; they believed in the Bible and found the answers for faith and life as needs demanded. This research eventually led to the manuscript, *A Pilgrimage of Faith*, which was finally published in 1993 (thirty-six years after the original assignment).

I withdrew from the Board of Reference and Counsel in 1960 because of the press of responsibilities with the Board of Foreign Missions. I had served for fifteen years. The tone of this period can be detected in the concerns raised in conference messages of the time.

In his "state of the conference" message at the 1954 Canadian Conference, B. B. Janz lamented the encroachment of dangerous tendencies: materialism, worldliness, thirst for honor, spiritual shallowness, disobedience of children and youth, lack of personal pastoral care (*Seelsorge*), weakening of church discipline, child conversions before maturity, and general spiritual decline.

By the time we celebrated the centennial of the Mennonite Brethren Church in 1960, there were deep concerns about our future. In his centennial conference message, G. W. Peters called for repentance and renewal. John A. Toews noted that our concept of salvation, our sense of separation from the world, and our view of scriptural authority were all suffering erosion.

Board of Missions and Services

I did not serve on any General Conference boards from 1960 to 1966. I was too busy implementing the missions policies of 1957. Some missionaries felt I was too dictatorial in establishing policies that limited individual liberties. One had to do with personal gifts to missionaries. Some of our overseas workers still accepted personal gifts from churches and individuals in addition to their mission board support, a carryover from before 1957. In some cases these private funds were quite substantial. We had to work hard to re-educate the missionaries and their donors to limit personal liberties and channel these gifts into the general treasury.

My resignation as executive and promotional secretary of missions in the spring of 1963 was an extremely difficult decision. I was anxious that the new leadership continue the progress we had made to forge a new partnership with the national churches. Missiologist Hans Kasdorf has suggested that our vision for "Partnership in Obedience" was far ahead of its time. In my view, not much progress has been made in this area since then.

In 1966, at the conference in Corn, Oklahoma, the Board of General Welfare and Public Relations was merged with the Board of Missions and renamed the Board of Missions and Services. I was urged to accept a six-year term on this board, 1966-1972.

These six years were difficult for me. For one thing, little attention was being given to the relationship to the national churches, as mentioned earlier. For another, the whole concept of missionary service was changing. The basic understanding of missions as a service performed with no guaranteed remuneration was abandoned. Until then, our missionaries had served with a mere allowance for basic needs rather than a stipulated salary. These allowances would vary according to circumstances and costs of living in the various countries.

The conference assumed the responsibility of providing for the missionaries' needs in retirement. For example, when the Jakob J. Dicks returned from the field because of illness, they settled in British Columbia. I negotiated the financial arrangement with the B.C. Conference, which built them a house with voluntary labor and assumed a portion of their support. The mission office provided a subsidy. Similar provisions were made for other missionaries. In the case of the Peter V. Balzers and John Lohrenz the conference support was minimal because they owned land with oil rights and did not need help.

Office personnel lived by the same policies. When I joined the mission staff in 1954 my allowance was $290 per month, at the time the highest allowance paid.

This all changed in the 1970s. Missionaries and administrators received regular salaries. A typical high school teacher's salary was accepted as the standard for a missionary, plus special expenses like travel, currency exchange and child support. Missionary service became a professional occupation, with standard financial returns.

For me, and for us as a family, this became a major issue. We had always believed strongly in the service concept. When I left the seminary presidency in 1972 my annual salary was $10,000. I had volunteered to serve with the limited income. Nettie and I were still committed to our 1932 covenant, "It is all right to be poor." My successor began his administration with a salary of $18,000.

The issue, however, was not dollars but rather dependence, trust and faith. I felt then, as I do now, that something was lost when we made the shift to a professionalized ministry.

A second issue for me while on the mission board was the introduction of the Good News Corps, a new opportunity for short-term service in missions. Even though I recognized the benefit such service could bring, I was troubled because it did not demand long-range commitment. To receive the benefit of one year of language study for two years of service with no long-term obligation was, in my view, not acceptable. As it turns out, very few Good News Corps workers have gone on to long-term missionary assignments.

These two concerns—the professionalization of the ministry and the short-term service program—led me to question my continued service on the mission board. Still, at the 1972 conference I was elected for another six years. I became uneasy as I contemplated this prospect. On the last day of the conference I asked the delegation to release me. I suggested they replace me with John Kliewer, long-time missionary in Zaire and at the time pastor of the Silver Lake Mennonite Brethren Church in South Dakota. The conference granted my request.

Continual Drift

As I reflect on my years in various levels of conference leadership, I continue to grieve over the relentless move toward greater professionalization of the ministry. I believe it has resulted in the institutionalization of the church. From a covenant people—a brotherhood—we have drifted to become a mere association of independent churches. This is partly due to the influence of American evangelicalism with its emphasis on the benefits of salvation without a consistent biblical theology manifested in the character of the church.

To have these changes take place during my years of conference leadership has been a most difficult experience for me. All attempts to mold the Mennonite Brethren fellowship appear to have been ineffective. The trend of accommodation was unstoppable, despite a Board of Reference and Counsel composed of strong leaders like A. H. Unruh, B. B. Janz, J. W. Vogt, H. H. Janzen and B. J. Braun in the 1950s and John A. Toews, David Ewert and Cornelius J. Rempel in the 1960s.

The death of John A. Toews while chair of the General conference in 1979 was a major loss in the historical struggle. The coming leadership of the 1980s was more from the ranks of professional pastors who were less interested in history and theology. Their concerns focused on their own positions in the local church and on evangelism. Church planting became the center of the conference program, with less attention paid to the spiritual qualities that the churches needed in order to be effective in reaching out to their immediate communities.

CHAPTER 20

In the Shadow of Death

Nettie and I spent considerable time apart in the summer of 1976. I felt it was necessary to take an extended visit to Africa to check the final draft of *The Mennonite Brethren Church in Zaire* with the national church. As a continuing teacher of history and theology, I also felt the need for a longer exposure to the world mission scene.

Nettie spent that summer with her sister, Grace, in Hillsboro. During the previous winter and spring she had complained of loss of energy, dizziness and general lack of well-being. While in Hillsboro, upon the urging of Grace, she went to the clinic at the Bethel Hospital in Newton. The diagnosis suggested a blood abnormality, perhaps even polycythemia (an over-production of red blood cells).

Back in Fresno we consulted her doctor, but he was unable to confirm the Newton diagnosis. Numerous tests failed to substantiate the possibility of polycythemia. Her doctor suggested we go to the University Hospital in San Francisco, which specialized in blood diseases.

Signals of Concern

We spent two days with the specialists in San Francisco. The Newton doctors had been correct. The verdict was polycythemia. We were openly told there was no cure for it. The suggestion was to have monthly blood tests. When the blood thickened, it was to be drawn to let the red blood cells multiply again. The doctors indicated that the condition would ultimately be fatal. The culmination would be either a rapid blood cancer or a series of strokes. The time frame they gave us was about two years.

Nettie, a nurse by training, took the news very seriously but characteristically did not panic. She was seventy-five at the time; I was seventy-two. Monthly blood tests were initiated immediately. At first it was necessary to draw blood only every other month. Very realistically, but calmly, Nettie began to express concern about the medical care that eventually would become necessary. In the spring of 1978 she suggested we sell our house and move into an apartment at Twilight Haven, a nearby retirement center with multiple levels of care. I did not feel ready for such a change, but agreed to her suggestion in light of my continued absences in ministries and teaching.

We applied for an apartment at Twilight Haven, only two blocks from our house, across the street from the Special Events Center of Fresno Pacific College. Nettie would feel more secure there during my absences, and help would be available if needed.

Nettie's disciplined diet, long walks twice a day, and monthly blood tests at the hospital sustained her. She did not want her condition to interrupt my ministry. Her ailment worsened as time went on. Soon it was necessary to take a pint of blood every month.

In December 1983 she suffered her first stroke, which left her slightly handicapped in her lower extremities. She recovered remarkably, so much so that she encouraged me to accept an invitation for a ministry in Russia in 1985. I went but my absence took a considerable toll on Nettie despite her earlier improvement.

The plan had been to spend three weeks in Russia followed by another three to four weeks of ministry in Europe. During the three weeks in Russia Nettie and I were completely cut off from communication as no private international calls were going through. The moment I arrived back in Frankfurt, Germany, on October 3, I called Nettie. Her first question was, "Are you still alive?" The three weeks of uncertainty had been too much for her. "John," she said with a pleading voice, "I need you."

I immediately canceled the engagements in Europe and made arrangements to catch the first plane out of Frankfurt to Los Angeles. By late evening the same day I was home. Nettie was relieved. During my absence she had suffered a light stroke.

While I was away an apartment in the same complex but on Winery Avenue, had become available. It was larger and somewhat closer to the library and seminary. We moved to the Winery apartment the next month. My schedule was revised to stay home, as Nettie was at a stage where I needed to remain close.

January 6, 1986

On January 6, the anniversary of the founding of the Mennonite Brethren Church in 1860, I was in San Jose for a weekend. Nettie was still waiting up for me when I returned. As we sat and reviewed the experiences of the weekend, she suffered another stroke, this one very severe. I carried her to her bed and called the doctor. He suggested we let her rest at home overnight.

She was transferred to the hospital in the morning. Several weeks of hospitalization followed. At times we expected her to die, but then she would rally. She regained full consciousness. By the end of January she had recovered sufficiently to come home. I took personal responsibility for her care with the help of a nurse who would come in when needed. February and March went well. It was very rewarding to care for her even though it was very taxing.

On March 23 her sister Grace in Hillsboro had a serious accident. A silk scarf she was wearing caught fire as she bent over the gas stove and she was badly burned. Grace, who had been such a vital part of our lives, was at the point of death. Since travel for Nettie was out of the question, it was decided that I would rush to the Wichita hospital to be at her side. Nettie was transferred to the Valley Convalescent Hospital for the time of my absence.

It was clear when I arrived in Wichita that Grace would not live long. I made arrangements for her funeral, selected the coffin, and advised the Hillsboro Funeral Home of procedures. I felt it best to fly home for a day and personally inform Nettie of Grace's condition, and than return to Kansas for the funeral. On the evening of my return, April 7, the message came that Grace had died.

The loss of our dear sister was too much for Nettie and me. I was hospitalized with heart irregularities. Nettie had another serious stroke. We were both in the hospital from April 7 to 14. Paul flew to Hillsboro to participate in Grace's funeral. I regained stability after a week of rest in the hospital. A few days later Nettie could be transferred to the hospital wing of Twilight Haven.

A Peaceful Homegoing

The time from May until October 15, 1986 was a very sacred period for Nettie, me and our family. John and Paul with their families were in Fresno; James was in Salem, Oregon.

In the providence of God, Hans and Irene Pankratz and their children, from Paraguay, were at the seminary. Irene, a nurse by profession, became a God-sent angel for us. Every day, Monday through Friday, Irene would come to Twilight Haven at 2:30 in the afternoon, help Nettie into a wheelchair and bring her home to our apartment. She would provide fellowship for Nettie and a measure of outdoor exposure by wheeling her to the seminary and college to dispel the atmosphere of the sickroom. I continued my regular schedule of work during the day, coming home at five for a supper prepared by Irene. I would care for Nettie during the dinner hour and roll her back to the hospital care unit of Twilight Haven for the night.

Periodically Nettie would have light strokes, but they did not affect her mental functions. Our communication remained vibrant through the final months of her illness. Many visitors called on her.

On Saturday, October 12, we again had our evening meal together. She looked at the daily paper. While sitting side by side we talked about family matters. Both of us had accepted the fact that our time together was growing shorter every day. After dinner we played a German record of the Janz quartet in Germany. The concluding hymn was, "I have a home that awaits me above, and I will not be a stranger there." Quietly Nettie wiped her tears. The music stopped. Silently we sat for a few moments, then she said, with eyes glistening, "I have a home above where Jesus is, and I will not be a stranger there." Neither of us realized this would be the last time we were together alone in our apartment.

Sunday morning, October 13, when I came to her bedside before going to church, the nurse in charge told me Nettie was running a low fever and could not go out that day. John, Paul, and their wifes came to her bedside Sunday afternoon and we visited with her. Her doctor came Monday afternoon to check the cause of the fever. His diagnosis was that her kidneys were failing. He called me to say he wished to send an ambulance to take her to the hospital for dialysis. I asked him to wait a moment.

Nettie, years before had requested no heroic medical measures to prolong her life. Now when I went to her bedside to tell her that her doctor wanted to transfer her, she calmly said, "Please let me stay here and don't take me to the hospital." The family concurred. I called the doctor and gave him the decision. The decision had been made. Quietly we waited.

Late Monday afternoon Nettie slipped slowly into a coma. The immediate family came to her bedside. There were moments when she would recognize those surrounding her. By evening she did not respond. The hour of separation was near.

We took turns at her bedside. At Paul's urging I went to the apartment at midnight to rest but could not sleep. In two hours I was back at her bedside and urged Paul, who had stayed with her, to go home.

I sat with her, my finger on her pulse, while she rested quietly. At 3:45 a.m. the pulse became irregular. Ten minutes later she took a deep breath, attempted a second breath, and her pulse stopped. I called our sons. They came quickly. Nettie's spirit had departed. It was 4:00 a.m., Wednesday, October 15.

The seminary was hosting a study conference that was to begin that afternoon and last until Friday. Nettie's funeral had to be delayed until Monday. All her life she had adjusted to the schedules of special meetings and conferences. This was true even in death.

Many guests who had come to the study conference postponed their departure from Saturday to Monday. A large contingent of conference leaders and guests was present at the service. The shadow of the Bell Tower, the spot she had selected for me at the time of my heart surgery seven years earlier, became her resting place.

A Serious Injury

Because of Nettie's condition I had delayed neck surgery that was necessary due to a car accident I was involved in while winding up our sister Grace's estate. Grace, who had died in April, left her entire estate to an endowment for the Chair of Missions and Evangelism at the Mennonite Brethren Biblical Seminary. I traveled to Hillsboro to look after the liquidation together with my brother-in-law, Isaac Unruh. An invitation for a weekend ministry at the Mennonite Brethren Church in Ebenfeld (Hillsboro) set the time for a weekend in June.

When I landed at the airport in Wichita on a Wednesday, my baggage was missing. Two days later we received a message that the baggage had been located and was now available at the airport. After a day's work sorting Grace's personal belongings, Isaac and I decided to drive to Wichita for the luggage.

The evening traffic on Highway 54 was heavy. We stopped for the last traffic light before the airport turnoff. Through the rearview mirror Isaac saw a car approaching at full speed. "They will hit us," he screamed. He did not finish the warning. The car, driven by two young people, slammed into our rear end resulting in a chain reaction involving three other cars in front of us.

I had not been prepared for the crash. When everything stopped I was unconscious. I had suffered severe whiplash from the rear impact. The collision with the car in front of us threw me forward so I shattered the windshield with my forehead. I have very little memory of what followed. I regained consciousness in the hospital.

Later, at my bedside, the physician asked about my previous neck injury. The X-rays revealed the injuries I had sustained many years ago, at the age of nineteen in Gnadenfeld, Russia. I spent three days in intensive care before I being transferred to the hospital ward. The need for major surgery was established.

As Nettie was then deteriorating, I could not think of staying in Wichita for any duration. Our son John came to Wichita to help me back to Fresno. My surgery would have to wait. I lived with heavy neck braces, much pain, and a loss of equilibrium.

A month after Nettie's burial I submitted to surgery. The recovery took many weeks. My equilibrium, for a time, was quite good. Gradually, however, I experienced increasing instability in mobility, and needed a cane for balance.

Surgery only one month after Nettie's death deepened the consciousness of her loss. Her tender care and undying affection, which had surrounded me in past surgeries and illnesses, was missing. Painfully, I had to process the reality that she was no longer at my side. She had been the center of our family life, and she was gone.

A burden for my brethren from Russia, the *Umsiedler* Mennonites who were immigrating to Germany, became one of my chief concerns. Annual ministries in Europe became a major focus of my life in the initial years of widowhood. The ministries in Europe, South America, U.S. and Canada became the substitute for the void in my life left by Nettie's passing.

CHAPTER 21

A Return Home

The 1980s presented two occasions for me to return to Russia. For safety reasons, I had turned down an earlier opportunity to revisit the land of my birth.

In the mid-1950s I had been invited by Harold S. Bender to join a Mennonite Central Committee delegation to Russia to gather information on dislocated Mennonites. During the 1930s many Mennonites, especially ministers and community leaders, had been persecuted. Some had been banished to Siberian labor camps; some had been executed. I declined Bender's invitation, as I had escaped only thirty years earlier while subject to military service and did not consider it safe to return.

My fears and suspicions had been fueled by an incident in 1940. While at the seminary in Portland, I had applied for a U.S. resident visa to accept an invitation to Freeman, College in South Dakota. The U.S. Consulate required a birth certificate. Because I had been born in Russia I wrote to the Russian Consulate in San Francisco. They demanded that I submit my passport, which they promised to return, as evidence of my Russian birth. Months later I was notified that my request for a birth certificate was denied. My passport was never returned. I took this to be a serious omen.

By now, in 1985, things were different. A new era was dawning in the Soviet Union. It seemed hardly likely that my escape of sixty years earlier would be a matter of concern.

David Redekop of Winnipeg, a veteran of several previous visits to Russia, had received an official invitation from the Mennonite Brethren churches in the Orenburg region through the channel of the All-Union Council of Evangelical Christian-Baptists of the U.S.S.R. The invitation was for us to visit and minister in the churches. Along with Johann Koehn, a former resident of the Orenburg settlement who had migrated to West Germany five years earlier, we traveled to Russia in September 1985.

If we needed any reminding, the customs inspection in Moscow quickly demonstrated that we were in a different world. At the suggestion of others who had visited among the Russian Mennonites I had packed books on Anabaptist faith and Mennonite history as gifts for our brothers and sisters in their search for identity after so many decades of isolation.

These included the works of Menno Simons, P. M. Friesen and A. H. Unruh. Now, however the customs officer declared all this material confiscated.

Johann Koehn stood by and watched. On the flight to Moscow he had informed us that he would not reveal his fluent knowledge of the Russian language. He had secured a German passport and did not want to let on that he was a former Russian. But he could not contain himself when he saw what was happening. In perfect Russian he burst out and challenged the customs officer. "We have come to your country as official delegates upon invitation of the Union Council of the Churches in Russia. The books that you confiscate contain the material which we came to present to the Russian churches. You have no right to confiscate official material that is being brought at the request of your own Russian organizations."

After a brief but heated exchange of words the customs officer backed off and returned all the books. The first round of confrontation with the Soviets had been won. The books were later given to Johannes Dyck a young historian in Karaganda and at the time the official historian of the union council.

As official guests of the council, we were met at the airport by Walter Mitz-Kovitch of the Theological Institute of the Evangelical Christians. Mr. Mitz-Kovitch remained our official host through the time in Russia. The union covered all our expenses in the Soviet Union.

Being back in the Russian environment was a test of how much of the language I had retained after some sixty years. I could still follow personal conversations, and understood the content of public presentations. But I did not have the vocabulary to personally respond to the conversations. I resorted to speaking through an interpreter.

The official leadership of the union was very cordial. A number of consultations were arranged and we participated in the celebration of the hundredth birthday of the first chairman of the union, Jakob Zhidkov, who had died some years earlier.

I was deeply moved by the public meetings in which we participated. I again felt the deep soul of the Russian people. Our arrival in Orenburg was celebrated with a welcome dinner. Daniel Janzen, leading minister of the church in Donskoye, Peter Enns, leader of the church in Orenburg city, and Victor Serpevski, the presbyter of the Orenburg region, served as our hosts for the visit.

The Orenburg settlement, consisting of fourteen villages, was established in the 1890s. The Mennonites of this area were not affected by World War II; they were not evacuated as were the Mennonites in the Ukraine. The villages were basically unchanged.

The heart of our visit were the public worship services. We were the first Mennonite delegation from abroad to visit Orenburg. Earlier visits had not been permitted to come to this area.

The services were moving. Our first public service was arranged for the evening of our arrival in Donskoye. Every seat in the church was filled. The windows were opened and people sat outside, many of them standing for the entire service, which lasted until after midnight. To meet our brothers and sisters who had been isolated for more than sixty years and find them strong in the faith was overwhelming. Several choirs participated in the service. A night lunch was served at 2:00 a.m.

A group of three people from the non-registered underground church asked to meet with me alone during the night to share their experiences. The underground church had suffered much persecution. The word of Christ, "I will build my church; and the gates of hell shall not prevail against it" (Matt. 16:18), was strongly confirmed in the testimony of these three who, like Nicodemus, had come during the night to find some encouragement.

In private conversations we heard many stories describing the suffering the Mennonites had endured during World War II; many of the men, fathers and sons, had been taken away, never to return.

Upon our return to Moscow Johannes Dyck was called from Karaganda for personal consultation. In several private conversations he gave me a picture of the status of the church. He represented the Mennonites who organizationally had identified with the Mennonite Baptist connection. I had read several articles in the *Bratskij Vestnik*, the paper of the Christian Baptist Union, outlining the historical roots of Anabaptism. All the books I had brought along were received with much gratitude.

Some of the tension in which Johannes lived was reflected in his insistence that we not visit in the hotel but rather talk while strolling along the streets of Moscow. He felt the need to protect his identity and to prevent the possibility of our conversation being recorded by hidden microphones in the hotel. These furtive conversations enlarged my consciousness of divine mercy in my escape sixty years earlier. Why had I been able to escape the suffering, isolation and death in the Siberian forced labor camps where most of my contemporaries ended their lives? The visit to Russia in 1985 was a powerful reminder of how fortunate I had been.

A Second Visit

Four years later, in the summer of 1989, it was my privilege together with my three sons and their spouses to make a second visit to Russia, this time as a tourist. On this trip I was able to meet some of the friends from my youth. Of course, none of these were men, only women. They had lost their husbands and sons to the cruelty of war, evacuation and persecution for being Germans and Christians.

The return to Moscow for the second time provided an opportunity to reminisce. I recalled the several weeks in 1926 when we hid and anxiously prayed for the change of my passport. The house where we hid, at that time the office of the Mennonite Center, is still there. Deep gratitude filled my heart that the process succeeded.

The twenty days in Russia on this second return provided two events that touched me deeply. The first was a visit to Karaganda. In the middle of the vast expanse of Asiatic Russia is the memorable region of Karaganda, known for its rich coal mines. When our people—mostly women and children—were displaced from the villages in the Ukraine they were brought to these regions and used as laborers in the mines.

The evening meeting in the Mennonite Brethren Church gave us the opportunity to meet a number of women from Alexandertal who had been part of my youth group. Now old and feeble, reflecting their years of grief over the loss of their husbands and sons, they sat before me in the audience.

I was asked to speak. Our group joined members of the choir and sang with them. Some faces looked familiar, though I could not identify them immediately. One was the wife of my spiritual mentor, David Reimer, to whom I owed so much. He was the one who negotiated my passport so I could escape. There was also Tina Reimer, one of our youth group from Alexandertal. The next morning, when I left the hotel for a brief walk, Liese Reimer sat at the door. We visited together for a time and reviewed the days of our youth. Again I wondered, why had I been spared the horrors that they had experienced?

The second moving experience was a visit to the villages of my childhood and youth. Halbstadt—now renamed Molochansk—was so familiar to me. Several buildings were still standing: the hospital where my mother had her eye operation, the *Kommerz-schule* (college) where my brother Aron studied, and the teacher's college.

In Gnadenfeld I found the campus of the Agronomic Institute, a satellite of the University of the Ukraine, where I had experienced the crisis that necessitated my escape. I also found the high school, adjoining the Agronomic College, where I taught chemistry and algebra while at the college. The buildings of the oil refinery, where I worked as a student, were gone.

The most touching experience came when we reached the village of Alexandertal. The school building in the center of the village, where I was born, was still standing though somewhat remodeled. The original buildings on our homestead across the street were gone, but the place still had the grand view of the river and the large meadow beyond the valley. The church of my childhood and youth was also still there. It had been remodeled as a community center. The sight of the church brought back memories of the events so important to my development. I recalled my early childhood, the Sunday school on Sunday afternoons, the young people's meetings, the weeks of Bible conferences. Here I had given my testimony before baptism and here I had preached my first sermon at the age of eighteen.

The next day we drove to Alexanderkrone, the birthplace of my father. The time was too short to absorb all the memories. The chance to return to the places of my birth, childhood and youth remains a highlight of my life. To make that visit together with my sons was all the more rewarding.

Interpreting the History

The broad exposure of many years of ministry and the search for historical records provided the setting for reactivating the assignment of the 1950s to write the theology of the Mennonite Brethren.

Following the trip to Russia, I committed myself to write two books. One of these was the spiritual pilgrimage of the Mennonite Brethren Church. It was published in 1993 under the title, *Pilgrimage of Faith*, and drew on my many years of reading, travelling and ministering in Mennonite Brethren churches in Europe, North and South America, Africa, Asia, and now Russia. The second book I committed myself to write was the story of my own pilgrimage, the book you now hold in your hands.

1978 celebration of the completion of translation and publication of P. M. Friesen's work: "Alt-Evangelische Mennoniten Bruderschaft in Russland, 1789-1910." Left to right: Peter J. Klassen, one of the translaters and editors, myself, Elmer Martens, member of the Board of Christian Literature and President of the Seminary.

Family picture in 1980.

Ebenezer — Our 50th anniversary, 1983.

Last formal portrait before Nettie's death.

Nettie's resting place under the shadow of the bell tower in the Belmont Memorial Park.

CHAPTER 22

Epilogue

M y lifespan (1906 to the present) has covered most of the twentieth century, a period described as a time of "breakneck changes, an era of the most troubled, unsettling, costly, adventurous and surprising time ever. More has changed and faster, more has been destroyed, more accomplished than in any comparable interval in the five thousand years since recorded history began."[12] It had been my fortune to live during this watershed of history.

Who would have thought, when I came on the scene, that life would change so quickly and dramatically. At first, our small Russian village was sheltered and serene, the cradle of a tight, culture-bound people with an unquestioning religious faith. But then, at the age of eight, the calm was brutally shattered as the First World War broke in like a thunderbolt and changed the course of history.

My life was abruptly transformed with the absence of my father for three years (1914-1917) and the revolution that followed. The stability of the past gave way to a boiling cauldron of civil war, starvation and political and social upheaval. There seemed to be no flickering light at the end of the tunnel of time.

The discipline and concentration required to complete my high school and university studies during this time of chaos strained me almost to the breaking point but equipped me with endurance and confidence that would serve me well. Though spiritually in a wilderness, I experienced the mercies of God even beyond mere survival.

It was my fiance, Nettie Unruh, a woman so totally unselfish and kind, who helped me come to terms with God's purpose for my life. Her words, "It is all right to be poor," freed me to submit in humble obedience. She provided a center with spiritual sensitivity and wisdom that marked the course of my life's ministry. As the mother of our three sons she was the heart of the family. She was the glue that held everything together during the weeks and months when my duties took me away from home.

The tumult of the twentieth century became the cutting edge of struggle in my sixty years of public ministry. The cultural revolution of the post-World War II years has tested my faith and commitment to the utmost. The Mennonite Brethren Church, torn from its spiritual, social and cultural isolation, was tossed into the tempest of most unprecedented change. Within a quarter century (1950-1975) a rural agricultural people was scattered into urban centers and integrated into a new milieu of professionalism. The central tenets of the church's faith and practice were shaken to the core. The interdependent fellowship of the Mennonite Brethren Church, in the midst of rampant individualism and pluralism, developed into an association retaining a structure of program in missions and education but with little abiding commitment to being a people in the world but not of the world. American evangelicalism, preoccupied with "being saved" and garnering the benefits of the gospel without the attendant costs in ethics and lifestyle, became our dominant model. Following this trend of evangelicalism, "there is a deemphasis of the more offensive aspects of the gospel: the nature of internal evil, sinful conduct and lifestyle, the wrath of a righteous and jealous God and external agony and death in hell."[13] The commitment to the absolutes of the Scripture in true discipleship—"take up the cross and follow me"—has become for many a mere matter of choice. Many years in leadership positions amid this environment created continuous tensions as I sought to remain true to my understanding of Scripture.

At this writing I have reached the age of eighty-eight. I must now face the prospect of concluding my ministry with Elijah under the juniper tree, saying it is enough, despite not seeing the seven thousand who remain confident that the Unchangeable One, "who has begun the good work in you (the Mennonite Brethren Church) will perform it unto the day of Jesus Christ" (Phil. 1:6).

The experiences of sixty years in ministry have equipped me with a fervent confidence that my God is a God of the impossible. The Mennonite Brethren Church, as it searches for spiritual renewal, will again find repentance and experience a new beginning to rise to the high purpose of its calling as a renewal movement within the biblical Anabaptist faith.

Under the tender watchcare of our three sons and their families in their respective services to the church and the larger society, and with the all-sufficiency of my Lord, I am content as I approach the transition from the things that are seen and temporal, to the things which are not seen and eternal.

The overarching response to my pilgrimage is well expressed in the words of Philipp F. Hiller:

What mercy and divine compassion,
Has God in Christ revealed to me!
My haughty spirit would not ask it,
Yet He bestowed it, full and free,
In God my heart doth now rejoice:
I praise His grace with grateful voice.

Eternal wrath should be my portion:
The Lamb of God for sinners slain;
Removed the curse and condemnation,
His blood atoned for every stain.
God's love in Christ on Calvary's tree
From guilt and shame has set me free.

Great God, accept my adoration,
Help me Thy mercy to confess;
In Jesus Christ is my salvation
He is my hope in life and death:
His blood, His righteousness alone
I claim before Thy judgment throne.

Thy bounteous grace is my assurance,
The blood of Christ my only plea,
Thy heart of love my consolation
Until Thy glorious face I see:
My theme through never ending days,
Shall be Thy great redeeming grace.[14]

Endnotes

1. David McCullough, "Extraordinary Times: Living in an Era of Breakneck Changes," *Life*, Fall 1986, 189.

2. *The Complete Writings of Menno Simons: c. 1496-1561*, trans. Leonard Verduin, ed. J. C. Wenger (Scottdale, Pa.: Herald Press, 1956), 307.

3. Thieleman J. van Braght, *The Bloody Theater or Martyrs Mirror of the Defenseless Christians*, trans. Joseph Sohm (Scottdale, Pa.: Herald Press, 1951).

4. Peter M. Friesen, *The Mennonite Brotherhood in Russia (1789-1910)*, trans. and ed. J. B. Toews et al. (Fresno, Calif.: Board of Christian Literature, General Conference of Mennonite Brethren Churches, 1978), 230-232.

5. D. M. Hofer, *Die Hungersnot in Russland und Unsere Reise um die Welt* (Chicago: K.M.B. Publishing House, 1924), 161-163.

6. John B. Toews, *With Courage to Spare: the Life of B. B. Janz (1877-1964)* (Winnipeg: The Board of Christian Literature of the General Conference of the Mennonite Brethren Churches, 1978), 55-56.

7. Paul Toews, "Henry W. Lohrenz and Tabor College," *Mennonite Life* 38 (Sept. 1983): 11-12.

8. Ibid.

9. Ernest R. Sandeen, *The Roots of Fundamentalism: British and American Millennarianism, 1800-1930* (Chicago: University of Chicago Press, 1970), 188-207.

10. For more extensive analysis of why it took so long to make this transition, see chapter of 18 of J. B. Toews, *A Pilgrimage of Faith: The Mennonite Brethren Church, 1860-1990* (Winnipeg: Kindred Press, 1993).

11. Interview in possession of author.

12. McCullough, "Extraordinary Times," 189.

13. James Davison Hunter, *American Evangelicalism: Conservative Religion and the Quandary of Modernity* (New Brunswick, N.J.: Rutgers University Press, 1983), 87.

14. "Mir ist Erbarmung Widerfahren," tr. Frieda Kaufman.